The Best of

NEW ORLEANS

Editor
Robert C. Fisher

Contributing Editors
Millie Ball, Gene Bourg, Tom Fitzmorris,
Vincent Fumar, Mary Gehman, Gregory Roberts

Associate Editor
Catherine Jordan

Additional editorial assistance
Christopher Caines

Editorial Director
Jim Burns

Prentice Hall Press Editor
Amit Shah

Operations
Alain Gayot

Directed by
André Gayot

New York ▪ London ▪ Toronto ▪ Sydney ▪ Tokyo ▪ Singapore

Other Gault Millau Guides Available from Prentice Hall Press

The Best of Chicago
The Best of France
The Best of Hawaii
The Best of Hong Kong
The Best of Italy
The Best of London
The Best of Los Angeles
The Best of New England
The Best of New York
The Best of Paris
The Best of San Francisco
The Best of Washington, D.C.

Published by Prentice Hall Press
A division of Simon & Schuster Inc.
15 Columbus Circle
New York, NY 10023

Please address all comments regarding
The Best of New Orleans to:
Gault Millau, Inc.
P.O. Box 36114
Los Angeles, CA 90036

Please address all advertising queries to:
Mr. Geoffrey Gropp, Vice President
Welsh Publishing Group, Inc.
300 Madison Avenue
New York, NY 10017
(212) 687-0680

Library of Congress Cataloging-in-Publication Data
The Best of New Orleans / editor, Robert C. Fisher ; contributing editors, Millie Ball . . . [et al.].
p. cm.
ISBN 0-13-084153-6: $16.95
1. New Orleans (La.)—Description—Guide-books. I. Fisher, Robert C., 1930- .
F379.N53B47 1990
917.63'350463—dc20 90-32610
CIP

Special thanks to the staff of Prentice Hall Press, Travel Books for their invaluable aid in producing these Gault Millau guides.

Printed in the United States of America

CONTENTS

INTRODUCTION

A FEAST FOR THE SENSES

Passionate, alluring and intoxicating, New Orleans is like the fiery barmaid or rough-hewn mechanic in a dangerous and impossible romance. It is bewitching and seductive, awash in indulgence and ripe with desire. At times it can be stylish and elegant, more often earthy and vital, and on occasion a bit tawdry and cheap.

An affair with New Orleans is neither wholesome nor sensible, neither well considered nor full of good prospects. For some, the bright light of the morning after falls too harshly on New Orleans, revealing the wrinkles beneath the rouge, the dirt beneath the fingernails. But for those who fall in love with the city, the flaws are not so much defects as signs of character—and the willingness to forgive them is a lesson in life.

The infatuation with New Orleans begins with the city's sensual extravagance. In the mornings, the rich, deep aroma of strong, dark coffee wafts from the roasters on Magazine Street or the steaming mugs at Café du Monde, the scent of jasmine and sweet olive seeps over a garden wall and the dank musk of the Mississippi creeps along the riverbank. At midday, a damp sticky blanket of heat and humidity wraps thickly around the skin, seeming to penetrate every pore. In the late afternoons, when rain washes the air clean, the luminous subtropical light slants on a crumbling ocher wall on Burgundy Street, silhouettes the simple grace of the cathedral spires, sifts through the leafy oaks of St. Charles Avenue and shimmers on the placid waters of Lake Pontchartrain. In the dark of night, Bourbon Street jumps to the blare of trumpets and the ruffle of drums, a bar on Frenchmen echoes with the husky rasp of a jazzman's song and a freighter's foghorn cuts through the heavy air. And day and night, uptown and downtown, the air is a feast of fragrances: spicy shrimp rémoulade, pungent and murky gumbo, luscious lemony crabmeat, succulent fried shrimp, cold oysters dashed with pepper sauce, fresh trout swimming in butter, red beans, rice, beignets, bread pudding and coffee, coffee, coffee.

Yet the city's appeal is more than the sum of its readily perceived parts. There is something deeper, something of the spirit and of the soul. It informs the city's distinctive approach to life as a mystery to be enjoyed, not a puzzle to be solved. New Orleanians stop to smell the roses, and they celebrate all of creation with unmatched zest and flair.

From one perspective, New Orleans is undisciplined and unambitious; but from another, it represents genius applied to the art of life. More than iron balconies or shrimp Creole or classic jazz, it is that joy in living—the knowing smile, the including embrace—that steals the heart.

VIVE LA DIFFERENCE!

New Orleans has long been recognized as a unique creature among American cities, and with good reason. To begin with, it has a distinctive pedigree. Other American cities were built by the English and other Northern Europeans or by their descendants, all deeply imbued with the Protestant work ethic. Even the cities of California and the Southwest were sleepy Spanish colonial hamlets before the Americans got there and started striving. But New Orleans was a lively and thriving Franco-Spanish city by the time it joined the United States with the Louisiana Purchase in 1803.

The French had founded New Orleans in 1718, consciously designing it in classical European style as the capital of their great province of Louisiana, which spread across the heart of the continent. They transferred it to the Spanish in 1763 and then got it back in 1801. After the sale of the territory to the fledgling United States two years later, Anglo-Americans flooded the exotic foreign metropolis, but the proud Creoles clung stubbornly to their heritage, coldly snubbing the uncouth newcomers.

The Mediterranean tradition of the early colonists remains pronounced in the city's culture. It is most visible in the annual celebration of Mardi Gras, a Catholic festival of last-minute self-indulgence on the eve of Lent. The imitation royalty of Mardi Gras and the gaudy floats of hollow papier–mâché reflect the Mediterranean taste for flamboyant make-believe, a preference for style over substance that has both enriched the city and hobbled it. It is the Mediterranean heritage that takes much of the blame for the city's well-known tolerance for political corruption—provided it is carried off with style.

The Americans were neither the first nor last immigrants to join the French and Spanish in New Orleans. Before them came African slaves in substantial numbers. New Orleans today retains more elements of African culture, heard in music and seen in parades, than does any other American city. The Franco-Spanish were far less racist than the Anglo-Americans, and until the Civil War, New Orleans was a relative haven for blacks in the South. The "free people of color" in antebellum New Orleans, many of whom sprang from interracial liaisons, practiced the building trades, studied art, music and literature, owned property (including slaves) and developed a cultured society that persists in many ways today.

In the nineteenth century, waves of European immigrants, many of them reinforcing the city's Catholic population, washed over the port city, Germans, Irish and Sicilians chief among them. The pattern was typical of the seaports in the Northeast but atypical in the South. A true Southern drawl is almost impossible to find among native New Orleanians today, a subject elaborated upon in our Citylore chapter.

The immigrations have continued: most recently, large numbers of Vietnamese have made their mark on the community. The great ethnic diversity of the population has immeasurably enlivened the city and added much spice to the cultural stew.

New Orleans long has tolerated—even prized—eccentricity. It may be because of all the mixing and blending. But there's another reason, one that explains much about the city's character: New Orleans is an island.

It is almost literally an island, geographically speaking. Perched a few feet above sea level on the narrow alluvial deposit of the riverbank, it is surrounded by lakes, streams and the trackless, marshy, mosquito-infested wasteland of the Mississippi's vast delta. (Those are the drawbacks of the site; the great overriding advantage is its location 100 miles from the river's mouth, as close as an eighteenth-century city could get without disappearing into the muck.) In fact, until the construction of bridges and causeways for railroads in the late nineteenth century and for roads in the twentieth, the only uninterrupted land route in or out of New Orleans clung to the tortuous path of the riverbank to the west.

Culturally, the city was an island as well. It was urban, Catholic and Franco-Spanish in a South that was rural, Protestant and Anglo-Scots-Irish. It was fun-loving and sybaritic in a hardworking and ambitious nation. Thus the city flourished gloriously aloof, a dazzling beacon of civilization in the wilderness, effortlessly enriched by its command of the great river, smug in its sense of uniqueness and superiority.

Modern technology has changed the face of New Orleans. Pumps have drained the swamps, allowing the population to disperse to the suburbs. Roads, bridges, the telephone and television have reduced the city's geographical and cultural isolation. Engineers even figured out how to build skyscapers in the muck, balancing them atop pilings driven 100 feet or more into the delta ooze. All of this has served to make the city less like the exotic Nouvelle Orléans of old and more like Atlanta or Dallas or Houston. Yet the citizens retain a sense of their difference, a shared identity they treasure and glorify.

A DISCLAIMER

Readers are advised that prices and conditions change over the course of time. The restaurants, hotels, shops and other establishments reviewed in this book have been reviewed over a period of time, and the reviews reflect the personal experiences of the reviewers. The reviewers and publishers cannot be held responsible for the experiences of the reader related to the establishments reviewed. Readers are invited to write the publisher with ideas, comments and suggestions for future editions.

RESTAURANTS

INTRODUCTON

JAZZ ON THE PLATE

New Orleanians still debate whether the city's paramount contribution to American civilization has been its music or its food. After all, the cradle of jazz also was the birthplace of gumbo, jambalaya and a multitude of earthy dishes that together constitute the remarkable, distinctive cuisine we call Creole.

One point on which both sides might agree is that jazz music and Creole cooking are founded on a unique set of principles and sensibilities. Judging the robust cooking of the Creoles against the refinements of modern French haute cuisine would be as absurd as making comparisons between Louis Armstrong and Mozart. For the visitor to New Orleans, the bottom line is this: accept this city's characteristic cuisine on its own terms, and there is considerable pleasure to be gained. Measure it against other, more fashionable, culinary styles and you may sometimes be disappointed. The centuries-old cooking of the South Louisiana Creoles and Cajuns, in its most basic forms, is neither subtle nor restrained. More often than not, dishes are boldly seasoned, deep-flavored and rich.

Food has been one of New Orleans's great obsessions almost from the city's very beginnings, more than two and a half centuries ago, when the local Indians showed the first French settlers what they could do with the aromatic herbs growing in the swampy, fertile soil along the banks of the Mississippi River. To this day, South Louisiana cuisine gives evidence of its earliest influences—French, African, Caribbean and Spanish. A typical bowl of gumbo, the souplike stew that is the quintessential Creole dish, will contain either okra, brought to the colonial city by African cooks, or ground sassafrass, a staple of the early Choctaw tribes inhabiting the area. The liquid will be thickened with a French roux (flour browned in lard or oil), but the roux will be spiced up with onion, garlic, parsley and a few other aromatics. In the gumbo you might also find a Louisiana version of France's robust andouille sausage, and the sweet peppers and tomatoes the Spaniards prized so highly, as well as Caribbean cayenne pepper.

The great European migrations of the mid-nineteenth to early twentieth century—especially from southern Italy—also left their mark. The end product is a hodgepodge of overlaps and crossovers, a melting pot in the literal sense of the term. And the fusing goes on unabated. All kinds of new ideas are entering contemporary New Orleans cooking. The 1980s saw the emergence of a new cadre of restaurant chefs with tenuous ties to the past, ready to break the old rules and, consciously or not, create a lighter, more elegant style.

RANKINGS & REVIEWS

As in all Gault Millau guides, New Orleans's restaurants are rated in the same manner that French students are graded: on a scale of one to twenty, twenty being unattainable perfection. The rankings reflect only the quality of the cooking; the decor, service, wine list and atmosphere are explicitly commented on within each review. Restaurants ranked 13/20 and above are distinguished with toques (chef's hats), according to the following table:

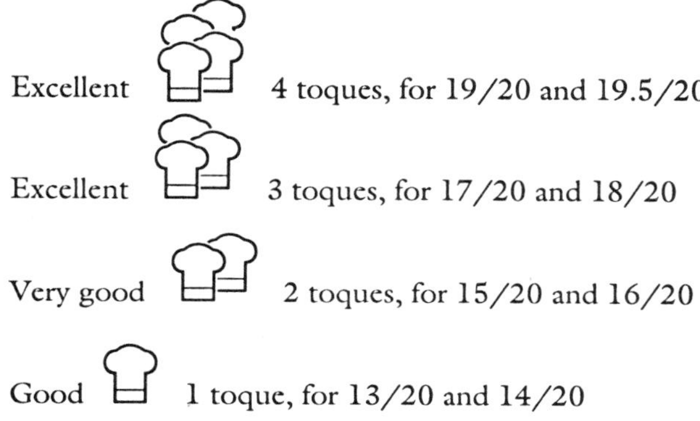

Excellent 4 toques, for 19/20 and 19.5/20
Excellent 3 toques, for 17/20 and 18/20
Very good 2 toques, for 15/20 and 16/20
Good 1 toque, for 13/20 and 14/20

Keep in mind that we are comparing New Orleans's restaurants with the finest in the world—just because the city's best restaurants don't get four toques doesn't mean they aren't exceptionally good. Also, these rankings are relative. One rank of 13/20 (one toque) is not very good for a highly reputed and very expensive restaurant, but it is quite complimentary for a small place without much culinary pretension.

PRICES

Unless otherwise noted, the prices given are for a complete dinner for two, including an appetizer, main course and dessert per person, as well as service and a bottle of wine. It is, naturally, difficult to estimate the cost of wine; for our purposes we've assumed it to be a modest bottle at a modest restaurant and a more expensive wine ($30-$40) at a more serious place. Lovers of the great Burgundies and Bordeaux will find their bills higher than our estimates. At many of the humbler restaurants, we quote the price for a dinner with beer or a nonalcoholic beverage.

SYMBOLS & ABBREVIATIONS

Les Lauriers Du Terroir: Creole and Acadian cooks have given the world a cuisine that, since the early nineteenth century, has endured as the foremost definable regional cooking style in mainland America. This grand tradition, we believe, deserves to be not only respected but also preserved. Gault Millau is therefore awarding certain New Orleans restaurants its laurel wreath, the same ***laurier du terroir*** we have used to recognize those restaurants in France that specialize in the country's diverse regional cooking styles. This marks the first time outside of France that Gault Millau so recognizes a country's regional cuisine. A laurel wreath accompanying the rating of a New Orleans restaurant means that the kitchen either is helping to preserve the traditional Creole-Acadian culinary style or is using traditional Creole and Acadian ingredients in new and creative ways.

André Gayot

Credit cards are abbreviated as follows:

AE: American Express and/or Optima
D: Discover
DC: Diners Club and/or Carte Blanche
MC: MasterCard
V: VISA

A WORD ABOUT FOOD

Categorizing the city's culinary diversity can be an exercise fraught with pitfalls. Menus in most of the better-known eateries cover a vast amount of local culinary territory. Keep in mind that these styles often overlap. Don't be surprised to find a decidedly traditional seafood gumbo being served alongside contemporary, inventive New Orleans–style food. After all, it is this kind of borrowing and blending that gave South Louisiana cooking its charmingly diverse character in the first place. Still, some distinctions can be made, and the brief guide that follows may be of help:

TRADITIONAL CREOLE

This is the earthy style of Creole cooking that fueled generations of New Orleanians at every socioeconomic stratum. Staples are gumbo, often made with combinations of seafoods or with chicken and sausage; red kidney beans cooked down with herbs, seasonings and ham or sausage and served with steamed white rice; jambalaya, which is a paella-like concoction usually containing shrimp, sausage, chicken or any number of other meats and seafoods in varying combinations; and grillades, which translate in New Orleans as escallops of veal cooked down in a roux-based gravy seasoned with tomatoes, onions and peppers. The ultimate Creole dessert: bread pudding.

CLASSIC CREOLE

In general, this food has a more elegant, urbane cast to it. Classic Creole cuisine began to develop in the mid-nineteenth century, when newly arrived French cooks began introducing butter and cream sauces. Fish and meats in these restaurants often arrive today under various improvisations of such rich embellishments as bearnaise, marchand de vin, ravigote, hollandaise and bordelaise. Typical dishes are shrimp rémoulade, a cold appetizer of spicy boiled shrimp in a peppery, oil-based dressing; oysters Rockefeller, baked on the half-shell in a puree of aromatic greens spiked with anisette liqueur; and trout meuniére, lightly floured and sautéed, then served with the browned butter and a bit of lemon. Desserts: crème caramel or crème brûlée.

CONTEMPORARY CREOLE

What began in the 1950s as a movement toward more creativity in New Orleans cooking blossomed during the 1970s and 1980s into a revolution of sorts, as restaurant kitchens grew bolder in their experimentation. Now, the old Creole rules are being broken, or at least bent, in a frenzy of improvisation. In a contemporary Creole restaurant, fried oysters might arrive on a green salad or swathed in Brie or in an herbal butter. Pasta has come to the fore as a natural companion for the region's shellfish and a great medium for richly herbed sauces. Fish is grilled and brushed with seasoned stock reductions rather than sautéed and drenched in cream.

CAJUN

Originally, it was the rough-hewn, country-style cooking of the trappers and fishermen descended from the French Acadians who settled southwestern Louisiana's bayou country in the mideighteenth century. Typical ingredients were pork, rabbit, turtle, game birds and the immense varieties of finfish and shellfish. Stewing in readily available herbs and spices and panfrying were the principal cooking methods. In the 1980s, Cajun cooking became a national hit, although the citified version bore scant resemblance to the real thing. Typical dishes in today's Cajun restaurants are fried shellfish, crawfish étouffée (basically a thick, spicy stew), dirty rice (a rice stuffing made with pork, beef or chicken), cochon de lait (roasted young pig) and pecan pie.

A GLOSSARY OF FISH (AND FRIENDS)

New Orleans owes most of its culinary fame to the thousands of shelled, finned, valved and web-footed creatures that live in the Gulf of Mexico, Lousiana's bays and bayous, and its more than four million acres of lakes, lagoons, rivers and marshes. Both commercial fishing and sportfishing are a vital part of life in Louisiana, and with a year-round average temperature of 67 degrees (F), the fishing "season" never ends. Following are those that are most likely to turn up on your plate:

CRAB - Most commonly the blue crab (or Atlantic crab), which flourishes in the brackish waters on Louisiana's coastline. Best blues measure four to eight inches from point to point (from the left to the right side of the shell).

CRAPPIE - This white perch, fished in local freshwater habitats, was also dubbed by the Creoles *sac-à-lait*, or "bag of milk."

CRAWFISH - Called a crayfish elsewhere, this small, lobsterlike crustacean lives in fresh water, and is prepared by local chefs in a variety of ways. Don't confuse it with its saltwater relative, the spiny lobster.

FROG - Native Creoles called it *ouaouaron,* an onomatopoeic term that approximated croaking. Only aquatic or pond frogs are eaten, and only their hind legs; the smallest are the most tender.

OYSTER - Usually the local Blue Point. New Orleans's most famous contributions here are oysters Bienville and oysters Rockefeller (the latter invented at Antoine's). Contrary to old beliefs, this tasty mollusk can be eaten safely year-round.

POMPANO - Highly prized everywhere for its firm, rich flesh. Described by Mark Twain as "delicious as the less criminal forms of sin."

REDFISH - Served blackened and spiced, this saltwater dweller was the staple item of the Cajun craze of the 1980s. New Orleans still loves it. Also called red drum, channel bass, *poisson rouge.*

SHRIMP - The Gulf and the mouth of the Mississipi River form one of the country's most important shrimping grounds. Can be white, brown, pink or red.

SPECKLED TROUT - Not really a trout at all, but a saltwater-dwelling member of the squeteague-weakfish family (a relative of the redfish). Also called spotted sea trout.

TURTLE - What you'll find in your bowl most likely will be a diamondback terrapin, which dwells in salt marshes, or the enormous loggerhead, a sea dweller. Increasingly rare and protected elsewhere in the country. If you can swallow your guilt, try a local favorite: thick, creamy turtle soup spiked with sherry.

SOME ADVICE & COMMENTS

- **BEWARE OF BRUNCHES**: Many of the better-known restaurants serve what is called a Sunday jazz brunch. It's often a buffet, with accompanying live jazz music, and prices are usually very low. However, don't expect to find the kitchen operating at its best, since quantity, rather than quality, is the draw at these affairs.
- **. . . AND LUNCHES**: In any city, dinner is when a restaurant serves its best food. It's especially true in New Orleans. Lunching in upscale restaurants has seen a considerable decline in recent years, a reflection of problems in the local economy since the early 1980s.
- **AVOID THE HORDES**: Big tourist events in New Orleans—such as the Super Bowl and Sugar Bowl football games, the Mardi Gras season, the annual jazz festival—always result in packed dining rooms at the better-known restaurants. These are generally not the occasions when they perform at their best. The preoccupation is more likely to be getting the hordes seated and fed without major complaints. Savvy locals rarely eat out in expensive restaurants in the heart of the city during major conventions and other such events.
- **MYSTERIOUS MENUS**: Despite the international reputation of the city's restaurants, many of them have not taken the trouble to devise menus that explain the local culinary curiosities. Servers are generally conversant with the menu, so if words like ravigote and rémoulade mean nothing to you, don't hesitate to request a translation.
- **PEAK SEASON**: Generally speaking, the peak restaurant season in New Orleans is October through April. Getting into the most famous places can be difficult. Reservations are often a must, and sometimes they should be made days, or even a couple of weeks, in advance. The best policy is to reserve as soon as you know on which nights you will be dining out.
- **NO-SHOWS ARE A NO-GO**: The city's most popular, high-profile restaurants are beginning to experience an increasing number of no-shows, people who reserve and fail to appear. An apparently common practice for some diners is to book tables at several restaurants on the same night and to choose one at the last minute. The practice, in addition to being uncivilized and inconsiderate, is tempting more and more restaurateurs to overbook, much as some airlines do.
- **TIPPING**: For larger groups of diners, usually eight or more, some New Orleans restaurants add a service charge to the bill. This can range from 12 to 20 percent, but it usually is 15 percent. Very rarely is a service charge added for groups of six or fewer. Common local practice is to tip 15 percent at moderately or low-priced restaurants and 20 percent at the very luxurious places. As in other cities, the amount of the tip is often lessened or raised when service is uncommonly poor or uncommonly good.

TOQUE TALLY

16/20

Bayona
Gautreau's
Henri

15/20

Emerald
Emeril's
Grill Room

14/20

The Bistro at Maison de Ville
Brigtsen's
Commander's Palace
Galatoire's
Hautreaux
La Provence
Versailles

13/20

Andrea's
Bayou Ridge Café
Christian's
Clancy's
Constantin's
La Gauloise Bistro
Lafitte's Landing (*West Bank*)
Mr. B's Bistro
La Riviera
Upperline

12/20

Arnaud's
Brennan's
China Blossom
Crozier's
Drago's
Flagons
La Gauloise
Ichiban
Le Jardin
K-Paul's Louisiana Kitchen
The Little Greek
Louis XVI
La Louisiane
Mr. Tai's
Mosca's
Rib Room
Ruth's Chris Steak House
Sazerac
Seb's
Tandoor
Trey Yuen

11/20

Absolute Bar & Grill
Alex Patout's Louisiana Restaurant
Annadele's
Antoine's
Bangkok Cuisine
Bon Ton Café
Bouligny
Cabin Restaurant (*East Bank*)

Café Sbisa
Casamento's
Chez Pierre
China Blossom
Crozier's
La Cucaracha Café
Dooky Chase's
Doug's
L'Economie
Gambrill's
Ichiban
Kabby's
Kung's Dynasty
Lena's Steak House
LeRuth's
Mandich's
Morton's of Chicago Steak House
Nuvolari's
Patout's
Peking
Sal & Judy's
Shogun
The Steak Knife

10/20

Alberto's
Antoine's
The Beef Room
Caribbean Room
Chehardy's
Chez Hélène
La Crêpe Nanou
Crescent City Steak House
La Cuisine
Delmonico
Drago's
Garces
Genghis Khan
Isadora
Maestro's
El Patio
Santa Fe
Tony Angello's
West End Café
Winston's

9/20

Bart's
Begue's
Impastato's
Jack Dempsey's
Liuzza's
Old N'Awlins Cookery
Pascal's Manale
Ralph & Kacoo's
Tavern on the Park
Taylor's

8/20

Copeland's
Court of Two Sisters
Moran's Riverside
Tujague's

LAURIERS DU TERROIR

Alex Patout's Louisiana Restaurant
Arnaud's
Bon Ton Café
Brennan's
Brigtsen's
Cabin Restaurant (*East Bank*)
Chez Hélène
Christian's
Commander's Palace
Copeland's
Dooky Chase's
Galatoire's
K-Paul's Louisiana Kitchen
Lafitte's Landing (*West Bank*)
Louis XVI
La Louisiane

BY CUISINE

AMERICAN

Absolute Bar & Grill
Bayou Ridge Café
Constantin's
Grill Room
Sazerac
Winston's

CAJUN

Alex Patout's Louisiana Restaurant
Bon Ton Café
Brigtsen's
Cabin Restaurant (*East Bank*)
Copeland's
K-Paul's Louisiana Kitchen
Patout's
Ralph & Kacoo's

CHINESE

China Blossom
Kung's Dynasty
Mister Tai's
Peking
Trey Yuen

CREOLE

Traditional Creole

Alex Patout's Louisiana Restaurant
Bon Ton Café
Cabin Restaurant (*East Bank*)
Chez Hélène
Copeland's
Dooky Chase's
K-Paul's Louisiana Kitchen
Kolb's
Lafitte's Landing (*West Bank*)
Mandich's
Taylor's
Tujague's

Classic Creole

Annadele's
Antoine's
Arnaud's
Brennan's
Caribbean Room
Chehardy's
Chez Pierre
Christian's
Court of Two Sisters
La Cuisine
Delmonico
Galatoire's
LeRuth's
Louis XVI
La Louisiane
Olde N'Awlins Cookery
Sazerac
Tchoupitoulas Plantation

Contemporary Creole

Bayona
Bayou Ridge Café
Bouligny
Brigtsen's
Café Sbisa
Clancy's
Commander's Palace
Doug's
Emeril's
Flagons

Gambrill's
Gautreau's
Isadora
Le Jardin
Kabby's
Mr. B's Bistro
La Provence
Seb's
Upperline

Italian Creole

Moran's Riverside
Mosca's
Nuvolari's
Pascal's Manale
Sal & Judy's
Tony Angello's

CONTINENTAL

Begue's
Rib Room
Versailles

CUBAN

Garces

FRENCH

Caribbean Room
La Crêpe Nanou
Crozier's
L'Economie
La Gauloise Bistro
Henri
Louis XVI
La Provence

GERMAN

Kolb's

GREEK

The Little Greek

INDIAN

Tandoor

INTERNATIONAL

The Bistro at Maison de Ville

ITALIAN

Alberto's
Andrea's
Annadele's
Impastato's
Liuzza's
La Louisiane
Maestro's
La Riviera

JAPANESE

Ichiban
Shogun

KOREAN

Genghis Khan

MEXICAN

Garces
El Patio
Santa Fe

SEAFOOD

Bart's
Casamento's
Drago's
Jack Dempsey's
Ralph & Kacoo's
Tavern on the Park
Taylor's
West End Café

SOUL

Chez Hélène
Dooky Chase's

SOUTHWESTERN

La Cucaracha Café

STEAKHOUSE

The Beef Room
Crescent City Steak House
Lena's Steak House
Morton's of Chicago Steak House
Ruth's Chris Steak House
The Steak Knife
Tavern on the Park

THAI

Bangkok Cuisine

YUGOSLAVIAN

Drago's

RESTAURANTS

Absolute Bar & Grill
5300 Tchoupitoulas St.
(Riverside Marketplace)
• 899-7008
AMERICAN

11/20

Being all things to all eaters is not easy, but the Absolute certainly tries. The hodgepodge ranges from peanut-butter-and-jelly sandwiches to a quarter-pound sirloin strip, and from old-fashioned milk shakes to Napa's latest releases. For a casual shopping-mall restaurant, the kitchen's ambitions—and its success rate—are higher than you might think. Gimmickry is at a blessed minimum. A grove of potted tropicals separates the bar from the sprawling dining rooms, which have the look (and sometimes the sound) of a suburban high school cafeteria—hardwood floors, spare blond furniture and splashy, polychrome posters. French doors under wide fanlights lead to the partly enclosed patio, pleasant in balmy weather. The wonderful potato chips are made on-site from scratch. Buttery sauces on the grilled fish and chicken are well composed. The meat in the appealingly grilled hamburger is of good quality. Components in the overstuffed sandwiches (a typical one includes hot baked ham, melted Cheddar, grilled onion and tomato on whole wheat) are fresh and classy. And desserts, especially the multifaceted chocolate "Corruption," are worthy of much fancier restaurants. Noise levels usually are low at night, but they escalate at lunchtime. Dinner for two shouldn't exceed $45.

Open Mon.-Thurs. 7 a.m.-11 p.m., Fri.-Sat. 7 a.m.-1 a.m., Sun. 9 a.m.-3 p.m. Cards: MC, V.

Alberto's

611 Frenchmen St., Faubourg Marigny • 949-5952
ITALIAN

10/20

No one climbs the single flight of stairs to this quaint and colorful little neighborhood place expecting to be coddled. Neither is one looking for the latest trendy combinations. The staples are pasta, seafoods and chicken. Spanish olive oil, rather than butter, usually lines the sauté pans—a wise move, since enough cream sauce flows from the kitchen each week to coat a flight deck. In one dish, the cream might be zapped with fresh tomato or a few drops of anisette liqueur or a combination of fresh herbs. Under it might be fettuccine tossed with sautéed shrimp, or cannelloni with any of three fillings—shrimp, crawfish tails or a simple ricotta with basil. The fresh fish changes from time to time. A regular is sautéed filet of drum in a lemony sauce with capers. Garlicky steamed mussels ring a plate of fettuccine dampened with a nicely seasoned tomato sauce. Occasionally the monotony is broken with such a dish as medallions of pork tenderloin embellished with artichoke hearts, green peppercorns and shrimp. The time the owner-chef spent in Barcelona is reflected in a color-splashed mural in a severely angular Catalan style. The rest of the decor is serendipitous—tables crafted from ancient sewing machines, a stuffed parrot, devil's ivy and white latticework. Service is rudimentary. But the prices—about $35 for two—can prompt forgiveness.

Open Mon.-Fri. 11 a.m.-1:30 p.m. & 6 p.m.-11 p.m., Sat. 6 p.m.-11 p.m. No cards.

Alex Patout's Louisiana Restaurant

221 Royal St., French Quarter • 525-7788
CAJUN/ TRADITIONAL CREOLE

11/20 

Lots of sins have been committed in the name of Cajun cuisine, and Alex Patout's soul is not without a blemish or two, despite his certified bayou roots. Fortunately, Patout makes a mean roux, the browned-flour paste that much South Louisiana cooking is built on. And some of his food comes as close as any in New Orleans to the deep and lusty flavors of the Southwest Louisiana marshes. Cooked-down vegetables and piped-in country music are not what you might expect to find in this soft-edged dining room, with its faux-marbre friezes, frilly Austrian shades and inch-thick carpeting. The few mossy landscapes and game-bird prints look awkward against the chic apricot of the walls. Concentrate, instead, on the thick white-bean soup, zapped with bits of tasso, an intense, raw-cured Acadian ham. It has the marvelous blend of richness and simplicity that makes for exceptional country fare. But what's advertised as cochon de lait usually is nothing more than dry, chewy chunks of roast pork loin in a bit of drab-tasting gravy. Beware of overkill. It pops up in a filet mignon sliced in half, placed on fried eggplant

and lavished with crawfish tails. A strong cream sauce delivers the fatal blow. Seafood dishes are better. Oysters Alexander, in a peppery, gratinéed cream sauce with a bit of cheese, clicks. So does a mound of spaghettini tossed with crawfish tails, shrimp and scallion-dotted cream. A prix-fixe dinner for two costs about $60, lunch about $35, even with a wine list that's short on bargains.
Open Mon.-Fri. 11 a.m.-2:30 p.m. & 6 p.m.-10 p.m., Sat.-Sun. 6 p.m.-10 p.m. All major cards.

Andrea's

3100 19th St., Metairie • 834-8583
ITALIAN

The vast network of highways and shopping malls in suburban New Orleans is no place for an avant-garde restaurant kitchen. For upscale restaurateurs, survival in this territory means fancying up familiar cuisines like Italian or French with as many continental flourishes as the law allows. Andrea's complies with gusto. The result is capacity crowds in a sprawling cluster of low-ceilinged dining rooms lined with embossed, off-white wall coverings and laden with gilt-framed still lifes and crystal chandeliers. The menu is filled with evidence of Andrea Apuzzo's prior career as a hotel chef—complex sauces, a huge variety of main ingredients, luxurious combinations and so forth. Some of these, such as a sautéed roulade of chicken breast with prosciutto, spinach and cheese in mushroom sauce, come off marvelously. Others, such as beef tenderloin awash in a demi-glaze overloaded with sweet peppers, shrimp and mushrooms and flamed with brandy, don't at all. Apuzzo is at his best with dishes that resonate with the simpler pleasures of Italian cooking and the impeccable freshness of his ingredients. His antipasto misto is full of rustic spirit. A sauté of shrimp in olive oil, white wine, lemon juice and herbs exudes an elegant flavor. The taste of his paglia e fieno in cream with sautéed beef tips is much better than its mere list of ingredients would indicate. Steamed littleneck clams keep delicious company with lemon and green herbs in a briskly flavored light broth, and fork-tender osso bucco in an aromatic gravy is properly served with the accompanying marrow. Since the finer Italian wines are hard to find in New Orleans, the list at Andrea's is a standout, with eight Brunellos alone and a representative range from Chianti, Orvieto and other principal regions. The minimal table spacing is fine if you're in a gregarious mood. Dinner for two, with a moderately priced wine, should end up at $70 to $80.
Open Sun.-Fri. 11 a.m.-10:30 p.m., Sat. 3 p.m.-10:30 p.m. All major cards.

Annadele's

Off U.S. Hwy. 190, Covington
• 893-4895
CLASSIC CREOLE/ITALIAN

11/20

For seekers of restaurants that exude the fabled charms of the Old South, pickings are slim in and around New Orleans. Annadele's, situated on a leafy bank of the Bogue Falaya River across Lake Pontchartrain, delivers about as much antebellum atmosphere as you'll find anywhere that you sit down to eat. So, what if the columned, Greek Revival cottage dates from the 1920s, and the clapboards and shutters could have used some fresh paint the last time we stopped by? Still, the frilly, ground-floor dining rooms are done up meticulously, with considerable Victorian style, and the bosky views from the glassy Garden Room at the rear can be as soothing as Grandma's liniment. The kitchen does best with fish and lamb. A steamed filet of red snapper en papillotte is infused with the fresh flavors of the lemon, herbs and vegetables inside the little paper tent. Lamb chops are competently grilled, although a seasoning of mint and other herbs blazes no trails. Salmon steak is gently grilled before joining garlic pods braised in olive oil and a light veal stock. Panéed rabbit tenderloin and a dessert of banana fritters are among the few dishes with a solid Southern lineage, and they taste quite good. Finally, don't look for hoopskirts or boots and breeches on the congenial service staff. Annadele's, as you may have guessed, is not a theme restaurant. Dinner for two should be about $65.

Open Tues.-Fri. 11:30 a.m.-2:30 p.m. & 5:30 p.m.-10 p.m., Sat. 5:30 p.m.-10 p.m., Sun. 11 a.m.-3 p.m.

Antoine's

713 St. Louis St., French Quarter
• 581-4422
CLASSIC CREOLE

11/20

As a kind of gastronomic museum, Antoine's preserves more than 100 years of classic New Orleans cooking in a fascinating maze of ancient rooms and alcoves festooned with all kinds of memorabilia. For much of the city's iron-lace aristocracy, it's a temple, where rites of passage are often celebrated in the private rooms. As a restaurant, Antoine's is a prisoner of its own mystique, ferociously guarding traditions that other French Quarter restaurants abandoned decades ago. The showpiece dessert, a rather dry baked Alaska, is dispatched from the kitchen with *1840* (the year of the restaurant's founding) emblazoned on the dome of meringue. Every time a customer asks for baked oysters Rockefeller (created here in 1889, and still definitive), the order is entered in a registry; the tally is now well into the millions. Waiters are trained to commit the most complex orders to memory rather than write them down. They will usually recommend pompano en papillotte, a parchment bag holding a gray and mushy mix of fish in an undistinguished sauce. Local aficionados find

relatively safe haven in the shrimp rémoulade, crawfish cardinale and shrimp bisque. A buttery filet of broiled trout, brushed with lemon and garnished with sautéed lumps of backfin crab, can be delicious or humdrum, depending on how many curiosity seekers the tour buses have just dropped off. Siberia in this immense restaurant is the front dining room, which happens to be the brightest and handsomest, with its cream walls, sparkling old chandeliers and huge, ornately carved captain's desk. The well-tended wine cellar is among the country's largest, holding more than 30,000 bottles. Chances are about even that they'll be properly handled by the waiter. The service rarely approaches the finesse called for at these prices—usually $100 for two, with a modest wine.
Open Mon.-Sat. noon-2 p.m. & 5:30 p.m.-9:30 p.m. All major cards.

Arnaud's

813 Bienville St., French Quarter • 523-5433
CLASSIC CREOLE

12/20

During the 1930s and 1940s, this was one of New Orleans's leading restaurants. After 30 years of decline en route to Worst Restaurant in Town, the gigantic premises were bought by hotelier Archie Casbarian. He set upon a course of restoration—both architectural and culinary—that continues to this day. Arnaud's dining rooms now sparkle with their trademark floor tiles and beveled glass windows. While the menu is far too extensive for everything to be consistently good, the restaurant's specialties can be assembled into memorable meals. (Fortunately, the waiters are almost shockingly frank in their opinions about what's a specialty and what's not.)

Start with the shrimp Arnaud, an unsurpassed version of New Orleans–style rémoulade; the sauce is ruddy, mustardy and rich with oil. The several baked oyster dishes are fine across the board, particularly the bell-pepper-and-bacon oysters Suzette. Soup is a strong course; the turtle soup, shrimp bisque and oysters stewed in cream are all superb versions of those Creole classics. The famous seafood here is trout meunière.

Birds are a good bet, particularly the Cornish game hen with a smoky veal stuffing. The very popular veal Wohl, topped with crabmeat and crawfish sauces, is interestingly rich. They put out a very fine steak au poivre. The desserts are good, especially the dense, cinnamony bread pudding, bananas Foster (the only flaming dessert worth the trouble), and crème brûlée. The wine list is too expensive, but is otherwise one of the city's best. Lunch here is a bargain, and draws a strong audience of local businessmen. Dinner for two can total around $100.

Open Mon.-Thurs. 11:30 a.m.-2:30 p.m. & 6 p.m.-10 p.m., Fri. 11:30 a.m.-2:30 p.m. & 6 p.m.-10:30 p.m., Sat. 6 p.m.-10:30 p.m., Sun. 10 a.m.-2:30 p.m. (jazz brunch) & 6 p.m.-10 p.m. All major cards.

Bangkok Cuisine

4137 S. Carrollton Ave., Uptown
• 482-3606
THAI

11/20

The exuberance of Thai cooking comes through nicely in this bright and pleasant restaurant tucked into a small shopping center. Pale wall coverings, colorful posters and a few sprays of silk flowers mollify the effect of a window shortage in the deep dining room, usually filled with college professors, young professionals and other familiar types sniffing around for exotic fodder. What they find is often fresh and attractive, with a pepper content that can be raised or lowered to taste. A soothing chicken soup carries bits of white meat in broth laced with coconut milk and zapped with crunchy bits of scallion. Cold, springy rice-flour crêpes are filled with mild pork sausage, chicken breast, egg and crisp vegetables, then brushed with a vaguely peppery plum sauce. Fanciers of soft-shell crab should head straight for the Bangkok's big ones, fried in an eggy batter and nested in crunchy, stir-fried broccoli, snow peas and other vegetables. Filets of fried fish, greaseless and crisp, join straw mushrooms and bits of pork in a bracing sauce of ginger and pepper. Panfried shrimp and chicken are tossed with cellophane noodles in a bracingly spicy sauce. A *yum* salad lives up to its name, delivering a sea taste with no seafood, only noodles blended with a lemony, oniony dressing and a mild shot of chile. The service staff matches congeniality with organization. Prices—$30 for two, with a couple of bottles of Thai beer—are easy to swallow.

Open Mon.-Thurs. 11 a.m.-3 p.m. & 5 p.m.-10 p.m., Fri.-Sat. 11 a.m.-3 p.m. & 5 p.m.-11 p.m., Sun. 5 p.m.-10 p.m. Cards: AE, MC, V.

Bart's

8000 Lakeshore Dr., Lakefront
• 282-0271
SEAFOOD

9/20

Overlooking a tongue of Lake Pontchartrain and serving yachts from its dock, this large, modern, casual restaurant prepares a menu composed mainly of seafood, with a spotty record of consistency. The best shots here are the soups, particularly the rich, robust crawfish bisque; the grilled fish, crusty and interestingly seasoned; and the shrimp Clemenceau, garlicky and firm. Stuffed and sauced fare is much less promising, and the fried seafood is just average.

A large part of the premises—the part with the better view—is given over to a rather loud, youth-thronged lounge. Dinner for two, with wines by the glass, should come in for about $45.

Open Sun.-Thurs. 11:30 a.m.-10 p.m., Fri.-Sat. 11:30 a.m.-11:30 p.m. Cards: AE, MC, V.

Bayona

430 Dauphine St., French Quarter • 525-4455

CONTEMPORARY CREOLE

Very few New Orleans restaurant chefs have inspired the kind of loyalty enjoyed by Susan Spicer. She first gained attention from the city's serious eaters in 1983 at Savoir-Faire, a small Uptown bistro. Her menu was hardly a trailblazer, but at that time even a garlic-cream soup, seared beef rib-eye slathered with a sauce of aromatic vegetables, and sautéed fish in clever sauces added up to a breath of fresh air in the local sea of gumbo and hollandaise. Spicer's subsequent sojourns in France and California and elsewhere on the West Coast broadened her perspectives and sharpened her intuitive talents. The first evidence came in 1986, when she opened the Maison de Ville hotel's sleek and sassy Bistro in the French Quarter: it was a runaway success. In early 1990, Spicer struck out on her own with Bayona, fashioned from an ancient Creole cottage on a quiet Quarter street (called, during the Spanish colonial period, Calle de Bayona), far from the hubbub and glitz of the riverfront. She has lost little time in spreading her wings. Scattered around Bayona's menu are a good many Spicer classics—velvety potato gnocchi and wild mushrooms glorying in cheese-sharpened cream; peppery Acadian-style boudin sweetened with apples and onions; a beautifully executed sweetbreads grenobloise; and her tour de force, succulent, thumb-sized slices of duckling breast in an invigorating pepper-jelly glaze.

But there are newer options, too. Among them are a bracing sauté of crawfish tails, pan-roasted salmon with choucroute and Gewürtztraminer sauce, smoked fish with wasabi-marinated cucumbers, and a whole new collection of desserts, including a superb baked chocolate meringue. A flat-tasting paella-risotto (shellfish, chicken and sausage in saffron rice with cream) may suffer by comparison, but the Spicer repertory remains as diverting and brilliant as ever. And the setting for it is a handsome blend of the contemporary and the time-honored. Large photos of murky, almost surreal, Louisiana scenes line the wide main

BRACING BREW

No one can say the old Creoles didn't appreciate a decent cup o' java. To them, the perfect brew had to be *Noir comme le diable, fort comme la mort, doux comme l'amour et chaud comme l'enfer.* It simply wasn't coffee unless it was "black as the devil, strong as death, sweet as love and hot as hell."

dining room, brightened with two oversize urns holding bursts of fresh flowers. In a smaller, almost square room, verdant landscapes are framed by trompe l'oeil terracotta walls. The glass walls of the rear loggia, now a plush bar and lounge, offer views of the very pleasant brick-and-slate courtyard, where pleasant weather might allow an al fresco cocktail. Whites are the strength of the rather short but wide-ranging wine list, expertly put together by manager Michael Fisher, whose previous post was sommelier at the Windsor Court Hotel. Dinner for two, with a modest bottle—such as the Josmeyer 1987 Gewürtztraminer (about $17)—can be had for $75.
Open Mon.-Thurs. 11:30 a.m.-2:30 p.m. & 6 p.m.-10 p.m., Fri. 11:30 a.m.-2:30 p.m. & 6 p.m.-11 p.m., Sat. 6 p.m.-11 p.m. Cards: AE, MC, V.

Bayou Ridge Café

5080 Pontchartrain Blvd. (enter from Metairie Rd.), Mid-City
• 486-0788
AMERICAN/ CONTEMPORARY CREOLE

Some of the boldest experimentation in New Orleans goes on in this sleekly contemporary restaurant on the edge of town. Its seasonally changing menu draws on any number of styles. A no-reservations policy causes a nightly wrangle for tables by the hip loyalists, wrapped in the latest from Saks' racks, and standing hip to haunch in the tiny bar as the nearby wood-fired stove spits out designer pizzas. The chic extends to the food, a coming-together of New York Italian, Creole, Californian and whatever else has recently struck the kitchen's fancy. One of the rages at this writing is tiny cubes of venison, nestled inside a polenta cup, with a minimally sweetened gravy cascading into loganberries underneath. The chef's sense of humor and talent shine in a muffuletta pizza, topped with the ham, green-olive salad, provolone and salami found in the traditional sandwich of New Orleans's Sicilians. Louisiana meets Italy again in oysters saltimbocca, the oysters delicately fried in a thin batter, then placed on penne in a Creole meunière sauce (brown butter and lemon) and flecked with prosciutto and sage. But the originality rarely degenerates into wackiness. Roasted chicken with garlic and thyme glows with expert cooking. Grilled rabbit with mushrooms is another essay in earthy deliciousness. And the crackly crème brûlée is impeccable in its silky texture and flavor. If the vegetables blaze no trails, they at least are done with flair. Cubes or crescents of potato are excellently sautéed, and the butter sauce on julienned squash or carrot is zapped with a bit of onion and pepper. All of these are delivered by energetic servers, blessed with a detailed knowledge of ingredients and their cooking.

The wine list is comparatively brief—about twenty labels, mostly Californian and French. But the selection is both knowledgeable and accessible, with most bottles in the $15 to $25 range. The cost of one of those wines and three courses for two should not add up to more than $70, more than reasonable for the menu's marvelous balance of creativity and logic.
Open Mon.-Thurs. 11:30 a.m.-3 p.m. & 6 p.m.-10 p.m., Fri.-Sat. 11:30 a.m.-3 p.m. & 6 p.m.-11 p.m., Sun. 11:30 a.m.-4 p.m. All major cards.

The Beef Room

2750 N. Causeway Blvd., Metairie
• 837-0431
STEAKHOUSE

10/20

From the white iron lace at the entry to the black upholstery on the functional chairs, the Beef Room reeks of 1950s nostalgia. Ceilings don't come much lower than the one here. The color scheme is basic black, maroon and white, with dark wood accents; the dim lighting was designed with makeup in mind. The food is similarly retro, a tribute to the durability of meat and potatoes, supplemented with a sprinkling of familiar seafood dishes. It's what has kept the Beef Room alive for two decades, although you're not likely to see a packed house even on a Saturday night. If the filet mignon is saltier than it should be, it might also have enough flavor of its own to do without the butter sauce that comes with every steak. As it happens, the better cuts usually are the porterhouse, brought out in varying sizes for varying appetites, and the well-marbled sirloin strip. The cook and the waiters seem to be enough in sync to produce a medium-rare piece of beef when medium-rare is requested. Potato dishes are competently done, too. Lyonnaise potatoes are tender and oniony, and the mashed ones are real, a happy surprise in any restaurant these days. Don't look for much more than that. Since the clientele is almost exclusively local, expect to pay about $75 for two, with wine.
Open daily 4 p.m.-midnight. All major cards.

Begue's

Royal Sonesta Hotel, 300 Bourbon St.
• 586-0300
CONTINENTAL

9/20

New Orleans's most celebrated chef wasn't French, Cajun, Spanish or black. She was Elizabeth Kettenring Begue (pronounced beh-GAY), a German immigrant whose instinctive way with a stove eventually made Begue's in the French Quarter the sine qua non of Creole cookery in the late nineteenth and early twentieth centuries. Since then, a succession of local restaurants have traded on her name, the latest being the prestige dining room in the Royal Sonesta Hotel on Bourbon Street. The latter-day Begue's, despite the presence of a rémoulade and a gumbo on its flashy menu, is no paragon of Creole gastronomy. The kitchen dispatches a hodgepodge of hotel-quality food, mostly in the continental mode, and occasionally tosses a dash of cayenne or a pod of okra into the pot to convince the easily swayed that what they're eating can't be found in Boise or Buffalo. It's all served in rooms luxuriously swathed in blond wood veneer, frilly floral fabric and occasional frosted-glass partitions etched with another floral motif. A bank of French doors opens onto a large, leafy courtyard. In stark contrast is the interior collection of contemporary oils, most of them gloomy depictions of stairwells. The unkindest cut of all is the check, which, in a wink, can mount to $80 or more for two.

Open daily noon-3 p.m. & 6 p.m.-11 p.m. All major cards.

The Bistro at Maison de Ville

733 Toulouse St., French Quarter • 528-9206

International

Homesick Manhattanites should find a quick cure in this stylish little restaurant, squeezed into a narrow, old French Quarter townhouse. A phalanx of postage-stamp tables, spaced inches apart, runs along a lengthy bank of tufted leatherette. Paintings on the opposite, mirrored wall—just a few yards away —offer a clever pastiche of French Impressionism. Getting into one of the 40 seats usually means a forced introduction to at least two neighbors. The food is the last word in fusion cooking. What put the Bistro firmly on the map when it opened in late 1987 was the brilliant cooking of Susan Spicer, a young chef who had returned to New Orleans after on-the-job training in Provence, Paris, California and Houston. The end product was a highly personal cuisine, blending Louisiana and country-French earthiness with modern American sophistication. In early 1990, Spicer left the restaurant—actually part of the small, upscale hotel next door—to put together her own. In the care of sous-chef Margaret Marion, she left a collection of signature dishes that remain on the lunch and dinner menus, while Marion builds a collection of her own. Fans of Spicer's grilled duck breast in pepper-jelly glaze will find it intact, along with her salad of fried oysters and spinach in rosemary vinaigrette and her grilled shrimp in coriander sauce with black-bean cake and crème fraîche. Those with no ties to the past can revel in Marion's chicken breast, marinated in Indian spices and brushed with a raitalike cucumber and yogurt sauce. Shades of the American Southwest also crop up in such refreshing creations as a quesadilla topped with a julienne of smoked venison, sweet pepper, onion and pepper jack cheese, escorted by an ancho-chile mayonnaise. Another impressive newcomer is a brace of cornmeal pancakes injected with shrimp and scallops and garnished with cole slaw in a piquant rémoulade sauce. The food's composition and color show up especially well on one of the four tables in the diminutive courtyard out back, shaded in daytime by market umbrellas and banana fronds. The choice of wines is limited but informed, and there is always an especially interesting label or two among the several glass wines. Table service doesn't always match the food's polish. The cost of all this continues to be a decidedly moderate $70 or so for two.

Open Mon.-Thurs. 11:30 a.m.-2:30 p.m. & 6 p.m.-10 p.m., Fri.-Sat. 11:30 a.m.-2:30 p.m. & 6 p.m.-11 p.m., Sun. 6 p.m.-9:30 p.m. All major cards.

Bon Ton Café

401 Magazine St., Central Business District • 524-3386

CAJUN/TRADITIONAL CREOLE

11/20 

Blackened redfish wasn't even a twinkle in Paul Prudhomme's eye when Al and Alzina Pierce quietly opened the Bon Ton in 1953, hoping to lure workers at lunchtime from the nearby office buildings in New Orleans's Central Business District. The bait was Cajun-style crawfish étouffée and bisque, country gumbos, chicken stew and other lusty bayou fare. Until then, New Orleanians looked on most Acadian cooking as too rough-hewn for restaurant dining rooms. The Pierces's tenacity paid off, and their initially modest bill of fare has mushroomed into today's extensive Creole-Acadian menu, produced by their nephew and successor, Wayne Pierce. The subtleties that separate Louisiana's two sister cuisines often show up in the laid-back, meticulously maintained dining room. Here, a rémoulade sauce depends more on vinegar than pepper for its bite. The Bon Ton's rustic oyster omelet won't be found in any of the city's classic Creole restaurants. Gumbos carry the soft herbs of gentle country cooking. The crawfish jambalaya is seasoned with more garlic and green onion than a Creole cook might use. And the bisques and étouffées get their density and thickness from an Acadian reliance on flour, rather than the butter or cream of the Creoles. Still,

butter is by no means disdained in the kitchen. Broiled fish and shrimp usually show up awash in it. And that's the way the Bon Ton's midday lunchers, seersuckered and sipping on martinis at the open bar, like it. The veteran servers, amiable and fleet-footed, know each of them by name. Dinner for two, with a wine from the serviceable list, will run about $70.
Open Mon.-Fri. 11 a.m.-2 p.m. & 5 p.m.-9:30 p.m. Cards: AE, MC, V.

Bouligny

4100 Magazine St., Uptown
• 891-4444
CONTEMPORARY CREOLE

11/20

Bouligny, unveiled in 1982, was the forerunner of a New Orleans restaurant category that might be called Uptown Contemporary. The species is roughly defined by bentwood chairs, white linens, contemporary art hung on pastel walls and a menu that pays equal homage to the past (gumbo and rémoulade), present (pasta and radicchio) and future (any combination that flies). The restaurant's name comes from its location in the erstwhile Faubourg Bouligny, a neighborhood that evolved from a riverfront plantation. Its other connection to the past is the lofty, nineteenth-century firehouse that now forms the main dining room. The rest is pointedly up to date. Out front, glass walls feed sunlight to a little alley of weeping fig trees separating a dining area from the bar. Farther back, in the large main room, Expressionist splashes of color radiate from the wall art, reflected in mirror panels embedded in what once were tall, arched doorways. The kitchen hopscotches in numerous directions, with a few stops in Creole country. The starter might be a little clump of feta nestled in a thin ruffle of fried eggplant, garnished with sun-dried tomato and lemon juice—clever and delicious. Or it might be gyoza, tiny purses of Japanese noodle dough stuffed with delicately flavored bits of veal and Asian vegetables. Then again, it might be a creditable Creole turtle soup, spicy and lemony, or a Caesar salad enlivened with plump, fried oysters. Sometimes, excess rears its head, as in grilled chicken wings in a gummy glaze of hickory and honey or in a tomato soup struggling under too much tarragon. But simply grilled lamb chops or fork-tender filet mignon, brushed with a rich demiglaze and garlic butter, can stir the blood again. Moderation, in size and price, is the strength of the wine list, which usually includes interesting German and Italian vintages. The locals who haunt the place keep the menu

prices at a sane level, so two all-inclusive dinners will cost about $60, including wine.
Open Mon.-Thurs. 11:30 a.m.-2:30 p.m. & 5:30 p.m.-10 p.m., Fri.-Sat. 11:30 a.m.-2:30 p.m. & 5:30 p.m.-11 p.m., Sun. 11:30 a.m.-3 p.m. & 5:30 p.m.-10 p.m. All major cards.

Brennan's

417 Royal St., French Quarter • 525-9713
CLASSIC CREOLE

12/20

The famous meal here is breakfast—but it's not what you're thinking. Breakfast at Brennan's is as involved and expensive as dinner would be anywhere else in town; block out the whole morning or midday to do it properly. Start with the great soups (turtle, onion or oyster) or a single-yolk version of one of the many elaborate egg dishes. The best of those is eggs Sardou, with a fresh artichoke bottom, spinach and a good hollandaise. Some of the egg dishes—particularly those with a large flank of fish as an understratum—make satisfying entrées.

At dinner, the main draw at Brennan's is the wine list, easily the best in town, with old, well-stored Bordeaux and Burgundies at prices startling for their moderation. Current French vintages and California wines are also extremely well represented. The dinner menu is a somewhat unadventuresome Creole catalog, but well-rendered. The baked oysters Rockefeller or casino and the buster crabs (baby-soft shells) with pecans start things off very convincingly. The best entrées are beef, particularly the strip sirloin Stanley, with its red-wine-and-mushroom sauce, creamy horseradish sauce, and sautéed banana. Brennan's also prepares a very fine steak au poivre tableside. Veal Kottwitz (with artichokes and mushrooms) and trout Nancy (with lump crabmeat and capers) are the best of the lighter entrées. The restaurant invented a great dessert, bananas Foster: cinnamon, brown sugar, brandy, flames and ice cream. Brennan's prices, at this writing, are among the highest in town, a fact mitigated somewhat by the absurdly large size of the portions. The premises are romantic and distinctly New Orleans; the large central courtyard is a window away from most tables. Dinner for two is about $150, with wine.
Open daily 8 a.m.-2:30 p.m. & 6 p.m.-10 p.m. All major cards.

CHAMPAGNE
CLICQUOT
WERLE
Veuve Clicquot Ponsardin
MAISON FONDEE EN 1772
REIMS
FRANCE

BRUT
CLICQUOT
WERLE
Veuve Clicquot Ponsardin
REIMS
BRUT

Brigtsen's

723 Dante St.,
Uptown
• 861-7610
CAJUN/CONTEMPORARY CREOLE

Now that the blackening brouhaha and jalapeño hype have run their course, it may be time to discover the true virtues of South Louisiana cooking in all of its awesome variety and inventiveness. In New Orleans, there is no better place to start than in this small, unassumingly decorated frame cottage, hard by the Mississippi River in the sleepy old Carrollton section. The restaurant's progenitor is K-Paul's Louisiana Kitchen, where Frank Brigtsen spent almost eight years, progressing from kitchen helper to chef Paul Prudhomme's star disciple. Initially, the unceremonious opening of Brigtsen's in early 1986 caused little stir among locals. They assumed it was a copy of K-Paul's, where long lines, high prices, community seating and bare-bones service are the rule. Eventually, reality sank in: Brigtsen's was not a K-Paul's wanna-be, but a real restaurant, with tablecloths, a creditable wine list, tables for two and a reservations desk. The chairs were rudimentary enough to discourage lingering, but the moderate prices were a soothing balm. The seasonal menu not only was gimmick-free but contained some of the best Creole-Acadian food anywhere, with the Louisiana hallmark of rich, deep flavors, seasoned with balance and restraint. Today, a seat at one of the twenty or so tables means reserving at least a week—often two weeks—in advance, unless 5:30 p.m. or 10 p.m. is your preferred dinner time. The food is worth the wait. Frank Brigtsen's oysters Rockefeller soup is a marvel—plump, lightly poached Louisiana oysters in a blend of cream, oyster juice, puréed spinach, green seasonings and a whisper of Herbsaint, the Creoles' anisette. Beautifully boned duck meat arrives glowing with flavor and a magnificent, orange-tinged gravy under a crisp sheet of feather-light skin. Alongside it are a purée of fresh sweet potatoes and a mound of "dirty rice," heartily seasoned with chopped meat, herbs and spices. Tiny whole rabbit livers, dusted with sesame flour and sautéed, come glistening in their port sauce, escorted by little spheres of caramelized onion. Buttery, panfried sheepshead bass, subtle in taste and golden in color, is embellished with shellfish and a lemony Creole meunière sauce. What the menu calls blackened tuna is a beautifully textured filet—just pink at the center—carrying a deep, golden-brown crust. The sauce below is of smoked fresh corn, steeped

We're always interested to hear about your discoveries, and to receive your comments on ours. Please feel free to write to us, and do state clearly exactly what you liked or disliked.

with onion and sage in seafood stock and a touch of cream. The kitchen's stellar ice creams include a silky banana-pecan that shames many a fussier dessert. The homey atmosphere in the too-small dining room comes from flowery, tied-back drapery, small bouquets on simple mantels and comforting still lifes and landscapes, some of them painted by the chef himself, dating from his art-student days. Dinner for two, with one of the sensibly priced California or French wines, shouldn't be more than about $75.

Open Tues.-Sat. 5:30 p.m.-10 p.m. Cards: AE, MC, V.

Café Sbisa

1011 Decatur St.,
French Quarter
• 561-8354
CONTEMPORARY CREOLE

11/20

A few years ago, table-hopping at this smartly turned out, contemporary bistro was the favorite sport of the French Quarter art-gallery crowd, Uptown trendies and assorted hangers-on. Many have moved on to livelier territory, leaving the glittery dining room and wraparound mezzanine to a few local diehards and a melting pot of upscale out-of-towners. The lofty mural behind the bar, peopled by a cluster of bons vivants, was a reflection of the activity below almost every night. These days, the real-life celebrants are likely to be fewer and also out-of-towners. Still, the fried shrimp—really big, fresh ones—are unbeatable. The broiled oysters and bacon en brochette continue to work their magic, and the kitchen may manage a really inspired bouillabaisse or grilled salmon. It all depends on who's shaking the skillets on a given night. Café Sbisa has had a succession of chefs in its decade of existence, although the regular menu's main-course focus remains seafood—broiled, fried, sautéed or grilled—brought out with bowls of steamed new potatoes. Ingredients are generally fresh and competently done. Specials usually revolve around clever sauces, and desserts range from a warm and homey pecan pie to such curiosities as watermelon ice. The crowd may have changed, but the prices remain rather steep, with $80 not an unusual outlay to assuage two appetites. The prix-fixe lunches and weekend brunches, mostly regional dishes put together with imagination, are much more reasonable.

Open Mon.-Thurs. noon-3 p.m. & 6 p.m.-11 p.m., Fri.-Sat. noon-3 p.m. & 6 p.m.-midnight, Sun. 11 a.m.-3 p.m. & 6 p.m.-11 p.m. All major cards.

Caribbean Room

Pontchartrain Hotel, 2031 St. Charles Ave., Uptown • 524-0581
CLASSIC CREOLE/FRENCH

10/20

The glory years of the Pontchartrain Hotel's Caribbean Room were roughly 1950 to 1970, when its mile-high ice-cream pie and poached trout topped with gratinéed hollandaise and white grapes were the *dernier cri*. Twenty years, a revolution in American cooking and several major changes in the hotel's management have left their marks. The kitchen is still trying to play catch-up. A Creole/Provençal menu was initiated a few years ago, only to be scrapped after Uptown matrons and Downtown bankers kept demanding shrimp rémoulade and turtle soup. What replaced the aïoli and herbs is a pastiche. The dinner menu retains such old favorites as crabmeat Remick (backfin lumps baked en coquille in a spicy sauce), white veal in Madeira and broiled filet of pompano Pontchartrain, topped with a baby soft-shell crab. It also produces one or two of the Provence-inspired dishes of yore. Loyalists, mostly moneyed denizens of the Uptown neighborhood, still show up regularly. Comfortable elegance, circa 1965, pervades the soft and lofty dining spaces, separated by architectural suggestion and encased in boiserie and understated murals depicting fanciful tropical landscapes. The upholstery on the luxurious fauteuils is as caressing as any in town, so don't look for bargains. And don't blanch if dinner for two, with a good wine, comes to $100 or more.

Open Mon.-Fri. 11:30 a.m.-2 p.m. & 6 p.m.-10:30 p.m., Sat.-Sun. 6 p.m.-10:30 p.m. All major cards.

Casamento's

4330 Magazine St., Uptown • 895-9761
SEAFOOD

11/20

Enter this small, laid-back seafood house and discover what it might be like to dine in an operating room. A dental hygienist couldn't do a better job on the acre of gleaming white wall tiles. Every tiny ceramic octagon in the geometric floor looks as it probably did when it was laid in 1919, the year Joseph Casamento opened his no-frills restaurant and scraped the first oyster from its shell. More than seven decades later, it remains the favorite of Uptowners on the prowl for fat, salty oysters. They're served up either raw on the shell, delicately fried in a superfine corn flour, or lightly poached in buttery scalded milk, zapped with chopped scallion and parsley. These are the big draw, and justifiably so. But there are also dew-fresh shrimp, soft-shell crab and trout, all excellently fried and delivered with french fries or between toasted, buttered pan bread. The rest of the menu is downright primeval—soft spaghetti drenched in a purplish tomato sauce with either meatballs or tender slices of beef, ham and cheese sandwiches and a couple of

omelets. Dessert is a cheesecake shipped in from Chicago. The clothless tables in the oyster bar up front and the small dining room out back are serviced with a casualness that will appall the finicky. Others will shrug and take another swallow from the long-neck of ice-cold beer. A filling meal for two can be had for $45.
Open Tues.-Sun. 11:30 a.m.-2:30 p.m. & 5:30 p.m.-9 p.m. Closed early June-late Aug. No cards.

Chehardy's

3528 18th St., Metairie • 455-2433
CLASSIC CREOLE

10/20

Chehardy's defines a style of cuisine you could call Suburban Creole. The indicator dish is veal, steak or fish covered in a sauce thick with crabmeat, crawfish or shrimp—or all three—on top. The style is extremely popular in Metairie, New Orleans's most well-heeled suburb. And, as Chehardy's demonstrates, it doesn't have to be atrocious. The focus of Chehardy's cooking is its mesquite-fired grill, which somehow avoids the bitter flavors usually associated with that wood and generates instead a pleasant, subtle smokiness. This appears to great effect in thick prime steaks, large (two and a half pounds and up) Maine lobsters, and ample flanks of fish (the best species for the method are wahoo, grouper, amberjack and mahimahi). Much less good, but still decent, are the sautéed fish and veal dishes; the first-class sautéed trout with pecans is an exception. You don't need much in the way of starters or dessert here; the entrées tend to the very large side. Service is friendly. Each table is supplied with a live telephone. Many customers eat in the bar. Dinner for two, with wine, is about $75.
Open Mon.-Fri. 11 a.m.-3:30 p.m.; Mon.-Sat. 5 p.m.-11 p.m. All major cards.

Chez Hélène

1540 N. Robertson St., Bywater • 947-1206

De la Poste Motor Hotel, 316 Chartres St., French Quarter • 581-1200
TRADITIONAL CREOLE/SOUL

10/20

Whatever honesty remains in Creole cookery is largely due to the legions of black cooks who, over two centuries, preserved its grass-roots goodness by continually transforming proletarian ingredients into noble dishes. Chez Hélène, plain but proud, and almost hidden in a blue-collar neighborhood, makes the point nicely with food that fueled generations of New Orleans Creoles—black, white and everyone else. Chef Austin Leslie's piquant jambalaya—ham, sausage and shrimp steeped with onion, garlic and parsley in shrimp stock and rice—is a good example of the genre. The peppery broth of his steamy, reddish gumbo holds a bounty of flavors from pork sausage, shrimp, ham and chicken. And the creamy red beans and rice, stuffed bell pepper and mustardy potato salad carry

an authentic Creole birth certificate. Yet much of the menu—especially the fine fried chicken, cornbread muffins and collard greens—would be familiar to any dyed-in-the-wool Southerner. So would the atmosphere in the original restaurant, a cozy, low-ceilinged affair lined in wood paneling and furnished as a dining room in a simple home might be. A branch of the restaurant inside a French Quarter hotel is more upscale in its looks, and serves breakfast, but the lunch and dinner menus don't differ significantly from the those at the mother house. In either place, dinner for two can be had for about $50.
Bywater branch: open Mon.-Thurs. 7 a.m.-10 p.m., Fri.-Sun. 7 a.m.-12:30 a.m. French Quarter branch: open daily 7 a.m.-2 p.m. & 6 p.m.-10 p.m. All major cards.

Chez Pierre

No. 3 West Bank Expressway, Algiers
• 362-6703
CLASSIC CREOLE

11/20

Fans of the crabmeat St. Pierre and mandarine ice at LeRuth's will find carbon copies of them in the sparsely decorated rooms of this classic Creole restaurant, a stone's throw from the western exit of the Mississippi River bridge. That may or may not be because the proprietor-chef spent fifteen years on the LeRuth's service staff. In any event, Chez Pierre's kitchen manages to come up with enough unique touches to make things interesting for its clientele, a conservative breed who like cream in their sauces, butter on their bread and salt in their gumbo. The exterior of the bunkerlike building, plopped into the middle of a parking lot, is as unremarkable as the narrow, windowless dining room, neatly hung with an olio of prints and posters. Fancy decor, it seems, is sacrificed for low menu prices. In the evening, the prix-fixe, five-course meal, with about a dozen main-course options, is often less than $20. Fish is the strong suit. A fine sauté of shrimp and crabmeat straddles a fresh and fragile trout filet in lemon butter. And a trout en croûte in lobster sauce offers penthouse quality at a bargain-basement price. Meat dishes are a cut below, and vegetables sometimes show up soggy and drab. But the warm, crusty loaves of New Orleans--style French bread are produced in-house, as are the good ice creams and sorbets. The wine list won't have oenophiles smacking their lips, but it's not an embarrassment. Two people should get through the belt-busting five courses, with a decent bottle, for $70—or perhaps even less.
Open Mon.-Fri. 11:30 a.m.-2 p.m. & 6 p.m.-10 p.m., Sat. 6 p.m.-10 p.m. Cards: AE, MC, V.

China Blossom

1801 Stumpf Blvd., Gretna
• 361-4598
CHINESE

12/20

Chinese-American chefs haven't begun to plumb the seafood possibilities in a city regularly inundated with excellent fish and crustaceans brought in from the nearby wetlands and gulf. Only a few years ago, sweet-and-sour shrimp was about the best one could hope for, and a corn-and-crab soup was close to revolutionary. Slowly and sporadically, the attitude is changing. The evidence appears every day in this casual and refreshingly uncluttered restaurant, nestled inside a small suburban mall just across the Mississippi from New Orleans, free of the fire-breathing dragons and tasseled lanterns of yore. The menu is undeniably derivative. Still, such tired old warhorses as lemon chicken and smoked tea duck are rejuvenated somewhat by fresh ingredients and good technique. A leader among the worthwhile novelties is shrimp, big and tasty ones, marinated in sesame oil, garlic and pepper, then grilled with mushrooms. Crawfish tails, often overrated by locals, take on a new personality in a peppery stir-fry with a black-bean sauce. A whole trout, boned and deep-fried, arrives moist and flavorful, swathed in an excellently proportioned blend of soy sauce, sugar and vinegar. Succulent Louisiana oysters get the same treatment. The roster of Asian and domestic beers is a workable substitute for the perfunctory wine list. Service is attentive and well organized, and the cost of it all—$30 for two big eaters—would put a smile even on a skinflint's face.

Open Tues.-Fri. 11 a.m.-2 p.m. & 5 p.m.-10 p.m., Sat.-Sun. noon-10 p.m. Cards: AE, MC, V.

Christian's

3835 Iberville, Mid-City
• 482-4924
CLASSIC CREOLE

The idea looks like a gag, but Christian's is a thoroughly serious restaurant. Owner Christian Ansel is a scion of the family that owns Galatoire's, where he did time before opening his own place. Originally, Christian's was in the suburbs, but it did badly there, so Ansel looked for a location in town and found a small, empty church. The pews were turned into banquettes, the pulpit into a waiter's station. The food is understated and consistently satisfying, being a combination of Galatoire's-style dishes and the French creativity of chef Roland Huet. Start with the herbal oysters Roland, the big, zippy shrimp rémoulade or the buttery oysters en brochette. They always have a few great fresh fish for entrées here; the versions au poivre, meunière, and grilled are uniformly vivid. The chef likes to smoke seafood and comes up with not just smoked salmon and trout but smoked soft-shell crabs as well, which are so edible as to be nearly inhalable.

Filet mignon is treated to a gelatinous, intense, translucent demiglaze studded with peppercorns or to a stuffing and saucing with oysters—a fine, neglected old Creole specialty. Shrimp Madeleine has an old-style French richness with lots of cream. Veal is napped with another polished cream-and-demi-glaze sauce with morel mushrooms.

There are lots of good specials, particularly in crawfish season. The restaurant makes its own wonderful ice creams, which figure in most of the desserts. Service is competent, but unceremonious. The wine list, like the menu, offers many interesting surprises at attractive prices. Dinner for two, with wine, will add up to about $75.

Open Mon.-Sat. 5:30 p.m.-10 p.m. All major cards.

Clancy's

6100 Annunciation St., Uptown
• 895-1111
CONTEMPORARY CREOLE

It wasn't too long ago that this Uptown nouveau bistro was mired down in mesquite madness and mustardy sauces. A change in ownership and in the kitchen's direction broadened the clientele beyond the pincorded and seersuckered clique that once ruled the tables. The food now balances Creole lavishness with contemporary restraint. Atop the functionally white-linened tables sit impeccably fresh veal sweetbreads in a superb sauce of cream, mustard and basil; a classically proportioned Nantua sauce dampening a butter-soft filet of sautéed Gulf drum; and a coquille holding a cluster of crawfish tails in a light, zesty cream sauce zapped with flecks of jalapeño and intense Cajun ham. The character of the table service, delivered by tuxedoed servers with blank faces, lies somewhere between a real restaurant's and a hash house's, although wines from the sensible and interesting list are usually handled properly. The loyal Clancy's crowd, now a cross-section of Uptowners, can stand only so much experimentation. That may account for the presence of several uninteresting, smoked holdovers from the previous menu. On the other hand, the quality of raw materials and the expert cooking add sparkle to such familiarities as crisp sticks of sweet fried eggplant, fettuccine Alfredo, lamb chops with béarnaise and an old-fashioned lemon icebox pie. The more adventurous can have a crown of Brie melted on their fried oysters, or their rabbit sausage cloaked in puff pastry with a zesty mustard cream. What they can't have is any semblance of visual interest in the dining spaces, neatly fashioned from a blue-collar bar and beanery of the 1930s. Bentwood chairs, ceiling fans and

a band of mirrors above the gray, tongue-and-groove wainscoting are the only distractions. A twosome can escape for $65, and half that at lunch.
Open Mon.-Tues. 5:30 p.m.-10:30 p.m., Wed.-Thurs. 11:30 a.m.-2:20 p.m. & 5:30 p.m.-10:30 p.m., Fri. 11:30 a.m.-2 p.m. & 5:30 p.m.-11 p.m., Sat. 5:30 p.m.-11 p.m. Cards: AE, MC, V.

Commander's Palace

1403 Washington Ave., Garden District
• 899-8221
CONTEMPORARY CREOLE

Commander's Palace has thrived for years on New Orleans's Latin obsession with food and drink in their most festive aspects. It is no hushed gastronomic shrine, but a vibrant, spontaneous restaurant, in a tradition as grand as the big Victorian Garden District mansion it inhabits. Savoring its full impact takes a celebratory spirit and an open mind about the often brassy power of mainstream New Orleans food. The proprietors—Ella, Dick, Dottie and John Brennan—have assumed the awesome task of delivering, seven nights a week, blue-ribbon cooking in a range stretching from bedrock Creole to the kinds of light and clever improvisations that sprout in the city's sassily trendy bistros. In December 1989, chef Emeril Lagasse, whose energetic imagination helped set Commander's on an exciting new course, departed from the kitchen to strike out on his own. At this writing, the long-term effect is not certain. In the interim, Lagasse's former pinch hitter and disciple, Jamie Shannon, is more than holding his own, and Commander's continues to impress much more often than it disappoints. The menu's signature dishes cover a lot of familiar Creole territory. In most cases, the clichés have been forged into archetypes. Cakes of spicy Louisiana crabmeat glory in seasoned cream with oysters. Sautéed shrimp and mushrooms glisten in a spicy brown sauce that speaks for generations of Creole cooks, as does the lemon-pungent turtle soup, brick red and meaty. Speckled trout with pecans can rise from its gimmicky origins with the seductions of impeccable freshness and a beautifully balanced,

THE CRAWFISH

New Orleans natives have been netting, boiling and eating crawfish for more than 200 years, and, for that matter, the French have been eating them since the Middle Ages. But it wasn't until around 1984 that the rest of the country suddenly caught on. Now the small, succulent, lobsterlike creature (known as the crayfish elsewhere) is shipped to markets all over the country. Commercial crawfish farming is a booming business for Louisiana, and production grows every year, to a current bounty of ten-million pounds annually. It's no wonder—there are 29 known species of the spiny crustacean living wild in Louisiana alone. This also makes for excellent sportfishing, immensely popular with both locals and visitors. Every spring, a solid chain of parked cars crowds the 80-mile stretch of Airline Highway from Baton Rouge to New Orleans, while their owners joust for a fishing spot. This creature has a few other names: crawdad, grasscrab, stonecrab or mudbug.

winey reduction of seafood stock. The kitchen's make-it-from-scratch approach extends all the way to Worcestershire sauce and goat cheese. This self-sufficiency shows up best in the seasonal specials. One night's might be delicate pompano in saffron cream with fresh fennel, or a two-fisted gumbo of duck and andouille sausage or meaty blue crabs still in their soft shells, dressed minutes before they're dusted with seasoned flour and then flash-fried. The formidable square footage of the restaurant is diminished opticallly by a maze of dining spaces. Giant oaks cradle the building, and their sinuous upper branches wrap the glass-walled Garden Room on the second floor, turning it into a plush treehouse. Bayou flora and fauna are traced in delicate pastels in the paneled main room downstairs, the haunt of savvy regulars (they know its closeness to the kitchen oils the service staff's wheels, so to speak). Candlelight gives the lush courtyard the proper otherworldly glow. An eye-popping collection of California's most reputable Chardonnays and Cabernets take up much of the cellar space, along with some of the best from Bordeaux and Burgundy. Table service, based on a team system, usually hums along somewhere between studied precision and relaxed informality. Two people, ordering from among the prix-fixe choices and resisting the wine list's major temptations, can dine very well for $110. Lunch, at well below $40 per couple (and for several courses), is among New Orleans's biggest bargains.

Open Mon.-Fri. 11:30 a.m.-2 p.m. & 6 p.m.-10 p.m., Sat. 11 a.m.-2 p.m. & 6 p.m.-10 p.m., Sun. 10:30 a.m.-2 p.m. & 6 p.m.-10 p.m. All major cards.

Constantin's

8402 Oak St., Uptown
• 861-2111
American

Far from the fast track, in a dark red bungalow just a few blocks from the Mississippi, chef Patti Constantin draws on any number of inspirations for her cooking. It's filled with imagination and freshness, and a quick perusal of the lunch and dinner menus also shows she's a risk taker. If the combinations appear contrived or affected on the menu, more often than not they will prove to be disarmingly good. Constantin dares to plop a few batter-fried snails into her cream soup of roasted garlic and shallots. As it turns out, the soup's nutty-edged flavor works deliciously with the snails. She also comes up with a pâté of chicken livers bound with green-peppercorn mousse and garnished with white raisins, chopped egg, caramelized onion and cornichons. If that sounds like the product of a too-vivid imagination, it materializes as a delicious blend of flavors. Local cooks have been experimenting with trout. Constantin's novel treatment has lots of flair; the fish is dusted with almond flour and fried before it gets a ladling of hollandaise, with just a whisper of orange in it. Over-fussy construction sometimes intrudes, but in every instance, raw materials are exceptionally fresh. Herbs are plucked daily from a patch just outside the kitchen door, against the ancient fence of black cast iron surrounding the cottage. Inside are a spacious bar and two rather large dining rooms, their eggshell walls brightened with colorful fabrics and botanical prints. The attitudes here are correct, but casual. Fleet-footed servers in practical sneakers dart around, carrying little slabs of filet mignon brushed with a delicious artichoke-chive butter, or a homey butterbean soup with tasso. The domestic atmosphere is reinforced with the chef's marvelous pies, cookies and ice creams, the summit being Snappy's Polar Chip—alternating layers of paper-thin chocolate-chip cookies and vanilla ice cream, blanketed by a first-rate hot chocolate sauce. The price of dinner for two, with a discreet choice from the very serviceable list of wines, usually ends up at about $65.

Open Mon. 11:30 a.m.-2 p.m., Tues.-Thurs. 11:30 a.m.-2 p.m. & 6 p.m.-10 p.m., Fri. 11:30 a.m.-2 p.m. & 6 p.m.-10:30 p.m., Sat. 6 p.m.-10:30 p.m. Cards: AE, MC, V.

Copeland's

4338 St. Charles Ave., Uptown • 897-2325

701 Veterans Blvd., Metairie • 831-3437

CAJUN/TRADITIONAL CREOLE

8/20

The snowballing of the Cajun fad in the 1980s gave us such trend followers as this small chain of "Cajun American" cafés. Each holds enough Middle-American glitz—plastic plants, Naugahyde, cutesy nostalgic photos, stained glass and brass rails—for three or four more restaurants. Tackling the menu, with its staggeringly rich and spicy food, requires a digestive system in Olympic condition. At its heart is a roster of Cajun-Creole clichés—gumbo, red beans, oysters en brochette and seafoods in a Niagara of cream or butter sauces, intensely spiced. The short-sleeved mob that regularly fills the tables, some of them elevated and with bar-stool seats, feasts on such fodder as "Chic-crawdads" (grilled chicken breast in a crawfish sauce en papillotte), breaded veal with linguine in a condensation of cream with shrimp and tasso (Acadian-style ham) and "Caesar's Wife Salad" (there's a joke there, somewhere). A lighter group of dishes introduced a while back is easier to digest, but hardly distinctive. The

servings are immense, so any two people spending more than $40 here are likely to waddle their way home.
Open daily 11 a.m.-midnight. All major cards.

Court of Two Sisters

613 Royal St., French Quarter • 522-7261
CLASSIC CREOLE

8/20

In one of the French Quarter's most desirable restaurant properties stands this cavernous monument to mediocrity, which has thrived on the patronage of unsuspecting (or unselective) tourists for decades. The huge, enclosed courtyard once was one of the most impressive in the city. Now, on warm nights, the leaves of the pretty trees flutter in the wind of electric fans on pedestals. The waiter will suggest something on the order of trout meunière—in this instance an overcooked piece of fish drenched in Worcestershire sauce—or the shrimp Creole, in a tired old tomato sauce that is likely to reappear in another fish course. Le Coq à l'Orange is a pedestrian Cornish hen, resting with a gummy sauce on a bed of dark and mysterious "Cajun rice" and caressing between its knees a twisted slice of orange. Crabmeat Rector translates as stringy lumps of crab in a forgettable pimiento and green-pepper sauce. A "jazz brunch" is served daily from a steam line and a green plastic *pirogue* (the Acadian's canoe) filled with ice and food stale around the edges. With wine, the cost at dinnertime easily adds up to $90 for two.
Open daily 9 a.m.-3 p.m. & 5:30 p.m.-10 p.m. All major cards.

La Crêpe Nanou

1410 Robert St., Uptown • 899-2670
FRENCH

10/20

Uptown yuppies and victims of the oil bust line up nightly at La Crêpe Nanou, because it reminds them of the cheap and unpretentious little Left Bank bistro they stumbled on during their student days. Not much around here dates later than 1960, except for the Häagen-Dazs in the dessert crêpes and the arty photographs on the walls. Initially, the food focus was crêpes with a variety of fillings. Gradually, dining in its more familiar forms (appetizers, main courses, salads and desserts) took over. Still, a three-course dinner can be had for less than what it costs to fill up the Volvo. Fillet of salmon comes in a less than generous serving, but it's fresh tasting, correctly cooked and napped with a decent béarnaise sauce. Mussels marinière are competently done, although the broth may be thicker and more oniony than it should be. A trio of baked oysters on the half-shell score with their garnish, a garlicky mince of seasoned breadcrumbs and a thin topping of gratinéed cheese. Soups, especially the puréed lentil, are always reliable, as are lamb chops in cognac

sauce and panfried sweetbreads in lemon and capers. The small front dining room usually is livelier than the very long, very narrow one behind it, which lets you know what it's like to eat in an alley with a half-glass roof. Don't look for prestige labels on the wine list, but do look for value. Two can eat and drink their fill here for a total of about $45.
Open Mon.-Thurs. 6 p.m.-10 p.m., Fri.-Sat. 6 p.m.-11 p.m., Sun. 10:30 a.m.-2:30 p.m. & 6 p.m.-9:30 p.m. Cards; MC, V.

Crescent City Steak House

1001 N. Broad, Mid-City • 821-3271
STEAKHOUSE

10/20

This is a good place to keep in the back of your mind for New Years' Eve, Mardi Gras, Super Bowl or other times when all the well-known places are packed. About 55 years ago, the Crescent City originated the New Orleans–style steak—prime beef, served sizzling in butter. They still broil a great steak; particularly the strip and the porterhouse. But the restaurant's operation is a bit eccentric, and the fact that the place is usually nearly or totally empty is disconcerting. Dinner or lunch here, with wine, is about $60 for two.
Open Tues.-Sun 11:30 a.m.-11 p.m. All major cards.

Crozier's

3216 W. Esplanade Ave., Metairie • 833-8108
FRENCH

12/20

The Gallic sauces are retro to the core, and the gratinée (onion soup) is straight from the textbook. All of the menu's French words are spelled right (except perhaps for the absent diacritics). This, and other evidence, point to a kitchen preoccupied with solid French cooking in the traditional mode, attuned to the tastes of older locals who might have been weaned on cream. Owner-chef Gerard Crozier's strong Lyonnais roots show up everywhere in these meticulously maintained suburban dining rooms, squeezed into a suburban mall and lined in dark woods and green paisley. The béarnaise on both the sautéed shrimp and the subtle salmon mousse is authentically eggy, flecked with just the right amount of tarragon. A dense duck pâté carries the trademark flavors of the French countryside. The filet mignon and gratin dauphinois, with thin potato slices coated in garlicky cream, are close to perfection, and the poached flounder is securely tied down with hollandaise. In other words, don't look for lightness, all ye who enter here, unless it's in a lamb shank, braised in aromatic vegetables and accompanied by unadorned noodles, or a sensibly sauced trout meunière jazzed up with a bit of fresh fennel or a

few capers. Desserts induce nostalgia, as in fine versions of floating island, a custardy lemon tart and a springy crème bavarois. The *patronne* seems to have an instinctive talent for organizing a service staff, and she is always around to suggest a bottle from the comparatively modest and practical list—mostly French, of course, and Californian. The majority carry price tags of $20 or less, so expect the final tab for two to end up at about $80.
Open Tues.-Fri. 11:30 a.m.-2 p.m. & 6 p.m.-10 p.m., Sat. 6 p.m.-10 p.m. All major cards.

La Cucaracha Café

8511 Oak St., Uptown • 861-8053
SOUTHWESTERN

11/20

Southwestern cooking is about as easy to find in New Orleans as ham hocks in Tel Aviv. This tiny restaurant almost makes up for the lack with a collection of Hispanic-American dishes done in a very personal style. Getting to them can be a challenge. The restaurant is located in the farther reaches of Uptown. Its dining room, the size of a two-car garage, holds fewer than twenty seats, and no reservations are taken. Once these hurdles and the rough-edged service are cleared, the odds for good eating become quite favorable. The cactus patch outside and the meticulous decor inside evoke Taos or Phoenix. Pull up a slatted chair and try one of chef Raul Mier's first-rate paellas, the saffron rice dotted with green peas and whatever has found its way to the pot—any combination of shrimp, chicken, artichoke, sea scallops, spicy chorizo or fresh mussels. Shipped regularly in from a Pueblo reservation outside Sante Fe are blue corn for dumplings, Mexican oregano, whole hominy and chile peppers for posole and an array of other ingredients. The Spanish-style chicken pie, its spiciness balanced with nuts and raisins, can become addictive. A delicious mix of chorizo and mashed sweet potatoes is the filling for wheat-flour burritos. A creamy butternut squash soup is filled with fresh flavors. Enchiladas suizas deliver no thrills, but the pork burrito in chile verde sauce is marvelous. Fanciers of home-style desserts can revel in Mier's freshly made, all-American ones, especially the deep-dish pies of rhubarb, and plum or peach with raspberries, all in luscious natural syrups. One of the many domestic and foreign beers is appropriate with the often boldly spiced food. The outlay for dinner for two rarely exceeds $35.
Open Mon. 11 a.m.-2 p.m. & 6 p.m.-10 p.m., Wed.-Sat. 11 a.m.-2 p.m. & 6 p.m.-10 p.m. Cards: AE, MC, V.

La Cuisine

225 W. Harrison Ave., Lakeview
• 486-5154
CLASSIC CREOLE

10/20

La Cuisine is the kind of restaurant Orleanians feel very comfortable dining in. It's almost like a neighborhood café in its surroundings, service and prices. The food is uncomplicated but good. Begin with oysters Saladino, a small casserole of plump oysters baked in an Italianate sauce of olive oil, garlic, pepper and bread crumbs. The taste of this grabs you so firmly that you may be tempted to order seconds, or an entrée serving.

Crab gumbo and the salad of Creole tomatoes, Vidalia onions, ricotta cheese and olive oil are other fine starters. Shrimps are stuffed with mozzarella cheese studded with jalapeño chips, wrapped in bacon and broiled. Steaks are prime, enormous and ideally rendered. Trout and soft-shell crabs are done simply in butter and sent out still sizzling. There's just enough in dessert and wine to cover the bases. Two can eat here for $60.

Open Tues.-Fri. 11:30 a.m.-3 p.m. & 5:30 p.m.-10 p.m., Sat. 11:30 a.m.-10 p.m.; Sun. noon-8 p.m. All major cards.

We're always interested to hear about your discoveries, and to receive your comments on ours. Please feel free to write to us, and do state clearly exactly what you liked or disliked.

Delmonico

1300 St. Charles Ave., Central Business District
• 525-4937
CLASSIC CREOLE

10/20

The exterior of this century-old establishment suggests a much fancier restaurant than it really is. Inside, Delmonico's is an unpretentious, charming pair of antique Southern dining rooms, dominated by a large old mural depicting life on the Mississippi. The food is old-style Creole, with a heavy emphasis on seafood; the cooking has a way of turning out better than you expect, given the low prices. Soups here are especially good, with a wonderful turtle soup and seafood gumbo. Shrimp rémoulade, baked oysters with four different sauces, and the marinated vegetable salad are other safe starting points. The platter of fried catfish with meunière sauce with a pair of crabmeat-stuffed shrimp is typical of the restaurant's style. Broiled, grilled, and even blackened fish and shellfish emerge with a good texture and a nice hint of Creole spice. They're not afraid to serve chicken here; the broiled half bird is moist and interestingly seasoned. All the desserts are small and understated, and the chicory coffee is addictive. Service is unceremonious. Dinner for two, with wine, goes for about $55.

Open Mon.-Sat. 11:30 a.m.-9:30 p.m., Sun. 11:30 a.m.-9 p.m. All major cards.

Dooky Chase's

2301 Orleans Ave., Treme
• 821-2294
TRADITIONAL CREOLE/SOUL

11/20

Chef Leah Chase's brand of Creole cookery may be the closest a restaurant gets to the down-to-earth food that has fueled generations of New Orleanians. It has neither the greasy heaviness usually associated with the South nor the fussy sophistication found in the city's trendier restaurants. Dooky Chase's, founded in the 1940s by the chef's father-in-law, is the place to sample dishes like delicate-tasting okra, stewed with tomatoes and neither stringy nor mushy, or fresh sweet potatoes cooked until just soft in their own minimally sweetened juices. They're served in an environment that's much more elegant than one might expect in a midtown, blue-collar neighborhood. Canvases and prints by the city's best black artists enliven the several rooms. Soft gray millwork borders the pale plum walls in the finely proportioned main room. On weekends, neatly dressed families usually fill the place. The lengthy menu has its pitfalls—a pallid crawfish étouffée, forgettable onion rings, a dry stuffed potato. But winners outnumber losers. Among the former are the thick grilled pork chops, blanketed in rings of sautéed onion, a thick and peppery crab soup that speaks for a legion of Creole cooks, panfried escallopes of veal encased in crunchy breading, and shrimp Clemenceau, in a buttery sauté with potatoes, peas, mushrooms and whispers of garlic and pepper. A bare-bones wine list is no surprise, considering the menu's homey style. But the dessert list is much less exciting than it should be. The cost of dinner for two usually falls somewhere between $50 and $60.

Open Sun.-Thurs. 11:30 a.m.-midnight, Fri-Sat. 11:30 a.m.-1 a.m. All major cards.

Doug's

348 Robert Rd., Slidell
• 649-1805
CONTEMPORARY CREOLE

11/20

The rolling, piney country on the North Shore of Lake Pontchartrain has more than its share of rubber-stamp fried chicken and conveyor-belt hamburgers. It also has a handful of serious restaurants offering food that rises above the suburban norm. One such is this low-slung roadhouse, set far back from the highway, serving elaborate versions of Creole classics dating to the chef's salad days in the kitchen at Commander's Palace. Much of it is assembled with shrimp and crabmeat stuffings, lemon butter or a traditional sauce blending tomato, onion and sweet pepper. If they keep reappearing, they're also put to good use. Broiled oysters, mushrooms and artichoke hearts keep delicious company in the lemon butter, seasoned with thyme. The same sauce often flavors the grilled fish, dependably fresh and not overcooked. When the day's specials are recited, keep an ear cocked for "crawfish pie." It's a ramekin crowned with a flaky crust and filled with firm crawfish tails in a winning sauce redolent of bay leaf, thyme and scallions. Ingredients are fresh and technique is solid. Escallopes of breaded, panfried white veal are eminently compatible with fettuccine in pepper-tinged cream and romano. And the desserts—especially French silk pie with strawberries and a fluffy bread pudding with bourbon sauce—have a finesse usually found in environments much tonier than this sprawl of homey decor under low ceilings. In daylight, the long room looking onto the garden is especially pleasant. If table service lacks polish, it also can be attentively efficient. And the cost, which should end up at $50 or $60 for two, is more than reasonable.

Open Tues.-Fri. 11 a.m.-2 p.m. & 5 p.m.-10 p.m., Sat. 5 p.m.-10 p.m. Cards: AE, D, MC, V.

Drago's

3232 N. Arnoult Rd., Metairie
• 888-9254
SEAFOOD/YUGOSLAVIAN

12/20

The large Yugoslavian community in Southeast Louisiana dominates commercial fishing and oystering. A few Yugoslavians filtered into the restaurant side of the seafood business; they tend to have the best fried-seafood restaurants in town, mainly because the family connections assure good supplies of first-class fish and shellfish. Drago Cvitanovich has had a popular seafood restaurant for twenty years or so, offering all the local standards, such as seafood gumbo and fried seafood platters. Drago's has terrific oysters, both raw on the half shell and char-grilled, with a beguilingly smoky taste.

But what makes this restaurant really interesting is a large menu of authentic Yugoslavian dishes. You can sample an assortment of these through the agency of the Yugo platter; it includes cabbage rolls, marinated pork with peppers, grilled squid and a couple of other things. The dining room is a touch more formal than most such places are; for some reason, it's a favorite of the local pro football players. Dinner for two, with Yugoslavian wine, will cost you about $40.

Open Mon.-Sat. 11 a.m.-9:30 p.m., Fri.-Sat. 11 a.m.-10 p.m. All major cards.

L'Economie

325 Girod St., Warehouse District
• 524-7405
FRENCH

11/20

The name implies moderation, and that's what pervades this likable nest of modern French cooking in the trendy Warehouse District. Dealers from the nearby art galleries like the downscale chic of its low prices, bare-bones decor (centered on three big Expressionist oils and a few assorted palms) and offbeat color scheme—white stucco walls above deep green wainscotting and rusty red paint on the cement floors. Contrasting with these rough edges is the food, a pared-down collection of creamless, flourless dishes executed in the post-nouvelle style of proprietor-chef Hubert Sandot. Everything—from the tomato and shallots in vinaigrette to the brought-in pastries—is prettily arranged on big white plates. The day's chicken might be a lightened version of coq au vin or boneless breast in a gossamer reduction of wine and olive oil, flavored with apple, browned onion and a smidgen of bacon. Fish is sometimes poached in Chablis, with tiny bits of butter and honey added. Such fragile food often has surprising depth. Mushroom soup, despite the absence of butter or cream, is rich with flavor, as is the carrot and celery. A pair of tiny, but thick, spring lamb chops retain their juiciness inside a light crust of garlic, thyme and mint, and almost nothing else. When the dozen or so tables are full, Mme. Sandot and the chef himself join the service staff of one. Tables wear white cloths, but paper napkins help bring the price for two, plus a bottle from the modest list, down to about $45.

Open Mon.-Thurs. 11 a.m.-2 p.m. & 6 p.m.-10 p.m., Fri. 11 a.m.-2 p.m. & 6 p.m.-10:30 p.m., Sat. 6 p.m.-10:30 p.m. No cards.

Emeril's

800 Tchoupitoulas St., Warehouse District • 528-9393

CONTEMPORARY CREOLE

You could have cut the anticipation with a knife when Emeril Lagasse announced he was leaving the kitchen at Commander's Palace to open his own restaurant in the heart of the neomodern Warehouse District. During the six years Lagasse had spent as Commander's executive chef, he elevated the contemporary Creole style to previously unreached heights, with a gutsy, thoroughly modern brand of cooking, stunning in its range, variety and execution. The opening of Emeril's in early 1990 was more than worth the wait. Left completely to his own culinary devices, Lagasse is forging ahead at Emeril's with an energy-charged repertory that helps put New Orleans cooking squarely in the nineties. And the decor in the 140-seat dining room, colorful and hard-edged, is as avant-garde as you'll find in these parts—an angular and lofty space enclosed in expanses of glass, brick, hard woods and plaster and dominated by a single, dramatic, abstract expressionist canvas. Lagasse himself darts from burner to burner in his special open kitchen.

Seasonal lunch and dinner menus begin with impeccable raw products brought in by the area's top purveyors. They leave the kitchen in consistently sterling shape. Louisiana caviar (from choupique, a lowly fish of the swamps) is lavished on airy corn pancakes resting on peppery sour cream. Springy ravioli are filled with an elegantly seasoned asparagus purée. Lagasse's own velvety goat cheese joins fresh spinach in a purse of buttery phyllo dough. The soup list includes an updated gumbo rich with chunks of swordfish and a luxurious cream of oysters Rockefeller soup. Among the showpieces are roasted, semiboned quail stuffed with andouille sausage and several species of mushroom in port sauce, and salmon filet, sautéed to a moist turn before joining warm greens and a bracing, lemony vinaigrette. A distinctive regional consciousness is everywhere, even in desserts. One is a judiciously sweetened goat-cheesecake embellished with a refreshing Creole cream-cheese sauce. California wines are another preoccupation, and the floor-to-ceiling racks behind the bar are filled with nicely priced new releases and labels from small, obscure producers. Perhaps by now a serious acoustical problem has been corrected. If not, expect a noise level approximating that of a high-school gym during a championship game. Dinner for two is about $80, with wine.

Open Mon.-Fri. 11:30 a.m.-2:30 p.m. & 6 p.m.-10 p.m., Sat. 6 p.m.-10 p.m. Cards: AE, DC, MC, V.

Flagons

3222 Magazine St., Uptown
• 895-6471
CONTEMPORARY CREOLE

12/20

During the mid-1980s, this place was the ultimate yuppie hangout. It started as a first-class wine bar, then expanded to become one of the more adventuresome nouveaux Creole bistros. When nobody wanted to be a yuppie anymore, Flagons redefined itself, and it remains a great place to have an easy, interesting lunch or dinner. This is especially true if you're an oenophile; Flagons has some 60 wines, all in great shape, served by the glass, plus a thick book of by-the-bottle selections. The food lately has taken some tastes from parts of the South outside Creole-Cajun country. The pork tenderloin stuffed with andouille and napped with rosemary-scented butter is a great exmple of this trend. The chef cold-smokes his own meats, poultry and fish with a subtlety rarely tasted in a venue like this. Flagons has always grilled fish well, and the daily offering of three different grilled fish is as mind-expanding as it is tasty. You can start with the fine turtle and black bean soups, an exceptional rendition of rigatoni with four cheeses, or a selection of caviars, the latter very well presented. End the proceedings with the intense chocolate St. Emilion, the fruity bread pudding, or a glass of port. The wine bar section of the restaurant offers a snackish menu till around midnight. Cost for

dinner in the main room is about $75 for two.
Open Mon.-Thurs. 11:30 a.m.-2:30 p.m. & 6 p.m.-10 p.m., Fri.-Sat. 11:30 a.m.-2:30 p.m. & 6 p.m.-11 p.m. Wine bar open Mon.-Thurs. 11:30 a.m.-1 a.m., Fri.-Sat. 11:30 a.m.-2 a.m., Sun. 11:30 a.m.-midnight. Cards: AE, MC, V.

Galatoire's

209 Bourbon St., French Quarter • 525-2021
CLASSIC CREOLE

The menu is a relic, reserving a table is out of the question and the waiters are dictatorial. None of that, however, seems to matter to Galatoire's loyalists, who regularly line up outside at the mercy of the elements (there is no bar or anteroom) just to spend a few hours in the quintessential Creole bistro. Some have been known to arrive at 1 p.m. for lunch, stay through dinner and leave at 10, after the final morsel of Cointreau-soaked crêpe has been gulped down and the last crumb scraped from the over-starched white linen. After 85 years, the fascination with this stubbornly old-fashioned French Quarter institution seems stronger than ever, a reminder that innovation comes and goes, but durability can be a higher virtue. The old pressed-tin ceiling has been replaced by some innocuous acoustical material. In the 1970s, a baroque green wallpaper appeared above the ancient mirror panels and brass coathooks that border the single, deep dining room. The doorman now keeps several generic sportcoats handy for the occasional upstart who arrives in shirtsleeves. Otherwise, not much has changed under the bright lights of the polished brass chandelier. The supremacy of the rémoulade sauce, deep red from cayenne and paprika, remains unchallenged. The dense and spicy Creole bouillabaisse, to be ordered at least six hours in advance, seems more soul-warming than ever. From the depths of the vast menu come more definitive gems: sticks of slightly sweet fried eggplant, which the cognoscenti dip into powdered sugar (yes, sugar); fried oysters and bacon en brochette with a bit of brown butter; gulf pompano, boned and broiled too long, but lavished with delicious lumps of backfin blue crab or rosy crawfish tails sautéed with green onion and a miser's dose of garlic; a crawfish étouffée for the ages; and homespun versions of gumbo and oyster stew. The short, generic list of wines appended to the

PASS THE SPICE, PLEASE!

What creates the highly distinctive flavor of Creole cooking? Most often, a jumble of these spices, in myriad combinations: allspice, anise, caraway, cardamom, cinnamon, cumin, ginger, mace, mustard, nutmeg, black and white pepper, saffron and turmeric. And don't forget filé—a major ingredient in gumbo, (depending on whom you talk to)—used to flavor and thicken the stew. It comes from the tender green leaves of the sassafras tree, which are dried and ground to a powder.

menu is merely a starting point for a discussion with the waiter on what is available. Pointing to the inconsistencies of the Galatoire's kitchen is a favorite local pastime. The canned asparagus in the combination salad is, of course, laughable. The Rockefeller sauce on baked oysters can taste like little more than creamed spinach. And the Marguery sauce on the poached trout has, on occasion, been a floury glue. Those who manage to avoid such clinkers, and approach Galatoire's on its own quirky terms, will enjoy its considerable pleasures to the fullest, and end up paying a not at all unreasonable $60 or $70 per couple for a class New Orleans meal.

Open Tues.-Sat. 11:30 a.m.-9 p.m., Sun. noon-9 p.m. No cards.

Gambrill's

94 Friedrichs Ave., Metairie
• 831-6917
CONTEMPORARY CREOLE

11/20

Gambrill's straddles several dividing lines. It sits almost on the border separating New Orleans from suburban Metairie. The rooms of the frame cottage it inhabits combine down-home coziness with rather sophisticated decoration, and the kitchen attempts, often successfully, to match traditional Creole earthiness with contemporary subtlety. The soft peach walls of the downstairs double parlor add to its welcoming aspect, along with cheering greenery and pastel canvases. Colors are bolder in the smaller rooms upstairs, hung with dramatic art objects and canvases. The menu is no revolutionary's manifesto, replete as it is with well-executed Creole standbys like cold lumps of crabmeat in a piquant ravigote sauce, oysters Rockefeller, fish in buttery sauces and a play on Commander's Palace's bread pudding soufflé. But there's enough diversity around to ward off boredom. A salad of crisp strips of duck confit and green apple in walnut-oil dressing is bracingly good. Fresh basil updates a sauté of shrimp in wine and cream with a bit of onion and garlic. Breast of chicken in a vaguely bittersweet glaze of raspberry wine and currants make a nice impression, even in the company of sautéed spinach. The restaurant's signature crabmeat dish, a gratin featuring a hollandaise sauce further enriched with cream and fish stock, is good and tangy. The occasional misfire is usually not disastrous. The taste of crab lurks somewhere in the otherwise decent crab-and-corn soup. Fanciers of tournedos Rossini will have to settle for a more practical morel in place of the truffle and concentrate on the beef's good quality rather than the excess of so-so liver pâté. The wine list, modest but respectable, is democratically composed, although it

has the usual Chardonnay-Cabernet bias. And the cost of it all, around $75 for two, won't make you miss the next mortgage payment.
Open Mon.-Thurs. 11 a.m.-2:30 p.m. & 5 p.m.-10 p.m., Fri.-Sat. 11 a.m.-2:30 p.m. & 5 p.m.-10:30 p.m. All major cards.

Garces

4200 D'Hemecourt St., Uptown
• 488-4734
CUBAN/MEXICAN

10/20

This is the best of a fair number of Cuban/American restaurants in the city. It's a reliable source of homey Caribbean specialties, from earthily delicious black beans to a refreshing seafood-and-chicken paella. The roast pork with beans and rice is an understandable favorite. Others are the thin, full-flavored Cuban flank steak, competently fried fish, several versions of fried plaintains and marvelous Cuban-style milk shakes made with tropical fruits. The warm grilled sandwiches, made with lean pork, beef or ham on the local French bread, are among the city's best, and the coffee is not to be missed. Families fill most of the tables in the neatly maintained dining room, brightened with a color-splashed mural depicting pleasures of the homeland. For a quick refueling, there is a lunch counter at the rear, a few steps up.
Open Mon. 10 a.m.-9 p.m., Wed.-Sat. 10 a.m.-9 p.m., Sun. 1 p.m.-9 p.m. Cards: MC, V.

La Gauloise Bistro

Hotel Le Meridien
614 Canal St., Central Business District
• 527-6712
FRENCH

The atmosphere is hardly as bourgeois as the name implies, but this informal hotel restaurant puts out a number of authentic, old-fashioned French dishes, like a ragoût of sweetbreads with cèpe mushrooms, a meaty chicken leg in tarragon sauce and a hearty gratinéed onion soup. Less exotic are the surprisingly good hamburger and club sandwich. A few Creole-inspired dishes round out the menu. An especially good deal is the fixed-price luncheon buffet and Sunday jazz brunch, both of which have gained considerable popularity with locals for their impressive variety and quality. The environment on the two levels is defined by wood paneling, mirrors, floor tiles and brass fixtures. The bistro theme extends to the calf-length aprons on the service staff.
Open daily 6:30 a.m.-10 p.m. All major cards.

Gautreau's

1728 Soniat St., Uptown
• 899-7397
CONTEMPORARY CREOLE

From our perspective, the remarkable polish and sophistication of the food at Gautreau's is the logical culmination of a decade's progress in New Orleans restaurant cooking. Reckless exaggeration, some would argue. Skeptics are invited to search out this tiny, unprepossessing bistro in a prosperous Uptown neighborhood, camouflaged by trees and devoid of any identifying sign, save for an almost unnoticeable monogram imbedded in the concrete of the front step. Inside, they will find a collection of dishes that more than a few chefs with gilt-edged reputations might be proud to call their own.

The original Gautreau's, a clubby dispenser of excellent contemporary Creole food, had been shut down for several months when chef Larkin Selman, not yet 30, reopened with considerable financial backing. In short order, Selman proved himself a creative force to be reckoned with. Granted, he did not arrive on the scene unarmed. Growing up in food-obsessed New Orleans was no handicap. And behind him, too, were numerous apprenticeships, plus a year and a half working in New York with Jonathan Waxman at Jams and fifteen months under Alfred Portale at Gotham Bar & Grill.

The bottom line to all this is the menu at Gautreau's, which is contemporary American as its heart but also endowed with enough vaguely Creole flourishes to connect with local sensibilities. Selman's is the ultimate crabcake, loaded with delicate backfin lumps of Louisiana blue crab, in a restrained herbal seasoning, lightly blanketed in a lovely golden crust and dabbed with a superb basil mayonnaise. A few crisp pine nuts add the right crunchy note to a creamy purée of shiitake mushroom and celery root, glowing and earthy. Pan-roasted breast of guinea hen, as tender and juicy as anyone could ask, is layered in slices over a brown risotto redolent of prune and sage. A thick and hefty filet of salmon, seared to exactly the right golden point, is matched with the threads of a robust marmalade of red onion.

From pastry chef Christopher Renz comes a semiliquid crème brûlée, infused with orange essence, which may be unsurpassed in the city, a stunning lime pie with banana whipped cream and an excellent tart matching seasonal strawberries with a silky, lemon pastry cream. Aficionados of the original Gautreau's will find the tiny dining room's artifacts intact, from the old tin ceiling and ceramic tile floors to the nostalgic old photos and wall-to-wall rear cabinet holding liquors and glassware. The noise level, as

ever, can rise to uncivilized peaks. The new Gautreau's proprietors have brought a new clarity to the modest wine list, mostly California and French selections. Dinner for two, with a proper bottle, should add up to about $85, hardly exorbitant for the menu's quality and the commendable service.
Open Mon.-Sat. 6 p.m.-10 p.m. Cards: MC, V.

Genghis Khan

4053 Tulane Ave.,
Mid-City
• 482-4044
KOREAN

10/20

Owner Henry Lee has two passions: the food of his homeland, Korea, and classical music (he's a violinist with the New Orleans Symphony). His restaurant has doled out liberal quantities of both since the mid-1970s. Start with any of the tempuras, which range from oysters and pineapple to squid. The kimchee—spicy pickled cabbage, served cold as a palate perker—is a fine sample of the classic Korean appetizer. The milder spinach namul, with an oily, somewhat nutlike flavor, performs the same job just as well. Korean cuisine includes a great deal of marinated, grilled beef, and this is executed very well at Genghis Khan. But the dish everybody talks about is the stunning, grease-free, crusty, whole fried fish, brought forth with a light sauce. The chicken Imperial, moist and very spicy, lies in the direction of a Chinese dish, although the texture and flavor are distinctive. Service is very pleasant, as is the live music in the dining room most nights. Dinner for two, with beer, goes for around $40.
Open Tues.-Thurs. & Sun. 5:30 p.m.-11 p.m., Fri.-Sat. 5:30 p.m.-11:30 p.m. Cards: AE, MC, V.

Grill Room

Windsor Court Hotel,
300 Gravier St.,
Central Business District
• 523-6000
AMERICAN

The Windsor Court Hotel's unfettered bravado in the provision of luxury to its guests extends to its one and only restaurant, the Grill Room. The name, like most of the furnishings and the style of the hotel at large, is a reference to an English standard. The cuisine, while quite sterling, is harder to nail down. The three chefs who have run the place since it opened in 1984 have been remarkable as much for their eccentricity as their talent. The current man is the most unpredictable of all. His menus, which change daily, are as likely to include Indian, French, Chinese, Italian or even American dishes as English or Creole. From all this critic-maddening variability, a few specialties emerge. Start with oysters Peacock or Polo, both baked on the half shell with unique sauces (a very spicy, crusty one and a horseradish-and-cheese affair). The crabmeat ravigote—cold lumps in an intensely fresh mayonnaise-based sauce—is the best around. The house salad, a light variation on the Cobb idea, makes a great lunch or salad course. The grill is fired with wood, and from it come lovely, understated essays in fish, veal and beef. Rarely does anything come off that grill overcooked, and the intrinsic merit of the raw groceries is so fine that the eating is a subtle joy. A roast duck with a coffee sauce and a black, shiny skin is as delicious as it is handsome, and the variety of smoked-on-site vegetables, meats and fish make fine ancillary courses. The excellent array of cakes, tarts and pastries emphasizes fresh fruit. The Grill Room's wine cellar, begun with two large private Bordeaux collections, has grown over the years. Older vintages are in great shape and are very well served. Dinner for two, with a moderate wine, is $150.

Open daily 7 a.m.-2:30 p.m. & 6 p.m.-10:30 p.m. All major cards.

Henri

Hotel Le Meridien,
614 Canal St.,
Central Business District
• 527-6708
FRENCH

Everything at Henri is designed to dazzle, and dazzle it invariably does. The mauve cymbidium orchids on each table almost glow against the whiteness of the table covers and the warm, deep green of the walls. The formality of polished green marble, beveled mirrors and ornate, bronze-doré chandeliers is balanced by the colorful whimsicality of the little murals depicting strollers in a formal eighteenth-century garden. Add a menu created by chef Marc Haeberlin of France's illustrious Auberge de l'Ill and you have what is arguably the most accomplished French restaurant in the southern United States. For two weeks each year, Haeberlin himself appears at Henri to update the menu and prepare lunch and dinner dishes that have made his family's Alsatian establishment a leading light in modern French cooking. The rest of the time, resident chef Patrick Granito, who trained for several years at the inn on the River Ill, is in charge. The descriptions on the bill of fare have just enough bravura to whet curiosity and just enough mystery to sustain it. Soufflé de saumon Auberge de l'Ill is a revelation in the form of salmon filets, millimeters thick, resting under a huge puff of pale coral egg white infused with a whisper of seafood flavors and finally with a light-as-air cream sauce, gently gratinéed. A vast repertoire of herbs and seasonings flavors all sorts of similar masterly compositions—a salad of lobster and minced artichoke in coriander vinaigrette, little roulades of skate cloaked in aspic with a bracing cream sauce flecked with dill, caviar profiteroles adrift on

a velouté of cauliflower Dubarry, a circle of duckling breast slices in a brown sauce with Boletus mushrooms ready for absorption by tiny rice-and-corn pancakes. Fall and winter bring robust meat and game dishes. Braised venison arrives with a cluster of wild mushrooms and a mound of Alsatian cheese noodles. Intensity peaks with a boned breast of squab, stuffed with enough foie gras and truffle for at least another course and wrapped in a translucent cabbage leaf. Desserts are similarly sumptuous. Fresh raspberries, strawberries and cherries are submerged with vanilla ice cream under a gratineed sabayon. And the chocolate sampler of mousses, ices and pavés should impress the most jaded chocolate addict. If the wine list is by no means encyclopedic, the 100 or so labels are chosen with care, although one would expect Alsatian whites to be better represented. This outstanding kitchen has its price, which probably will end up at $150 for two.
Open Mon.-Fri. 11:30 a.m.-2 p.m., Sat. 6 p.m.-10 p.m. All major cards.

Ichiban

1414 Veterans Blvd.,
Metairie
• 834-1326
JAPANESE

12/20

The people who opened Shogun generated such crowds of sushi-heads that they moved Shogun to a new, bigger location and, in its place, installed this much lower-key, more ambitious Japanese restaurant. Ichiban's sushi bar is as good as any in town; the fish is pristine, carved with precision, and served at the ideal cool temperature. Away from the sushi bar, enjoy such famous Japanese dishes as sukiyaki, shabu-shabu (beef simmered in stock with vegetables) and yosenabe (the same, but with seafood). The marinated, grilled teriyaki meats, chicken and shrimp are also well accomplished, and the fried tempura dishes are fresh-tasting and greaseless. At dinner, Ichiban offers a kaiseki service—the lengthy dinner of many small courses, some quite exotic. The premises are casual and hard-edged, but the cuisine is grand. Dinner can be had for two for about $45.
Open Tues.-Thurs. 11:30 a.m.-2 p.m. & 5:30 p.m.-10 p.m., Fri. 11:30 a.m.-2 p.m. & 5:30 p.m.-11 p.m., Sat. 5:30 p.m.-11 p.m. Cards: AE, MC, V.

Impastato's

3400 16th St.
Metairie
• 455-1545
ITALIAN

9/20

This moderate Italian restaurant somehow became general headquarters for the football crowd—the players and coaches themselves, in addition to their following. Impastato's also plays to its regulars, of which there are many; you may have to wait awhile for a table. Once seated, you dig into some very good, if unambitious, cooking. This is New Orleans Italian, in which it's just

fine to cover a casserole of crabmeat or crawfish with cheese, and where fettuccine Alfredo (a very light version) made tableside is a big deal. The chef-owner spends the night visiting (and sometimes bussing, in more ways than one) tables, and stirring up that fettuccine. He assembles a dinner in which you have only to choose an entrée; they don't even tell you what's coming, but it's an interesting assortment in which everyone gets something different. The best entrées are the messy but fine osso buco, the veal with artichokes and mushrooms, and a buttery trout meunière. Service is very friendly, if not always attentive; the wine list is minimal. Dinner is about $60 for two.
Open Tues.-Sat. 5 p.m.-midnight. Cards: AE, MC, V.

Isadora

Energy Center,
1100 Poydras St.
• 585-7787
CONTEMPORARY CREOLE

10/20

Restaurants in large office buildings usually deserve their reputations for ghastliness, but not Isadora. It's an art-deco showplace with lofty ceilings, massive geometrical columns, and the best piped-in music in town (standards from the 1930s and 1940s). The original chef, who set the style, was a veteran of the hard-fought 1980s campaign to re-invent Creole cuisine in nouvelle terms. Start with the unbelievable grilled shrimp and artichoke coulis, a masterful combination of flavors. The rabbit Wellington, sweetbreads in the sauce of the day, and the pastas with seafoods also get things going encouragingly (and invite one to make a complete meal of appetizers). The entrée menu changes with great frequency, but standards included grilled fish and thick steaks of veal, each abetted with intense, reduced sauces studded with peppers, coriander, ginger, garlic or something else pleasantly pungent. The smoked rabbit with crawfish and wild mushrooms is a good blend of complementary tastes and textures. The wine list is short but quite good; the few desserts are rich and made here. Service is a little unsteady. Dinner will cost you about $60 for two, with wine.
Open Mon. 11:30 a.m.-2:30 p.m., Tues.-Thurs. 11:30 a.m.-2:30 p.m. & 6 p.m.-10 p.m., Fri. 11:30 a.m.-2:30 p.m. & 6 p.m.-11 p.m., Sat. 6 p.m.-11 p.m. Cards: AE, DC, MC.

Jack Dempsey's

738 Poland Ave.,
Lower Ninth Ward
• 943-9914
SEAFOOD

9/20

Lines form early outside the door of this very basic neighborhood eatery, which has no affiliation with the late boxing champion. It draws customers from all over town with a large inventory of fried seafoods delivered in servings fit for stevedores. Onion rings or stuffed mushrooms are good starters. The fried shrimp, fish and oysters come in gargantuan heaps, and a single seafood platter might feed three normal appetites. Seafood shunners have to make do with a broiled beef rib eye that is edible, if undistinguished. There's a small charge for styrofoam take-out cartons, and everybody seems to leave toting at least one of them. Those who pack the place nightly are not expecting finesse. Chairs are padded metal, specials are advertised on a big blackboard, and the predictable art on the wood-paneled walls is photography from the point-and-shoot school.

Open Tues. 11 a.m.-1:30 p.m., Wed.-Thurs. 11 a.m.-8:45 p.m., Fri. 11 a.m.-2:30 p.m. & 5 p.m.-10 p.m., Sat. 4 p.m.-10 p.m. Cards: AE, D, MC, V.

Le Jardin

Westin Canal Place Hotel, 1 Canal St.
• 568-0155
CONTEMPORARY CREOLE

12/20

It's hard to imagine a handsomer restaurant than the Westin's flagship eatery. Le Jardin is a step up from the hotel's eleventh-story lobby, and its enormous windows offer a great view of the French Quarter and the tricky bend of the Mississippi River. Even without the view, the three expansive rooms would be luxurious. In addition to all that, the food is quite good. The chef is European, but he's a great fan of Creole cooking and gives a Creole spin to every dish on the menu. Some of the food has an old-style richness that, these days, makes you feel a bit guilty. Crabmeat broiled atop avocado slices and napped with hollandaise is a magnificent little work with which to begin. Crawfish bisque breaks through its surfeit of heavy cream with a tantalizing crawfish flavor and spiciness. They are very good with fish here, preparing ample flanks of many fresh Gulf species in many delectable ways. The poached fish has particular merit; there may be no New Orleans restaurant that handles the technique better. Big chops of lamb, venison and veal are grilled and sent out with such delicious addenda as wild mushrooms. Much of the menu changes nightly, so there are plenty of surprises. The wine list is abbreviated, but always seems to contain at least one interesting oddity (Meursault rouge, for example). On Sunday, they mount one of the two or three best brunch buffets in town. Two people can eat dinner, with wine, for a touch under $100.

Open daily 6:30 a.m.-2:30 p.m. & 6 p.m.-10 p.m. All major cards.

Kabby's

Poydras St. at the Mississippi River (in the New Orleans Hilton's Riverside complex)
• 584-3880
CONTEMPORARY CREOLE

11/20

The towering glass wall of the New Orleans Hilton's cavernous, casual restaurant affords one of the most dramatic views of the Mississippi available anywhere. From the tables along the cantilevered expanse, diners can watch a tanker glide along the muddy water, or have a front-row view of one of the old sternwheeler pleasure boats that glide by. In daylight, the panorama is theatrical. At dusk or after nightfall, it's magical, as points of light from the vessels bounce along the rippling water. The menu covers a broad spectrum of seafood dishes and sandwiches (fried shrimp or oysters are the safest choices here) with strong New Orleans connections, as well as the usual array typical of big hotels that have to cater to every possible taste. Boiled crawfish, crabs and shrimp, after they're extracted from their shells, carry the appropriate Creole spiciness, along with the new potatoes steeped in the pot with them. Baked oysters Bienville and a seafood-okra gumbo wouldn't embarrass a local, homegrown seafood house. Each day's menu features specials by chef Louis Evans, whose locally honed instincts with seafoods inform the daily specials. One day it might be golden, buttery crabcakes, held together with pasta rather than breading. Another might bring lightly sautéed lemon sole under a thick crawfish sauce, or tuna (ours was on the flaky side) brushed with a flattering butter sauce with mustard and dill. Big, cold lumps of blue crab come off nicely in a mustardy white rémoulade sauce. If seafoods are out of the question, skip the flat-tasting grilled chicken breast bordelaise and splurge on the good-quality filet mignon, usually served with a decent, tarragon-flecked bearnaise. Desserts conform to the elaborate, excessive hotel style. The superrich Mississippi mud pie ends up being little more than mud. At least two different wines by the glass are offered. Dinner for two runs about $70.

Open Mon.-Sat. 11:30 a.m.-2:30 p.m. & 6 p.m.-11 p.m., Sun. 10:30 a.m.-2:30 p.m. & 6 p.m.-11 p.m. All major cards.

Kolb's

125 St. Charles Ave., Central Business District
• 522-5079
GERMAN/TRADITIONAL CREOLE

7/20

Until the unlikely day when traditional German cooking regains its long-lost stylishness, this pre–World War I museum of Teutonic culture probably will continue to languish in all its frayed Bavarian splendor. The few German dishes are nothing to yodel about. A dry, chicken-fried steak poses as Wiener Schnitzel. What the menu describes as sauerkraut is an acrid, mushy mound of chopped red cabbage. Sauerbraten is diner-quality pot roast, burdened with a pasty tan liquid of a deadening sourness. Potato pancakes have the taste and texture of cotton hockey pucks. In its glory days, which ended in the 1960s, Kolb's was a favorite lunchtime haunt of linen-suited business types who came for the good crawfish étouffee, red beans and rice and other assorted dishes from the homey Creole repertory. These days, an evening almost can be salvaged with one or two of the Creole-style dishes, but even they never rise above the mundane. New Orleans–style barbecued shrimp, in an herbal, peppery sauce, arrives atop slices of French bread that sop up the liquid nicely. For the tourists, there's the inevitable platter of fried seafoods, in this case oysters, shrimp, fish and a "crab ball"—all of which ultimately end up tasting alike. Time is more profitably spent contemplating the cat's cradle of pulleys overhead that activates the ceiling fans, the pretty old stained glass and the modest collection of beer steins. Expect to pay about $75 for dinner for two. *Open Mon.-Sat. 11 a.m.-2:30 p.m. & 5 p.m.-10 p.m., Sun. 5 p.m.-10 p.m. All major cards.*

K-Paul's Louisiana Kitchen

416 Chartres St., French Quarter • 942-7500

CAJUN/TRADITIONAL CREOLE

12/20 

Occasionally, in a driving rain, out-of-towners clad in plastic bags can still be spotted queuing up outside this very unimpressive French Quarter building. For them, K-Paul's is to New Orleans what the Great Wall is to China. As it turns out, penetrating either is not for the faint of heart. The now legendary rules on Chartres Street are ironclad: the place is dark Saturdays and Sundays; reservations are not accepted; no group is seated until everyone has arrived. When entry is finally gained, there are other hurdles: table-sharing is a necessity. The only cocktail is a "Cajun martini" laced with jalapeño peppers. A glossary would help for such menu terms as "mirliton" (vegetable pear), "tasso" (an intensely flavored Cajun ham), "seven steak" (a small T-bone) and "Cajun crawfish" (tails fried in a spicy batter). Don't clean your plate and you miss having a gold star pasted on your cheek by the server. Refuse to join the line of customers prancing to the piped-in Cajun music and you're a party pooper. And, at last, pay the hefty bill in the very nondescript dining room, lined in prefab paneling and drab linoleum. Is it any wonder that legions of hungry locals have never tasted a morsel of Paul Prudhomme's celebrated handiwork? Of those who have, many were no doubt impressed. The basket of fresh breads includes heavenly corn-flour biscuits. The intensely seasoned, murky gumbos are minor masterpieces of South Louisiana gastronomy. Double lamb chops and fresh tuna, in spicy coats

seared to a deep brown, are loaded with good flavor. Roasted duck has a fine, rustic taste, as does its accompanying rice, cooked in duck stock and dotted with giblets. Sweet potato–pecan pie is free of the sugary excesses that normally characterize such Southern desserts. Whether the food is worth the hassles, the gimmicks and the price tag—$80 to $90 for two—is something to ponder.
Open Mon.-Fri. 11:30 a.m.-2:30 p.m. & 5:30 p.m.-10:30 p.m. Cards: AE.

Kung's Dynasty

1912 St. Charles Ave., Lower Garden District • 525-6669
CHINESE

11/20

Inventiveness is not the strong suit in the city's Chinese-American restaurants. Kung's is one of the few that comes up with enough originality to separate itself from the crowd. It does so with occasionally novel treatments of oysters and crab, as well as dining spaces that are as bright and airy as any around. At midday, sunlight illuminates the classically proportioned rooms inside the graceful old Garden District cottage. On the off-white walls, between jade green curtains, hang a few Asian artifacts, admirably restrained in style and color. Tables are not generously spaced, but the effect, for once, is to lend some liveliness to the place. The menu's focus isn't very sharp, filled as it is with a hodgepodge of regional Chinese styles. Attention is paid to presentation, which means the platters usually arrive brightened by slivers of orange or tomato rosettes. Crackly spring rolls are filled with a moist and delicious mince of shrimp and earthy-tasting vegetables. Spirals of bean curd contain a mince of black mushrooms in a semi-sweet sauce with a wonderful nutty flavor. The signature squab dish features diced breast meat in a plum-type sauce with ginger root. Working our way through the rest of the lengthy roster, we came up with an excellent double-cooked pork, lean and flavorful in a spicy brown sauce with green pepper, mushrooms and bamboo shoots. A profusion of plump, lightly sautéed Louisiana oysters benefited deliciously from the pungency of a brown sauce with scallion. Finding the gems among the pebbles, however, takes work. Stick to the chef's specials and the payoff might be something like a grand roast duck Szechuan-style or delicious soft-shell crab marinated with ginger and garlic. The cost of it all, for two, rarely exceeds $40.
Open Mon.-Thurs. 11:30 a.m.-2:30 p.m. & 5 p.m.-10:30 p.m., Fri. 11:30 a.m.-2:30 p.m. & 5 p.m.-11:30 p.m., Sat. noon-2:30 p.m., Sun. noon-10 p.m. Cards: AE, MC, V.

Lafitte's Landing

Donaldsonville, La., at the western end of the Sunshine Bridge that crosses the Mississippi River, about 60 miles from New Orleans • 473-1232

CAJUN/TRADITIONAL CREOLE

A hankering for Cajun food on its home turf can be satisfied by driving up the Mississippi to Donaldsonville, where chef John Folse will ply you with his rich and intensely flavored repertory. Mussels or bay scallops in puff pastry with garlic cream is hardly a mainstay of bayou gastronomy, but there's enough rusticity in other dishes to keep the kitchen honest. The setting is a nicely proportioned, West Indian–style frame cottage, its upper-floor veranda supported by sturdy brick pillars. According to a restaurant brochure, the building dates from the eighteenth century and has vague connections to the legendary pirate Jean Lafitte. Meals are served on the ground floor, its brick walls festooned with a score or more of oils primitively depicting nearby landscapes. An occasional window makes the place look less like a dungeon, although it can sound like one when the clackety-clack of heels begins on the uncarpeted floor of the private banquet rooms overhead. What emerges from the kitchen combines French finesse with the rough-hewn style of South Louisiana. A sterling example is crawfish bisque. At bottom, it's a bowl of cream suffused with crawfish essence, gloriously spiced and seasoned. More elegantly subtle is a classic pairing of tender white veal with morels, in a cream sauce infused with the flavor of the mushrooms. The fumbles occur when basic details aren't attended to. A superabundant shrimp cocktail can arrive, pointlessly refrigerated to just above freezing. A dinner salad shows up with boring cherry tomatoes and a few canned black olives in a sweet vinaigrette. Escaping cream is rather difficult, but persistence might produce such winners as shrimp Malacher, in a fairly light butter sauce perfectly seasoned with green pepper, garlic and onion. Oyster aficionados can revel in the ones named Viala. Each oyster, fried just until its corn-flour coating begins to brown, rests on a big garlic crouton, with a nearly perfect brown meunière sauce. A wine list above the rudimentary is one of the pleasant surprises. Stick with a modest one, like Jean-Pierre Moueix's full-bodied St. Emilion, and dinner for two probably will come to around $80.

Open Mon. 11 a.m.-3 p.m., Tues.-Sat. 11 a.m.-3 p.m. & 6 p.m.-10 p.m., Sun. 11 a.m.-8 p.m. Cards: MC, V.

BRACING BREW

No one can say the old Creoles didn't appreciate a decent cup o' java. To them, the perfect brew had to be *Noir comme le diable, fort comme la mort, doux comme l'amour et chaud comme l'enfer.* It simply wasn't coffee unless it was "black as the devil, strong as death, sweet as love and hot as hell."

Lena's Steak House

1801 Stumpf Blvd., Gretna
• 362-1855
STEAKHOUSE

11/20

Broiling ovens and deep fryers are the indispensable tools of the New Orleans steakhouse, and both get a real workout at Lena's. USDA prime beef and definitively fried seafoods are the headliners, and both are done with enough savoir faire to keep the place humming with shirtsleeved carnivores and shellfish freaks. Everything else is in place, too. Veteran servers dart across the dark green carpeting with trays holding industrial-strength cocktails, oversize baked potatoes and hefty wedges of pecan pie. The functional environment turns on burnished wood walls, sturdy oak furniture and brass shades on the lamps. The beefsteak doesn't languish in the kitchen, but arrives bubbly hot. On it is just enough lightly seasoned butter to enhance the meat's flavors without overloading them. The cuts are filet mignon, sirloin strip and rib eye, in sizes ranging from eight to eighteen ounces. The filet, beautifully trimmed and broiled until a char forms at the edges, is especially reliable. As for accompaniments, the only rival of the tasty onion rings is thick disks of fried, breaded eggplant. The breading reappears in most of the fried seafoods, and is best with shrimp. A new wrinkle is spinendata, a broiled strip steak stuffed Italian-style with tomato, garlic, mushrooms, cheese and breadcrumbs. If the warm pecan pie isn't your bag, there are decent alternatives in the form of a chocolate parfait, and vanilla ice cream crowned with strawberries and laced with Grand Marnier. About $80 will cover dinner for two. *Open Mon.-Fri. 11:30 a.m.-2:30 p.m., Sat. 5:30 p.m.-10:30 p.m. All major cards.*

LeRuth's

636 Franklin Ave.,
• 362-4914
CLASSIC CREOLE

11/20

Faded glories abound in this former paragon of French/Creole creativity. The recipes that gave LeRuth's its preeminence in the 1960s are still there, but they are now executed with a matter-of-factness more common to motel dining rooms. It wasn't too long ago that hordes lined up on the porch of the small, raised Victorian cottage in the suburbs for the ethereal potage of oyster and artichoke, and the incomparable soft-shell crab blanketed in an herbal sauté of more crabmeat. Today, access to a table comes in a trice. Have a meal or two in these once proud rooms, still hung with handsome prints and oils, and the reasons become evident. Pommes dauphine, which once upon a time were models of lightness and flavor, have deteriorated into something that would get thumbs down in a McDonald's test kitchen. Fried trout Oliva, roasted rack of lamb with fried parsley and filet de boeuf LeRuth, three dishes that in the restaurant's heyday set the local standards, have turned lackadaisical. The reality not yet faced at LeRuth's is that time does not stand still, especially for restaurants, and the stewed banana served with every main course for 25 years has turned into a ridiculous anachronism, as have the little foot cushions shoved under the feet of women customers after they're seated. A wine list that once challenged both the palate and the imagination has become a perfunctory addendum to the menu. The veteran waiting staff occasionally shows a glimmer of enthusiasm, but it's never enough to dispel the clouds. Dinner for two should add up to $100 or so. *Open Tues.-Sat. 5 p.m.-10 p.m. All major cards.*

The Little Greek

2051 Metairie Rd., Metairie
• 831-9470
GREEK

12/20

The scarcity of Greek restaurants in the Creole capital is corrected in one fell swoop by this exceptional, family-operated place just outside the city limits. It began as a neatly turned out hole in the wall, but its following snowballed until expansion became necessary. Most of the familiar dishes are there—moussaka, dolmas and roasted lamb, and they're supplemented by original dishes that taste good in any language. Utterly fresh fish filets are sautéed with garlic and other seasonings, then baked inside lacy phyllo dough with lemon, wine and butter. Other good choices are lamb chops roasted with feta cheese, and sliced leg of lamb in an herbal gravy. Shrimp Aegean matches the delicious shellfish with olive oil, sherry, garlic and lemon in a refreshing paprika sauce. Skewers of tasty marinated beef or chicken are served with springy orzo pasta. The appetizers include fresh and excellent renderings of such traditional spreads as taramosalata, hummus and skordalia. The place is meticulously maintained, and service is casual but good. A couple of nights a week, there's live traditional Greek music. The dry white wines on the list are drinkable evidence that Greek vintners have progressed well beyond the cloying retsinas of yore. With a bottle, the bill for two will be about $60.
Open Tues.-Thurs. 11 a.m.-2 p.m. & 5 p.m.-9:30 p.m., Fri.-Sat. 11 a.m.-2 p.m. & 5 p.m-10 p.m., Sun. noon-8 p.m. Cards: DC, MC, V.

Liuzza's

3636 Bienville, Mid-City
• 482-9120
ITALIAN

9/20

Liuzza's is the apotheosis of the back-street New Orleans neighborhood restaurant. In one room there is a bar where large, heavy, frozen glass goblets are filled with beer or root beer. Most of those are passed through a small window into the second, smaller room, where, at Formica tables, the neighborhood gang chows on the basics. Roast beef po' boys, fried seafood and platters of red beans and rice are nothing but delicious. The menu's specials include some offbeat and often disappointing homestyle dishes, frequently with an Italian accent. Lunch or dinner for two will be under $20.

Open Mon.-Sat. 10:30 a.m.-11:30 p.m. No credit cards.

Louis XVI

St. Louis Hotel,
730 Bienville St.,
French Quarter
• 581-7000
French/Classic creole

12/20 

In the tourist-infested French Quarter, a French restaurant that ignores the Creole classics is asking for trouble. Louis XVI, ensconced on one of the district's prettiest courtyards, succumbs with such palliatives as a peppery rémoulade on its shrimp and crab, Rockefeller sauce on its oysters and the brick red turtle soup that defines the local genre. But the cooks seem much more comfortable with their slightly updated versions of Gallic sauces and combinations. Very little here is throbbing with imagination. The kitchen's lack of courage with both the classical Creole and the classic French probably comes from the independently owned restaurant's location inside a medium-size hotel, the kind of place where experimentation is frowned on. The registration desk out front also accounts for the presence of breakfast at Louis XVI every morning, despite the absence of lunch. The real action, of course, starts at sunset, when the banana fronds just outside the windows start wafting in the evening breeze. The views of the elegantly understated courtyard, with its graceful, gurgling fountain and welcoming garden furniture, are as soothing as a back rub, or a bottle of Clos de Vougeot or Montrachet from the list of 100 or so wines. Similarly relaxing is the interior environment—a tasteful mix of period and contemporary luxury, with heavy draperies framing the row of French doors overlooking the courtyard. The best starters are a grand velouté of oysters garnished with a few threads of crisp vegetables, very satisfying feuilletés of sweetbreads in Madeira or shellfish in cream, and a veal and pork terrine backed up by puckery cornichons. Slices of duckling breast grand veneur appear in a nutty-tasting reduction of stock and cream. The lightly sautéed salmon regularly appears in a creditable, coral-hued Nantua sauce. And desserts naturally lean toward the baroque. The cost will come to about $100, for two, with a wine that won't insult the food.

Open Mon.-Fri. 7 a.m.-11 a.m. & 6:30 p.m.-10:30 p.m., Sat.-Sun. 7 a.m.-noon & 6:30 p.m.-10:30 p.m. All major cards.

La Louisiane

725 Iberville St.,
French Quarter
• 523-4664
CLASSIC CREOLE/ITALIAN

12/20

This ancient fixture of the French Quarter has changed hands any number of times since 1881, when it was first transformed from an elegant Creole town house into a small but luxurious hotel, with a Creole dining room. Since the 1950s, the handsome old building with the gorgeous entrance of iron lace and beveled, leaded glass has been classified as a "Creole/Italian" restaurant, although what eventually appears on the table is closer to "Lavish Continental." So is the look of the front bar and cluster of rooms, with a plethora of cut-glass prisms, damask wall coverings and huge vases of silk flowers. The atmosphere doesn't reach the fussiness of Miami rococo, but it comes close. Pasta dishes have such familiar monickers as Alfredo, carbonara and al pesto, and they're generally done competently. The best of the lot is a homespun malafatta, where spinach gnocchi keeps company with prosciutto, peas and onions in a refreshingly good Alfredo sauce. Baked oysters Elmwood, served on the half-shell under a coat of bread crumbs seasoned with olive oil, bacon and pepper, are a safe bet, too. Good-quality white veal comes in thick chops blanketed under a cognac-and-cream sauce and woodsy-tasting morels, or in three big cubes of tenderloin, each carrying a different butter sauce. Bread pudding enthusiasts can relish a piping-hot one here, submerged under a translucent brandy sauce sweet enough to make their teeth hurt. The veteran servers, holdovers from the days when La Louisiane buzzed with city politicians on expense accounts, aren't much help with the wines, a manageable collection of mostly French, Italian and Californian bottles. The three-course, prix-fixe dinner, for two, with wine, tax and tip, should run to about $80. Ordering à la carte for two means adding another $20.

Open Mon.-Thurs. 11:30 a.m.-10:30 p.m., Fri. 11:30 a.m.-11 p.m., Sat. 5 p.m.-11 p.m. All major cards.

Maestro's

714 N. Rampart St.,
French Quarter
• 581-5453
ITALIAN

10/20

Maestro's ambitions, defined by complex variations on the rich, southern Italian theme, are not always fulfilled. And its makeshift decor, the result of a move to a defunct art-deco palace stripped of its glories, hardly flatters the food. Sauces are the mainstay, and they often show up in amounts that overwhelm whatever delicacy the main ingredient might have had. What saves the chef's reputation is his treatment of local seafoods, especially shrimp, and a few of the pasta dishes. In the best of the shrimp creations, big and rosy ones are deftly sautéed in a garlicky herb butter. As a garnish, they're sprinkled onto grilled fish with a compatible mix of artichoke, tomato and basil. Properly cooked capellini, dotted with sumptuous white-veal meatballs, joins a bracing tomato sauce with basil. Other sauces are usually layered combinations of cheeses, herbs, cream and spices. Oysters are competently fried, but whether they belong on a bed of creamed spinach, mozzarella and hollandaise is another issue. Too many sweet peppers in too much sauce sabotaged one night's special, a brace of thick pork chops of excellent quality. The better appetizers include little panfried rice cakes, seasoned with ham and cheeses. Operating less than two years, in a part of town that has seen livelier times, Maestro's deserves a chance to develop an identity. Removing some of the clutter from the menu and creating a more definable atmosphere would be good for starters. Until then, $60 isn't an unconscionable price for two. *Open Tues.-Thurs. 11:30 a.m.-2:30 p.m. & 5 p.m.-midnight, Fri. 11:30 a.m-2:30 p.m. & 5 p.m.-1 a.m., Sat. 5 p.m.-1 a.m. Cards: AE, MC, V.*

Mandich's

3200 St. Claude Ave., Ninth Ward
• 947-9553
TRADITIONAL CREOLE

11/20

Aficionados of this rough-cut gem, in the heart of a blue-collar neighborhood, ignore the rudimentary wall art and make-do decor. The magnet is food, specifically classic New Orleans cooking with a home-style edge to it. Getting to it means overcoming a number of obstacles. The quirkiness of the operating schedule (dinner twice a week and lunch four times) is aggravated by a no-reservations policy that usually means a wait of a quarter hour or longer in a usually crowded, working-class bar that only the most gregarious will find comfortable. Yet the wood-veneer dining room, lit by an assortment of fixtures, is one of the best places to sample down-to-earth New Orleans cooking. At lunch everyone from the local cops to the young and idle rich enjoys such basic fare as white beans and rice, shrimp stew and veal parmigiana. At night, the fare rises considerably in sophistication, although the excellent seafood po' boys are still available. A house specialty is trout Mandich, sautéed in a floury coating that is exceptionally crisp outside, but can be rather soggy inside. On both the appetizer and entrée lists is one of the kitchen's best offerings —fried oysters with garlic butter, flecked with parsley and scallion. Ignore the pinkish, salad-dressing–type sauce garnishing the grilled shrimp and andouille sausage and enjoy their grand, spicy flavors. A star attraction is the "high-hat filet," a bulbous nine ounces of top-quality beef tenderloin, beautifully char-broiled and brushed with a subtly seasoned butter sauce.

The best accompaniment is Boston potatoes, a crisp-edged, layered cake of thin potato slices sautéed in garlic and butter. Wines are displayed on a counter near the kitchen, each bottle ringed with a price tag in big black numbers. Mainstay desserts are serviceable versions of bread pudding and cheesecake. Prices are higher than you would expect in such unpretentious surroundings. Dinner for two, with a modest wine, can easily cost $80.
Open Tues.-Thurs. 11 a.m.-2:30 p.m., Fri. 11 a.m.-10 p.m., Sat. 5 p.m.-10 p.m. Cards: MC.

Moran's Riverside

In the French Market complex near the intersection of Decatur & Dumaine Sts.
• 529-1583
ITALIAN CREOLE

8/20

Eating in a restaurant that names its dishes after business and sports figures is always risky business. This pretentious, flashy place has more than its share of pitfalls. Refinement is scarce at Moran's Riverside, despite its elegantly proportioned dining room, flanked by big, fan-light-topped windows overlooking the Mississippi River, and the pretty baroque banquet room leading to the al fresco bar. Between a starter of spiritless "shrimp scampi" and a main course of cooked-to-death trout, you will be served a supersweet sorbet. The owner is the city's "king of fettuccine," a title that he bestowed upon himself for strands of unremarkable pasta with tiny clumps of Parmesan clinging to them in a watery pool. Safer harbor might be found in osso bucco, an extra-large, extra-tender veal shank excellently braised in aromatic vegetables. Aside from the humdrum salads, the only other vegetables around are potatoes and mushrooms. A smoky-tasting rack of lamb can rise to acceptability, and the turtle soup is not embarrassingly bad. Any further search for distinction usually results in a succession of dead ends in this tired and tiring throwback to 1950s chic. Two should not expect to escape for less than $120, with a decent bottle of wine.
Open Mon.-Fri. 6 p.m.-11 p.m., Sat. 6 p.m.-midnight. All major cards.

Morton's of Chicago Steak House

402 N. Peters, in the Jackson Brewery Marketplace
• 523-4965
STEAKHOUSE

11/20

Morton's is revered in its hometown for serving state-of-the-art steak and lobster, a reputation it steadfastly maintained during a nationwide expansion. Until it got to New Orleans. The Morton's here is no less good than any of the others. But since New Orleans has been a great steak town for decades (this fact gets little publicity, but it's true), Morton's doesn't stand out quite as much. Start with the giant shrimp from somewhere else, or the beef-steak-tomato salad. The steaks are prime and well aged. They are broiled in one hell of a hot roaster until they have a thrilling, lightly charred exterior—even at the rare degree of doneness. The superlative cuts are the porterhouse for one or three and the strip, but the filets and ribeyes are also first-rate. The broiler also crusts up fine, juicy chops of lamb and veal, as well as very large and expensive Maine lobsters (that charred-shell aroma and flavor adds a wonderful new dimension to the crustacean). The premises are simple and comfortable. Service, once you get past the show-and-tell display of the goods for sale, is efficient. The wine list is excellent, and some local nobs have their private stocks in prominently displayed lockers in the foyer. Dinner for two, with wine, will set you back $100. *Open Mon.-Fri. 11:30 a.m.-3 p.m. & 5:30 p.m.- 11 p.m., Sat. 5:30 p.m.-11 p.m., Sun. 5:30 p.m.-9 p.m. All major cards.*

Mosca's

4137 U.S. Hwy. 90, Waggaman
• 436-9942
ITALIAN CREOLE

12/20

Rustic Italian cooking with distinctive Creole flourishes is the stock-in-trade of Mosca's. Since 1946, it has remained the quintessential diamond-in-the-rough, couched inside a clapboard building and surrounded by marshy woods and an expanse of crushed clamshells that serves as a parking lot. The late Lisa Mosca, better known to her army of admirers as Mama, crafted the repertory of herbal, garlicky seafoods and fowl that first made the place's reputation. Almost nothing has changed over the decades, except perhaps the consistency of the cooking. The dish called "Italian oysters"—an aluminum pie pan holding oysters baked in a breadcrumb dressing with olive oil, garlic and herbs—inspired dozens of imitations. When it's done right—which is about 50 percent of the time these days—it still beats all the competition. "Italian shrimp"—which translates as big, fresh, unpeeled ones in a warm sauce of butter, olive oil and spices—also spawned a legion of imitators. Chicken à la grande (roasted after a swabbing with olive oil, white wine and rosemary), can be a model of succulent tenderness or a dried-out disappointment. Whole cracked crab, steeped in a homey Italian marinade with pickled vegetables, has a better track record. The made-from-scrach spaghetti aglio e olio is usually overcooked, but the flavors hold up nicely. Delicious home-style Italian pork sausages, lavished with anise seed and other spices, lend their flavor to the chunks of potato they're roasted with. The setting is appropriately no-frills. Bare wood floors extend from the spacious bar into the single dining room, hung with folkloric art and window-unit air conditioners. The collection of mismatched flatware and crockery must go back to World War II. Table

service amounts to taking orders and delivering food—no more. The very small wine list, a footnote to the menu, is even more basic. Expect a wait of about 30 minutes for main courses and a financial outlay of about $60 for two.
Open Tues.-Sat. 5:30 p.m.-9:30 p.m. No cards.

Mr. B's Bistro

201 Royal St., French Quarter • 523-2078
CONTEMPORARY CREOLE

Throbbing with sassy energy, Mr. B's is the best of the upscale, contemporary Creole bistros that began sprouting in the 1970s. Although strong traditional undercurrents run through the cooking, most of it sparkles with a fresh approach. The atmosphere in the dining spaces, sectioned off with low partitions of polished wood and etched glass, is clubby and convivial. A strategic location on the French Quarter's busiest corner attracts a steady stream of tourists, but locals like the place enough to wink at the shirtsleeves and Reeboks. The kitchen's focal point is a hickory-fired grill. From it come impeccably fresh fish in bold and lustrous sauces, glistening shrimp and andouille sausage, hefty steaks and quail bulging with flavorful stuffings. The proprietors are Ralph and Cindy Brennan, sibling members of the Commander's Palace branch of the Brennan family of restaurateurs. The family's trademarks include well-organized service and a wine cellar loaded with the most respected names in California. Finding room for the bottle can be difficult, though, when four diners sit elbow-to-elbow at one of the small tables. Chef Gerard Maras's creations are fervently international in spirit. A typical salad matches warm goat cheese with duck confit, crunchy pecans, an herbal vinaigrette and leaves of Bibb, radicchio, endive and watercress. Maras's albacore tuna might arrive lightly sautéed in olive oil and embellished with succulent plum tomatoes and onions atop wilted romaine. Filet mignon is sometimes swathed in a shimmering, mellow raisin sauce. Pasta pinch hits for rice in the signature jambalaya, blending bits of chicken, duck, spicy sausage and shrimp with spinach fettuccine in a refreshing sauce of duck essence. The New Orleans–style barbecued shrimp, unpeeled and wading in a grandly spiced liquid, are unbeatable. The fusion of traditional and contemporary extends to desserts, such as the knockout bread pudding with Irish whiskey sauce and the silky brownie of white chocolate with vanilla ice cream and hot-fudge sauce. Avoid the loftier-priced wines, and the bill for two should be about $80.
Open daily 11:30 a.m.-3 p.m. & 5 p.m.-10 p.m. All major cards.

Mr. Tai's

Old Metairie Village,
701 Metairie Rd.
• 831-8610
CHINESE

12/20

The opening of Mr. Tai's in 1986 was one of the first signs of progress along New Orleans's chopsticks circuit, littered over the years with wonton and fried rice. Hunan and Szechuan cooking is the preoccupation in this elegantly understated suburban restaurant. The deep, often spicy flavors of Hunan cuisine come through consistently well in a festival of sauces. Major seasonings are sesame, garlic, anise, pine nuts, chilis and ginger, ingredients that may be humdrum on the East and West coasts, but ground-breaking in these parts. Hunan duck rises above the cliché with its grand flavor, redolent of camphor and tea leaves, and a tangy plum sauce that's notable for the balance of its complex tastes. Another winner in the Hunan category is spring lamb, in wafer-thin slices interlaced with threads of white onion and a bracingly peppery brown sauce zapped with vodka. A pungent black-bean sauce moistens a dice of quail breast, ready for wrapping in crisp lettuce leaves that bring an interesting contrast of textures. From the steamer comes a row of six large, rosy shrimp, ready for a coolly delicious mustard and ginger sauce. The night is not without its risks, however. Too much sugar can deflate the taste of a corn-and-crab soup, and crawfish tails might show up in a dark red, sweetish liquid reminiscent of ketchup. Helping fill the two elegantly understated dining rooms are handsome, red mahogany chairs, a few softly colored prints and wisps of silk flowers in stem vases. Their colors show up nicely against deep green table liners and eggshell walls with a delicate brushstroke motif. Dinner for two, with wine or one of the Asian beers, runs about $45.

Open Tues.-Thurs. 11 a.m.-2 p.m. & 5 p.m.-10 p.m., Fri. 11 a.m.-2 p.m. & 5 p.m.-11 p.m., Sat. 5 p.m.-11 p.m., Sun. 5 p.m.-10 p.m. Cards: AE, MC, V.

Nuvolari's

246 Gerard St., Mandeville
(north shore of lake)
• 1-626-5619
ITALIAN CREOLE

11/20

Nuvolari's old brick building has the interior look of a fern restaurant, but the cooking is serious. Chef Tim Eihausen creates food that's mostly Italian, but with unexpected twists, Creolisms and other points of interest. The pairing of escargots and crawfish in a peppery demiglaze is as promising a start as any. Shrimp rémoulade served in an avocado and a corn-and-crawfish chowder are other inspired starters. Italian standards such as lasagna and veal Parmigiana include layers of fresh spinach—not classic, but delicious. Lamb T-bone steaks with jalapeño sauce, roast duck with both cherries and green peppercorns, and a strip steak with a Scotch whisky and demi-glaze sauce all make for satisfying eating. Side dishes of pasta, Caesar salad, minestrone and the like are all even better than expected. The wine list will delight the curious oenophile; there are always a few bottles whose presence is a nice surprise. Service is cheery and good. The place is popular, and waits for a table are almost inevitable at busy times. Dinner for two can be had for about $60, including wine. *Open Mon.-Wed. & Fri.-Sat. 5 p.m.-10 p.m., Thurs. 11 a.m.-2 p.m. & 5 p.m.-10 p.m., Sun. noon-10 p.m. Cards: AE, MC, V.*

Olde N'Awlins Cookery

729 Conti, French Quarter • 529-3663
CLASSIC CREOLE

9/20

The original chef here was the first of many spinoffs from K-Paul's, back when that restaurant was a trendsetter. Although the fellow has long since moved on, he established a style of cooking here which has continued to hold great appeal for the masses of tourists passing the front door. The Cookery has a decent local following, too. The menu is on a blackboard and includes ample, very full-flavored versions of jambalaya, barbecued shrimp, fried trout with pecans and meunière sauce, red beans and rice and a handful of other dishes. Unfortunately, the consistency record is not particularly good. The restaurant has a certain chaos about it and the noise generated by the staff in the name of free-spiritedness is insane. The premises—brick inside, and pleasant courtyard outside—could be a lot cleaner. Dinner for two, with beer, is about $45. *Open daily 11 a.m.-11 p.m. No credit cards.*

Pascal's Manale

1838 Napoleon Ave., Uptown • 895-4877
ITALIAN CREOLE

9/20

It wasn't too long ago that local lawyers in white linen and post-debs in discreet jewelry packed the spacious, cluttered bar of this Uptown institution. If they were on the "short list," they'd be ushered into one of the low-slung, densely furnished dining rooms ahead of anybody who wasn't wearing a familiar face. The scene is much changed today. The bar's paneled woods still sport an archive of sports photos, snapshots of regulars and Mardi Gras memorabilia. But the crowd is much more likely to be a mishmash of professional types from Chicago, Atlanta and Denver, in town for a convention or the Sugar Bowl. What probably drove the locals away was a combination of a pecking order that got out of hand and a kitchen that became increasingly unloyal to its original standards of quality. Now, the bar is posted with a boldly lettered warning: "Please pay when served. Cash only." Hanging from the ceiling are T-shirts, umbrella hats and baseball caps carrying the restaurant's advertising and price tags. Very good food can still be gotten at Pascal's Manale, but the probability of that grows slimmer by the

year. The original barbecued shrimp—a bowlful of unpeeled shrimp in a buttery, spicy bath—remain the safest bet. The rest of the territory is a minefield, ranging from excellent fried eggplant and onion rings to a harsh, undercooked Rockefeller sauce, and cream sauces with the consistency of library paste. White veal dishes and fried oysters are usually satisfying, too, if they're not sabotaged by another of the production-line sauces. And you may find the dining room neat and clean one night, littered and messy the next. Whatever the room's condition, the cost of dinner for two, with wine, is about $90.
Open Mon.-Fri. 11 a.m.-10 p.m., Sat. 4 p.m.-10:30 p.m. All major cards.

El Patio

3244 Georgia Ave. (at 33rd, a block from Williams Blvd.), Kenner
• 443-1188
MEXICAN

10/20

Jorge Rodriguez has owned a series of Mexican restaurants around town for over twenty years, but this little café in Kenner (the suburb where the airport is located) is the culmination of his efforts. The entire Rodriguez family is involved in all aspects of the place: cooking, waiting tables, playing guitar and singing. Amazingly enough, they're all pretty good at every one of those endeavors. Black bean soup here is perfect in texture, seasoning and aroma, and the avocado-and-tortilla soup is almost as good. The ceviche of marinated raw Gulf fish is tart, cold and fresh. Amid the usual array of tortilla dishes and combinations thereof, you find some more ambitious fare. Mexican seafood dishes are in gratifying abundance. The best of them is a plate of crabmeat-stuffed, white-sauce-napped squid, sharpened with cilantro. Baked fish with a Veracruz-style sauce of tomatoes and peppers is also wonderful. A mole poblano—the peppery chocolate-based sauce—abets a fine roasted chicken. Puerco y bifteck asada is also savory stuff, aromatic with garlic and herbs. Arroz con calamares—rice with squid—is better than the paella. For dessert, don't miss the creamy flan, made with the highly distinctive flavor of Mexican vanilla. A *comida corrida para dos* (meal for two) is about $40, with beer.
Open Mon.-Thurs. 5 p.m.-10 p.m., Fri.-Sat. 5 p.m.-11 p.m. Cards: AE, MC, V.

Patout's

1319 St. Charles Ave., Uptown
• 524-4054
CAJUN

11/20

The baby-boom generation of the large, New Iberia–based Patout family has been aggressive in capitalizing on the demand for Cajun restaurants, and very successful in getting the Patout name spread about. The Patouts serve authentic Cajun food, but in a style that leaves you wondering whether you've missed something. You haven't. Authentic is not always good. They have a penchant for cooking food—particularly vegetables—to death. They also overwhelm the flavors of fish, veal and even steak with rich, creamy, buttery sauces studded with crabmeat, crawfish or both. Despite the kitchen's unreliability, a good meal is possible at the New Orleans edition of Patout's; the basic raw materials are fresh and good, and if you ask them to grill a fish lightly and send it out with the sauce on the side, you get a delicious dish. The soups are uniformly wonderful, especially the corn-and-crab bisque. They roast fine chicken and duck. In season, the crawfish étouffée has a finely-balanced spiciness and richness. The restaurant is in the back of a hotel, which it serves as the house eatery. Dinner comes to about $130 for two, with wine.

Open daily 11 a.m.-2 p.m. & 6 p.m.-10 p.m. All major cards.

Peking

6600 Morrison Rd., eastern New Orleans • 241-3321
CHINESE

11/20

You won't overdose on theatrics or spectacular presentation in this cozy and likable place, couched in a shopping mall far from the central city's hubbub, and much of the food would pass muster with a finicky fan of Chinese cooking. The spicy and meaty dumplings, steamed and fried, are the best in town, bolstered with a sauce that would do any Asian chef proud. Peking duck, to be ordered in advance, also makes a good impression, with subtle contrasts of textures and flavors. This is a family operation, which may account for the earnest, down-to-earth qualities of such dishes as dry-cooked string beans with pork or shrimp, and a crisp and greaseless fried whole fish with brown sauce. The usual regional styles are represented. Crispy egg-roll wrappings, thin as onionskin, hold a delicious mince of softly seasoned shrimp. Layers of chicken breast, lobster and ham fill a crunchy crust in Phoenix chicken. Scallions and ginger add their zip to the delicious brown sauce that's served with slices of lightly floured, braised fish. Ribbons of sweet eggplant are artfully arranged with pork strips in lively Szechuan seasonings. Service is cheeringly informal, and if the gilt and red paint of the decoration look much too familiar, they don't interfere with the honest goodness of the food. Two people can enjoy the Peking's best without spending more than $45, including beer.

Open Tues.-Sat. 11 a.m.-10:30 p.m., Sun. noon-9:30 p.m. All major cards.

La Provence

Across Lake Pontchartrain on U.S. Hwy. 190, Lacombe, La.(about 35 miles from central New Orleans)
• 626-7662
FRENCH/CONTEMPORARY CREOLE

At its best, the very personal cuisine of Chris Kerageorgiou represents the most admirable qualities of French country cooking—earthy, yet elegant, full-flavored, but not lacking in subtlety, and executed with the knowledge that freshness and simplicity are high virtues, indeed. Kerageorgiou's Greek-French parentage and the formative years he spent near Marseille obviously shaped his sensibilities, which often come to full flower at La Provence, his charming little restaurant in the piney woods on the northern shores of Lake Pontchartrain. No chef in the region puts Louisiana's bounty of finfish and shellfish to better use, and none understands better the value of balancing richness with lightness. Everything you will find around the dining room's huge, welcoming hearth is impeccably fresh. It begins with a little pot of rillettes, ready for spreading on the just baked country bread. Next might come a trio of plump and salty oysters, baked on the half-shell, each in its own sauce—one a squiggle of aïoli, another a mayonnaise lightened with oyster juice and herbs, the third a mince of green pepper and andouille sausage. A saddle of rabbit glories in lavender and hints of other provençal herbs. The jambalaya des gourmets is a revelation—pieces of boldly seasoned sausage, shrimp and chicken, trading flavors in the pan before ringing a mound of rice dotted with crabmeat and sweet pepper in a little pool of Nantua sauce. Utterly fresh soft-shell crab is sautéed in butter and graced with bits of tomato and snips of basil. A soul-warming chowder of catfish and artichoke flatters both the fish and the vegetable. A rack of lamb niçoise, lean but juicy, gains in seductive power with a dark, herbal sauce. Wines are not an obsession here, although the list contains enough prestige labels to keep the food from being insulted. For dessert, there might be a St-Honoré, classically constructed with fine puff pastry, almond cream and crème anglaise, or a tulip of thin cookie dough resting on a coulis of strawberries and filled with a definitive chocolate mousse. A litany of dishes does not do justice to Kerageorgiou's intuitive technique. This is food that transcends the trendy or fashionable without getting bogged down in monotony or boredom. Occasionally, the patron himself will take a minute or two to troubleshoot and table-hop. It's consistent with the relaxed informality of the place, brightened with naive Provençal landscape paintings. Dinner for two, with wine, costs about $100. *Open Wed.-Sat. 5 p.m.-11 p.m., Sun. 1 p.m.-9 p.m. Cards: AE, MC, V.*

Ralph & Kacoo's

519 Toulouse St.,
French Quarter
• 522-5226

601 Veterans Blvd.,
Metairie
• 831-3177
CAJUN/SEAFOOD

9/20

More than 50 seafood dishes crowd the menus of this small chain of casual restaurants. They may not win prizes for innovation, but they're marketable enough to attract crowds that fill the cavernous dining rooms. Everything coming from the deep fryers and sauté pans will be familiar to most diners, and in both the French Quarter and suburban branches, thousands of meals are delivered to the tables every night with a minimum of fuss and a maximum of efficiency. Take a number in the bar or anteroom and wait your turn for a crack at the huge, mix-and-match selection of fresh, intensely seasoned Louisiana seafood dishes. In the French Quarter restaurant, a fishing-boat hull dominates the bar. In suburban Metairie, the decor is less colorful and the proportion of youngsters at the tables is higher. In either place, a good way to start is with boiled shrimp, crab or crawfish, still in their shells and carrying the authentically spicy taste of the bayous. The raw oysters, freshly shucked, are reliable, too. The best of the several gumbos may be the crab, infused with good sea tastes and seasonings. The trout meunière is no embarrassment, either. Space does not allow a listing of the major occupants of the fried-seafood platter; suffice it to say that everything usually is fresh, hot and reasonably greaseless. Some time ago, the roster of artery cloggers was supplemented with a nice variety of "heart-healthy" meals, each adding up to about 800 calories. In these, boiled potatoes replace the french fries, salads come with low-calorie dressings, and butter and oils are kept out of the seafoods and chicken. The service staff is trained to feed the hordes quickly and painlessly, and that's what it does. The cost of it all for two is about $40 or less.
French Quarter: open Mon.-Thurs. 11:30 a.m.-10:30 p.m., Fri.-Sat. 11:30 a.m.-11 p.m., Sun. 11:30 a.m.-9:30 p.m. Metairie: open Mon.-Thurs. 11:30 a.m.-10 p.m., Fri.-Sat. 11:30 a.m.-10:30 p.m., Sun. 11:30 a.m.-9 p.m. Cards: AE, MC, V.

Rib Room

Royal Orleans Hotel,
621 St. Louis,
French Quarter
• 529-7045
CONTINENTAL

12/20

The rear wall of this expansive cube holds a bank of rotisseries, slowly turning loads of big shrimp, oysters, chickens, ducks, quails and a few other things. The rotisserie was meant to update the Rib Room, which, although it resides in one of the best hotels in town, is surprisingly unswank. The eponymous prime ribs, a holdover from the 1960s, remain pretty good.

Dishes originating on the rotisserie are, however, much more interesting—especially the shrimp and the birds. You may wish the Rib Room would make even greater

use of this resource. The remainder of the menu is a pastiche of Continental and Creole specialties. The crab bisque, pink and spicy, is one of the city's best. A second good starter is the rich linguine forestière, with a tan cream sauce studded with wild mushrooms. A stack of romaine topped with a gigantic slice of sizzling, crusty panned veal, dressed with an Italian vinaigrette, is one of the best dishes in the house and a simple thrill. The Rib Room's recipe for dense chocolate mousse is unparalleled locally; the dessert cart has a further wealth of sweets. Service is rather casual, given the prices and pretension of the menu. Dinner for two, with wine, costs about $95.
Open Mon.-Sat. 11:30 a.m.-3 p.m. & 6:30 p.m.-11:30 p.m., Sun. 11 a.m.-3 p.m. & 6:30 p.m.-11:30 p.m. All major cards.

La Riviera

4506 Shores Dr., Metairie
• 888-6238
ITALIAN

"Northern Italian" is how you'll usually hear La Riviera's style described. That label ignores the restaurant's profusion of southern Italian tomato sauces and the heavy reliance on garlic, oregano and basil. Still, there are enough delicate white sauces, flavored butters and gentle cooking here to keep everybody happy. Best of all, what emerges from the stoves represents, more often than not, some of the most satisfying Italian/Creole food in or around New Orleans. Choose wisely, and you will be presented with a dish or two that properly reflects veteran chef Goffredo Fraccaro's Genoese roots—something along the lines of springy ravioli stuffed with mildly seasoned crab in a silky and elegant cream sauce, or a golden broth carrying the very compatible flavors of artichoke and lightly poached oysters, or a sauté of shrimp in a magnificent sauce of garlic and basil, bound with white wine and olive oil, then reddened with a bit of paprika. These lighter dishes lend authenticity to the art on the white, embossed wall coverings, a series of large, nostalgic oils that dreamily recall some of the picturesque towns along Italy's Ligurian coast. Midweek usually finds the pace at dinner much more relaxed than on weekends, when the tuxedoed waiters and bus staff race by like decathlon competitors, loaded down with plates of red snapper, topped with crabmeat and glistening in a fragile beurre blanc, or medallions of white veal piccata. The nightly specials usually include very good treatments of pasta with seafood, such as crawfish tails in herb butter with spaghettini. Occasionally, oversalting mars a sauce or pasta, and it seems to happen when Parmesan or Romano cheese is an ingredient. Choosing a wine has become

more interesting since a good number of premium Italian labels were added to the cellar. Two diners concentrating on the prix-fixe menu will pay about $70. The à la carte route means an additional $20 or so.
Open Mon.-Thurs. 5 p.m.-10 p.m., Fri.-Sat. 5 p.m.-11 p.m. All major cards.

Ruth's Chris Steak House

711 N. Broad, Mid-City • 486-0810

3633 Veterans Blvd., Metairie • 888-3600

STEAKHOUSE

12/20

For reasons rooted in the proximity of the horse racetrack to a pair of expensive steakhouses, New Orleanians are accustomed to eating prime, well-aged beef when they go out for a steak. This tradition is of such long standing that a New Orleans style of steak cookery has evolved. It involves a butter sauce—not a brushing of it, but a lake of sizzling butter in which the steak all but floats. As crazed a surfeit of fat as that sounds, the aroma and flavor of a steak done this way is irresistible. Ruth's Chris, the standard by which all other steakhouses in New Orleans are compared, packs them in at both its locations, and has also done extremely well in its expansion to other American cities. The steaks are of unimpeachable pedigree; the best cut by far is the strip, with a tight, tender texture and aged flavor. The filets are also good, but are cut oddly. The porterhouse involves a stretching of the definition of that cut, and the ribeye is a bit much—the normally fatty cut goes over the edge when it's prime. Ruth's is an excellent all-around chophouse, with lamb, veal and pork chops near tops. Side dishes are huge and very good, particularly the shrimp rémoulade, the salad (with a unique hot-paprika dressing) and any of the dozen or so potatoes. The service is very attentive and friendly, the wine list selected and priced attractively. Ruth's on Broad Street—the original—is *the* hangout for the local politicians and other power brokers. Lunch costs under $50 for two; double that for dinner.
Open daily 11:30 a.m.-11:30 p.m. All major cards.

Sal & Judy's

U.S. 190, Lacombe (north of the lake) • 1-882-9443

ITALIAN CREOLE

11/20

This is a roadhouse in the center of a small town across the lake from New Orleans. The premises are ramshackle, but the place is so popular that getting a table usually involves a substantial wait. Both the wait and the drive are worthwhile, particularly if you get a special kick out of paying laughably low prices for above-average eats. The printed menu will not impress you; it's a collection of very basic Italian food. Order one of the day's specials, many of which involve fresh seafood prepared expertly. A best bet is trout belle meunière, sautéed to a moist texture and sauced with the ideal lemon butter. Variations on this with shrimp, mushrooms or artichokes in the sauce are also fine. Italian sausage is made on the premises and grilled to a thrilling crunchy skin; the flavor, redolent of anise, is a fine foil for the roasted peppers and spaghetti aglio olio alongside. Chicken cacciatore has a lusty, chunky tomato sauce with no small amount of pepper. First courses include the herbal, oil-enriched baked oysters Cinisi, grease-free fried calamari and a good oyster-artichoke soup. Service is country-style friendly; roll up your sleeves. For dinner for two, plan on $50, with wine.

Open Wed.-Thurs. 5 p.m.-10 p.m.; Fri.-Sun. 12:30 p.m.-11 p.m. Cards: MC, V.

Santa Fe

801 Frenchmen St., Faubourg Marigny • 944-6854

MEXICAN

10/20

Occupying the gastronomic region lying somewhere between a chili parlor and a chic Southwestern café, Sante Fe attracts a young, with-it crowd by updating Tex-Mex with a number of novel twists. It does so in roomy, whitewashed spaces done up with restraint—a few handsome Indian rugs and blankets, greenery, cushioned rattan seats and wall mirrors in the slightly baroque style of colonial Mexico. Arranged on the woven-straw placemats are various deviations from the Tex-Mex mainstream. Both the beef and turkey chilis have character, chock-full of meat and slightly peppery. Gazpacho is a thick purée of tomato and fresh-tasting vegetables. A variety of nachos with occasionally clever toppings, such as pine nuts and raisins, are other good starters. The combination plates are usually filled to capacity, each element spilling over into the other. In the one with seafood, crabmeat, crawfish and shrimp lurk somewhere under the garnishes of egg, poblano sauce, guacamole, scallions, sour cream, cheeses and nuts. Pepian translates as a baked chicken breast coated in crushed pumpkin seeds and topped with a pleasant mix of cheese, cream and poblano sauce sprinkled with herbs. If the greeting at the door can be matter-of-fact, service is efficient enough, and frozen margaritas arrive in a flash. The chef's European origins come to the forefront in the competent desserts, such as white- and dark-chocolate mousses, a satiny flan and a checkered coconut pie. Dinner for two, with beer or a couple of glasses of wine, usually costs about $50.

Open Mon.-Fri. 11 a.m.-11 p.m., Sat. 5 p.m.-11 p.m. Cards: AE, MC, V.

Sazerac

Fairmont Hotel,
University Place ,
Central Business District
• 529-4733
AMERICAN/CLASSIC CREOLE

12/20

If you've just been promoted from president to chairman, this superplush, neorococo watering hole is where you're likely to be fêted. And what better place to feast on expense-account goose liver, Russian caviar and turbot in champagne than this paragon of old-fashioned hotel luxe? The table covers are white lace, the curvilinear banquettes are tufted red velvet and the gilded-bronze chandeliers glistening overhead add their fairytale touch. If these aren't sufficiently otherworldly, go on a night when the gowned harpist plucks away. Until a couple of years ago, the lunch and dinner menus were overloaded with dishes from the nineteenth-century catalogue of French classicism, spiced up with an occasional Creole dish from the same era. Today, as historical personages look down from the huge, stately oil portraits, tuxedoed waiters deliver food that often has a New American look. The decently grilled soft-shell crab shows up in a "light Creole butter sauce," nesting on winter greens. Diced veal sweetbreads are tossed with pasta threads. Cool slices of lobster are joined by a bracingly good relish of papaya and basil. Four huge grilled shrimp appear with enoki mushrooms in a nest of frisée lettuce. A murky Creole gumbo sits cheek-by-jowl with a warm salad of pheasant and spinach. All are meticulously done, often to good effect. Sometimes, the atmosphere gets downright operatic, as flames shoot from a gueridon at one table, while molded-ice swans as big as chickens are brought out holding scoops of sorbet between their wings, illuminated from below by flashlight bulbs. To bring you down to earth, there are dessert soufflés with a floury texture to remind you that you are, after all, in a hotel dining room. Dinner for two, with a proper wine, should come to about $120.
Open Mon.-Fri. 11:30 a.m.-2 p.m. & 5:30 p.m.-11:30 p.m., Sat.-Sun. 5:30 p.m.-11:30 p.m. All major cards.

Seb's

600 Decatur St.
(Jackson Brewery Millhouse,
5th level),
French Quarter
• 522-1696
CONTEMPORARY CREOLE

12/20

The sleek and immaculate spaces at Seb's may be the ideal antidote for anyone who has overdosed on iron lace, peeling paint and seedy crawfish joints. And the fifth-floor views of the French Quarter and Mississippi River are sensational. Against the neutral tones of the walls, sculpted ribbons of seaweed undulate, and beautiful sea-green sculptures depict pairs of gaping catfish, their tails intertwined in baroque curves. These contrast nicely with the crisp, neomodern lines of the architecture, which dovetails with the design of the building the restaurant inhabits, the Jackson Brewery Millhouse. A restaurant in the Quarter's densest concentration of tourists has to have

some range, and Seb's complies with both Creole and Continental sauces on its seafoods and meats. Crabmeat gets the respect it deserves in a couple of the appetizers, one featuring a cool, peppery mayonnaise similar to a Creole ravigote sauce, the other a warm mix of crabmeat, prosciutto and scallions in a light cream sauce. Baked oysters Rockefeller are several cuts above average, thanks to a sauce of puréed spinach that's marvelously fresh and balanced. For more contemporary tastes, there's Elysian endive, braised and wrapped in ham, then lightly bathed in raspberry vinaigrette. Fresh fish is a major attraction, and several species are always on hand. They are grilled or sautéed, and served up with any number of garnishes and sauces, ranging from a tart brown butter with lemon to Creole mustard with shrimp and artichoke added. The simpler renditions work best. Meats are not always successful. Good filet mignon is overworked in its two thick sauces, one a rich brown one, the other a blue-cheese concoction. Lamb chops are expensive and can be fatty. The best desserts are the superb flourless chocolate cake and the "5th Floor Pie," containing enough ice cream, meringue and chocolate sauce for at least two people. The bill for two, with wine, comes to about $80.
Open Mon.-Sat. 11:30 a.m.-2 p.m. & 5:30 p.m.-10 p.m., Sun. 11 a.m.-4 p.m. & 5:30 p.m.-10 p.m. All major cards.

Shogun

2325 Veterans Blvd., Metairie
• 833-7477
JAPANESE

11/20

The town's sushi fanatics, a loud bunch, are pretty much in agreement that Shogun leads the New Orleans sushi-bar league. The rather large restaurant has a sushi bar so long you can hardly see from one end to the other. The fish, both raw and cooked, is selected, sliced and presented with care and elan. The volume is so great that the fish is always vivdly fresh. In assortments of sushi or sashimi, Shogun always includes a species or two that one rarely encounters elsewhere in town. The cooked specialties at the table are also good—even those sneered upon by the sushi addicts: crisp, mellow tempuras and piquant grilled teriyaki meats and seafood. Since the death of the local Benihana, Shogun has shouldered the load of teppanyaki cookery, installing those tables with the hot grill in the center. But nothing here tops the works of the sushi bar. Dinner, with beer, for two runs around $35, although you could quite effortlessly run up a bill higher than that in sushi for one.
Open Mon.-Thurs. 11:30 a.m.-2 p.m. & 5:30 p.m.-10 p.m., Fri. 11:30 a.m.-2 p.m. & 5:30 p.m.-11 p.m., Sat. 5:30 p.m.-11 p.m. Cards: AE, MC, V.

The Steak Knife

6263 Marshal Foch St., Lakeview
• 488-8981
STEAKHOUSE

11/20

The neighborhood known as Lakeview is hardly a hotbed of thrill seekers, and The Steak Knife fits right in with the middle-of-the-road attitude of the families who fill the brick bungalows surrounding it. Burnished-wood walls are there to placate, not to excite. A collection of prints idealizing old-timey New Orleans provokes no arguments. What the kitchen produces occupies similar middle ground. The menu is a roster of steaks and homey dishes drawn from the local Creole and Italian hit parades, the kind of fare that has to compete with whatever sitcom is on the tube on a given night. Steaks are the probable bestsellers, because the meat's quality is good and the charbroiling is more than competent. The ribeyes and sirloin strips are delivered in the form locals prefer, right from the broiler and gently brushed with a lightly seasoned butter. Filet mignon and porterhouse are the most dependable cuts. The beef's chief rivals are a thick veal chop with the right lean-to-fat ratio and a four-chop rack of spring lamb, just pink and presented in a nest of watercress beside a ramekin of warm butter sauce with a little mint. Appetizers and soups travel a familiar road. There are sound versions of shrimp rémoulade, fried eggplant and fried onion rings. Seafoods are a hit-and-miss proposition. Fried shrimp can be excellent, but ordering anything more elaborate is asking for trouble. Both wine labels and prices are geared to middle-range incomes, which means dinner for two can be had for about $60.

Open daily 5 p.m.-11 p.m. Cards: V, MC, AE.

Tandoor

3000 Severn Ave., Metairie
• 887-7414
INDIAN

12/20

Visually, it's a mix of suburban America and mysterious India. Gastronomically, it's a creditable Indian restaurant, serving a wide array of authentic and well-prepared dishes—spicy curries, mildly seasoned stews and succulent meats roasted in a flash in the superhot clay ovens that give the place its name. A good way to begin is with the spicy, fritterlike pakoras with vegetables or chicken, followed perhaps by a sizzling platter of lamb, shrimp and sausages on a bed of onion strips. The curries, mild or peppery, include good shrimp, chicken or beef, as well as the navrattan, with nine vegetables in a luscious red sauce. Aficionados of searingly hot peppers should head for the shrimp or lamb vindaloo, in a fiery red sauce that will bring a tear to just about any eye. Bread lovers can feast on paper-thin papadums, made with lentil flour; onion kulcha, soft and buttery; or naan, made with unleavened dough and used to scoop up sauces. At this writing, table

service desperately needs upgrading. Servers have been seen emerging from the kitchen wearing two plates of food and a puzzled look, then plopping them down on the table before a couple of customers to see if the dishes elicit the right reaction. While you're waiting for the curry to arrive, you can contemplate what a mural depicting a Hindu myth is doing in the same room with steakhouse lighting fixtures.
Open Tues.-Sun. 11:30 a.m.-2:30 p.m. & 5:30 p.m.-10:30 p.m. All major cards.

Tavern on the Park

900 City Park Ave., Mid-City • 486-3333
STEAKHOUSE/SEAFOOD

9/20

Tavern on the Park is for eaters hankering for recognizable food in unusually pleasant surroundings. These handsome spaces, crafted from a big, nineteenth-century coffeehouse on the edge of City Park, can be a soothing respite from the clatter and crowds of more centrally located restaurants. Just across the street from the main room's windows is City Park's dense grove of ancient, legendary oak trees. A recent renovation has given the old building lots of sparkle—polished Siena marble floors, mirrored support posts, burnished woods and simple brass accents. Dominating the menu are unadventurous steaks and fried or sautéed seafoods and salads. The kitchen succeeds most often with the basics—shrimp rémoulade, oysters Rockefeller, breaded veal cutlets and broiled lobster tails. Steaks rarely rise above the acceptable. Fried shrimp and oysters, and broiled trout with herbed butter and scallions are the most reliable of the fish dishes. Desserts are perfunctory versions of bread pudding, crème caramel and ice cream with praline sauce. The restaurant's most valuable assets remain its handsome environment, well-organized service staff and overall congeniality. Dinner for two, with wine, can be had for an all-inclusive $75.
Open Mon.-Thurs. 11:30 a.m.-10 p.m., Fri. 11:30 a.m.-11 p.m., Sat. 5 p.m.-11 p.m. All major cards.

Taylor's

2708 N. Hullen St., Metairie • 888-6422
TRADITIONAL CREOLE

9/20

The proprietors of Taylor's entered the Metairie scene a few years ago, convinced that there was still room in the New Orleans suburbs for a restaurant specializing in shrimp rémoulade, oysters bordelaise, corn-and-crab soup, crabmeat au gratin, fried shrimp and onion rings. For better or worse, time has proved them correct. The reasons why are still rather unclear. Maybe fresh blueberry muffins have a wider following than we thought. In any event, Taylor's does come up with acceptable versions of just about every cliché from gumbo to bread pudding.

Every now and then, something unusual pops up. One such is oysters Michael, breaded, panfried, plopped onto oyster shells and topped with sautéed shrimp and crabmeat. Another is the "Cajun skillet," holding four-ounce portions of beef filet mignon, fish, shrimp and chicken breast, all on the dry side for having undergone the tortures of blackening, but all still quite tasty. And we must admit that the shrimp-and-sausage jambalaya is more edible than most. Other minor attractions are the neat and airy dining room, brightened with tropical greenery and jazz-related artifacts, and the refreshingly positive attitude of the service staff. Prices are easy to cotton up to also, with dinner for two running about $60. *Open Mon.-Thurs. 11 a.m.-10 p.m., Fri.-Sat. 11 a.m.-11 p.m. All major cards.*

Tchoupitoulas Plantation

6535 River Rd., Westwego
• 436-1277
CLASSIC CREOLE

7/20

The building is old (1812) and quaint, but not nearly as historic or impressive as many another plantation on the river. There is an enjoyable feeling of being out in the countryside of about 50 years ago; from the windows of the porchlike dining room, you see turkeys, chickens and guinea fowl running around in the yard. The food here is much less a landmark than are the premises. The best dish is an almost-soup of oysters in a rich brown sauce (a distinctive Creole taste: seafood with brown sauce). The rest of the offerings are standard Creole dishes, mostly seafood, in versions surpassed by those of many, many other restaurants. The service is by old waiters who seem more interested in doing a good routine than in serving you. The tab for two dinners with wine is about $60. *Open Mon.-Fri. 11:30 a.m.-3 p.m. & 5:30 p.m.-9:30 p.m., Sat.-Sun. 5:30 p.m.-9:30 p.m. All major cards.*

Tony Angello's

6262 Fleur de Lis Dr., Lakefront
• 488-0888
ITALIAN CREOLE

10/20

A rich and intense tomato sauce fairly gushes from the kitchen of this large, but darkly cozy, restaurant. It's in a low, sprawling brick building that looks like one of the hundreds of low-slung, suburban cottages that cluster into neighborhoods along the New Orleans Lakefront. Inside, the ornately homey furnishings and wall art add to the place's domestic feeling. The simpler pasta dishes—stuffed shells, spaghettini in garlicky olive oil, lasagne—are the better ones, and the broiled meats, especially the white veal chop, are juicy and flavorful. Curiously, the best dishes in this mostly Italian establishment are the baked oysters Bienville, a Creole dish, and the filet mignon. Lemon icebox pie and cassata are the desserts to order. Portions are large and prices are eminently affordable, which helps keep the bar and anteroom packed. Reservations are accepted, but don't expect immediate seating. Platoons of the restaurant's army of regulars are usually around to claim preference. A couple ordering à la carte, with a sensibly priced bottle of wine, can escape for about $65. Those reckless enough to choose from the fixed-price menu of Italian-style dishes will pay $15 or $20 less. *Open Tues.-Thurs. 6 p.m.-11 p.m., Fri.-Sat. 5:30 p.m.-11 p.m. Cards: AE, MC, V.*

Trey Yuen

600 Causeway Blvd., Mandeville • 1-626-4476
CHINESE

12/20

Chinese food in New Orleans was relegated strictly to the neighborhood café level until this place opened across the lake. It's a palace, filled with Chinese antiques. The cooking, while not especially more mind-blowing than the best of the cafés, has a fine degree of polish and uses first-class, sometimes unusual ingredients. Trey Yuen's best dishes involve South Louisiana foodstuffs such as soft-shell crabs, alligator, crawfish and oysters. Most of these—particularly the alligator—lend themselves well to Szechuan treatments. A particularly good range of dishes at Trey Yuen involves a slightly sweet, moderately spicy, thickish, translucent brown sauce called tong-cho; this is great on almost everything it touches, from seafood through duck to pork. The "lettuce flower" is a big leaf of iceberg with a very moist, nutty concoction of minced quail; you roll this up and eat it as an appetizer. Maine lobster is cooked whole with a great ginger sauce. The tea-smoked duck is aromatic and beautifully savory. The wine list includes quite a few sparkling wines, which are great with Chinese food. Service is more informal than the place. (A newer location in Hammond is no less good or grand.) Dinner for two, with wine, costs around $65. *Open Mon.-Tues. & Thurs. 5 p.m.-10 p.m., Wed. 11:30 a.m.-2 p.m. & 5 p.m.-10 p.m., Fri. 11:30 a.m.-2 p.m. & 5 p.m.-11 p.m., Sat. 5 p.m.-11 p.m., Sun. noon-9:30 p.m. All major cards.*

Tujague's

823 Decatur St., French Quarter • 525-8676
TRADITIONAL CREOLE

8/20

Were the food's quality brought up several notches, this would be a fine example of bourgeois Creole cooking from the turn of the century. The restaurant dates from 1856, when Guillaume Tujague, recently arrived from France, began to offer no-frills breakfasts and lunches to the tradesmen and shopkeepers from the bustling French Market, just across Decatur Street. Later, it thrived on its reputation for down-to-earth cooking and low prices. Today, the ornate French bar imported by the founder still dominates the adjoining saloon, and the two small

downstairs dining rooms have enough leftover charm to lend the place a rough-edged nostalgia. The menu is a variation on table d'hôte, five courses sandwiched between loaves of crusty, New Orleans–style French bread, and a shot glass filled with chicory-laced coffee carrying an unpleasantly bitter edge. Anyone with a horseradish allergy will have to forgo the initial two courses, both cold. The first is peeled shrimp in a rémoulade sauce that is basically horseradish and Creole mustard. The second is a little strip of boiled beef brisket, accompanied by a sauce made with seemingly equal parts of ketchup and horseradish. If you're lucky, the soup course will be a passable crawfish bisque; if not, it will be the pasty crab with spinach. Three main courses are offered, usually chicken, beef or seafood. Again, the range is from edible (crawfish on pasta) to forgettable (stewed chicken). Bread pudding in cranberry sauce and garden-variety pecan pie are frequent desserts. The cost for two, with a wine from the serviceable list, ranges from about $70 to about $80.
Open Mon.-Thurs. 11 a.m.-3 p.m. & 5 p.m.-10:30 p.m., Fri.-Sat. 11 a.m.-3 p.m. & 5 p.m.-11 p.m. All major cards.

Upperline
1413 Upperline St., Uptown • 891-9822
CONTEMPORARY CREOLE

Upperline is the epitome of Uptown. It straddles the cutting edge of contemporary New Orleans cooking, embracing whatever influences happen to fuse with its basically Creole sensibilities. Its most disarming quality may be its delightful tendency to bend the old rules and come up with a surprise or two. The night's cold soup might be vichyssoise, with sweet peppers deliciously pinch-hitting for leeks. The salad might be a starburst of endive leaves, each carrying a tidbit of fresh orange, a sprinkle of julienned beet and a ginger-tinged vinaigrette. The fish course, a soft and moist filet of drum, will have its subtlety perked up with a buttery sauce flavored with pecans and roasted garlic. The guiding lights are chefs Tom Cowman and Jason Clevenger, one a seasoned veteran, the other a youthful experimenter. Cowman's cold and creamy trout mousse, ready for spreading on slightly garlicky croutons, remains in a class of its own. His baked oysters on the half-shell in five sauces breathe new life into a Creole standby. Clevenger can be counted on for such innovative turns as crawfish enchiladas in a heartily seasoned cream sauce. He also uses novel approaches to pasta. The Upperline's smart, up-to-date look is appropriate to its eclectic menu and the upscale local clientele it regularly attracts. Bursts of color from the wall art enliven the pale gray expanse of the three dining

rooms. The lack of clutter brings out the hints of geometry in the occasional art-deco accents. Bentwood chairs around starched white linen-covered tables add a certain timelessness to it all. The kitchen covers its bases, too, with a number of more traditional treatments. You'll find a creditable trout meunière here, and also the restaurant's signature trout Lacombe, bedecked in an addictive cream sauce flavored with dill and brandy. Sautéed calf's liver with orange is dependably good, as are the frequently appearing curries. Lemon mousse, coconut-banana cake and a tropical rum trifle are the desserts to get. The wine list is composed with some care, but it's short (usually fewer than twenty labels) and mostly domestic. Prices are geared to keep the locals coming, with dinner for two running about $75, possibly a bit less.
Open Mon.-Sat. 6 p.m.-10 p.m. All major cards.

Versailles

2100 St. Charles Ave., Uptown
• 524-2535
CONTINENTAL

Classically trained European chefs seem to revel in Louisiana's almost limitless supply of fish, crabs, oysters and shrimp. None of them does it with more grace than Gunter Preuss, New Orleans's leading practitioner in the lush Continental style. The point is made and remade in the all-encompassing plush of Versailles, his restaurant in the Lower Garden District. Snowy lumps of top-quality backfin crab are nimbly tossed with salt and pepper in a light vinaigrette to become a lesson in the values of simplicity. Warm crawfish tails luxuriate in fish stock and cream energized with a bit of Dijon mustard and dill. A trout filet is gently sautéed to a crisp turn before joining artichoke bottoms and a modicum of capers in a seasoned beurre blanc. Bouillabaisse is reinterpreted as an elegant broth, with whispers of Pernod and saffron, and the bolder flavors of shrimp, oysters, crabmeat and fish. Versailles's old-world polish and finery—wrapped in billowy draperies, lace tablecloths and damask wall coverings—have a hotel dining room look, but with enough personality to make it unique. The tables along its front wall of glass afford pleasant views of St. Charles Avenue's streetcars clanging by. To bring the place into the late twentieth century, the kitchen relies on reductions rather than flour to deepen the tastes of its sauces, although, more often than not, they're bound with cream or butter. Basil bolsters the delicacy of beurre blanc in poached salmon Argenteuil, garnished with fresh asparagus and tender artichoke bottoms. The best treatment of beef may be the filet named Madagascar, in a peppercorn sauce on a bed of braised onion. Finding an acceptable wine for less

than $30 takes some work, but it can be done. Desserts don't clash with the rest of Versailles's Continental flourishes. There are very good versions of Bavarian cream, hazelnut mousse and lemon soufflé. Let caution be your guide through the wine list, and the cost of dinner for two should be about $110.
Open Mon.-Sat. 6 p.m.-10 p.m. All major cards.

West End Café

8536 Pontchartrain Blvd., Lakefront • 288-0711
SEAFOOD

10/20

Fried seafood is the mainstay in the restaurants that cluster around Lake Pontchartrain's southern shore. This is not fertile territory for adventurous eaters, the type who regularly prowl around for the latest vegetable to arrive from the West Coast. The dozen or more seafood restaurants grouped along the western edge of the Lakefront include this sassy newcomer, which breaks no new culinary ground, but produces a very good line-up of down-to-earth dishes, competently executed. The homey gumbo, stuffed crab, cold and spicy shrimp rémoulade and shrimp salad are generous and fresh-tasting. The boiled crabs, crawfish and shrimp in the shell, usually served warm, are expertly seasoned. Frying is likewise exemplary. The family-style menu is sensibly priced, with a few pasta dishes, a good hamburger steak and other familiar entrées. The casual, but spotless, surroundings include a sports bar, where baseball and football fans gather regularly.
Open Sun.-Thurs. 11 a.m.-11 p.m., Fri.-Sat. 11 a.m.-11:30 p.m. Cards: AE, MC, V.

Winston's

New Orleans Hilton, 2 Poydras St., Central Business District • 584-3900
AMERICAN

10/20

A spacious, cushy dining area, open to the lobby atrium and its concomitant noises, started out as a dining parlor with an English atmosphere and confusing food. After several rethinkings of the style and menu (the one around 1986 was pretty good), Winston's has become a rather stiff, unimaginative steak-and-chops house, with prices at about the peak level for such places locally, and humdrum execution. You can find a better restaurant elsewhere in the hotel (Kabby's), to say nothing of elsewhere in town. Dinner for two, with wine, will probably reach or exceed $85.
Open Sun.-Thurs. 6 p.m.-10 p.m., Fri.-Sat. 6 p.m.-11 p.m. (Schedule varies, depending on the number of people in the hotel). Cards: AE, MC, V.

QUICK BITES

CREOLE, CAJUN & MORE

Wherever there is a strong local cuisine—like New Orleans's Creole and Cajun—some of the best examples of it are found in plain, inconspicuous, and even frivolous-seeming venues. Great eating in New Orleans historically came from the bottom up, a tradition that continues today. Indeed, it's a cherished belief among Orleanians that the only difference between neighborhood cafés and the most renowned restaurants concerns atmosphere and price, not food. It is not at all a bad strategy to decide against donning a jacket and tie or other fancy dress for any meal in New Orleans. Thus unarmed, so to speak, you can sally forth to any but the most rigorously regulated establishments, and still find excellent dining.

CAFES & DINERS

Coffee Pot

714 St. Peter St., French Quarter • 523-8215

A favorite hangout of French Quarter residents, this is the parlor and carriageway of a nice nineteenth-century building turned into a pleasant café. The menu reaches to the point of cliché in presenting the staples of home-style Creole cooking, but the cooking is considerably better than that of the myriad tourist joints in the vicinity. Red beans and rice, seafood gumbo, fried seafood, po' boy sandwiches, bread pudding and the daily specials are all good, inexpensive eating. Avoid, however, the fried chicken. The Coffee Pot serves breakfast all day, including a culinary relic: calas. These are crusty, cinnamony, spherical rice cakes, served hot with syrup. The coffee, oddly enough, is terrible. Dinner for two should run about $18. *Open daily 8 a.m.-2 a.m. No cards.*

Eddie's

2119 Law, Gentilly • 945-2207

Here is the textbook backstreet kitchen, New Orleans–style. The place consists of a raffish dining room on a street so obscure that even lifelong Orleanians have trouble finding it (all the cabbies know the place, however). The menu is what they used to call soul food, which in New Orleans is indistinguishable from good Creole home cooking. The gumbo is spicy and full of chicken and seafood. The fried chicken and fried seafood are crusty and well-seasoned. Red beans and rice with hot sausage and daily platters of pot specials also fill the stomach convincingly, deliciously and very inexpensively. Dinner

for two should cost about $12.
Open Mon.-Thurs. 11 a.m.-10 p.m., Fri.-Sat. 11 a.m.-11:30 p.m. Cards: AE, MC, V.

Gumbo Shop

630 St. Peter St.,
French Quarter
• 525-1486

In the attractive antique dining room, the namesake specialty is delicious in both of its common forms: seafood gumbo (chockablock full with shrimp, crabs, oysters and okra) and chicken gumbo (with andouille sausage, rice and the aromatic ground sassafras leaves called filé). They also turn out excellent versions of the other neighborhood specialties, with a particularly savory rendering of red beans and rice. In recent times, the Gumbo Shop's menu also has included some pretty good grilled or blackened fish and chicken. Dinner for two runs about $16.
Open daily 11 a.m.-11 p.m. All major cards.

Liuzza's

3636 Bienville St.,
Mid-City
• 482-9120

Liuzza's is the apotheosis of the back-street New Orleans neighborhood restaurant. In one room is a bar, where large, heavy, frozen glass goblets are filled with beer or root beer. Most of those are passed through a small window into the second, smaller, room, where, at Formica tables, the neighborhood gang (which includes a large contingent from the big hospital across the street) chows down on the basics. Roast beef po' boys, fried seafood and platters of red beans and rice are nothing but delicious. The menu's specials include some offbeat home-style dishes, frequently with an Italian accent. Lunch or dinner for two will probably be under $10.
Open Mon.-Sat. 10:30 a.m.-11:30 p.m. No cards.

Mandina's

3800 Canal St.,
Mid-City
• 482-9179

Mandina's neon-splashed dining room, dominated by an antique bar at which you will probably stand for a while waiting for a table, feels like a classic New Orleans neighborhood restaurant. The food can be delicious, too. The menu covers an almost absurd amount of territory. Seafood and daily plate specials are the best eating; the Italian food is forgettable. Service is a bit careless, sometimes borderline rude. But the scene is engaging—colorful characters from every stratum of New Orleans society hang loose here—and the prices are very low. Dinner for two should cost about $18.
Open Mon.-Thurs. 11 a.m.-10:30 p.m., Fri.-Sat. 11 a.m.-11 p.m., Sun. 3 p.m.-10 p.m. No cards.

Miss Ruby's
539 St. Philip St., French Quarter
• 523-3514

This funny little café occupies one corner of an otherwise abandoned paper warehouse. Miss Ruby differs from her competitors in serving Southern food—a very different thing from Creole or Cajun. On the handwritten menu of the day, you'll find outstanding fried and baked chicken, terrific fried fish and an assortment of unpredictable, but consistently satisfying, pot specials. The dessert list is dominated by homemade pies—a rarity in New Orleans. Two should spend about $15.
Open Mon.-Fri. 11:30 a.m.-4 p.m. & 5 p.m.-10 p.m., Sat. 11 a.m.-4 p.m. & 5 p.m.-10 p.m. No cards.

DESSERT & COFFEE

Angelo Brocato's
214 N. Carrollton Ave., Mid-City
• 486-1465

537 St. Ann St., French Quarter
• 525-9676

Around the turn of the century, Mr. Brocato, recently arrived from Sicily, set about making the ice creams of his homeland. From that day to this, Brocato's has set the standard for Italian frozen desserts hereabouts. The most spectacular items are lemon ice, spumone, torroncino (vanilla ice cream crunchy with almonds and cinnamon—a beguiling flavor) and the made-to-order cannoli (crusty pastry tubes stuffed with sweetened ricotta cheese, chocolate and jellied fruits). All of this is made from scratch and served in the most unprepossessing way by Angelo's grandchildren. Brocato's antique ice cream parlors also have imported candies, homemade Sicilian cookies and espresso, all delightful. Ice cream and espressos for two runs about $6.
Mid-City: open Mon.-Thurs. 9:30 a.m.-10:30 p.m., Fri.-Sat. 9:30 a.m.-10:30 p.m., Sun. 9:30 a.m.-10 p.m. French Quarter: open Mon.-Thurs. 10 a.m.-6 p.m., Fri. 10 a.m.-10 p.m., Sat. 10 a.m.-11 p.m., Sun. 9 a.m.-9 p.m. No cards.

Aunt Sally's Original Creole Praline Shop
810 Decatur St., French Market
• 524-5107

Pralines are the native Creole candy, made of caramelized sugar, pecans, cream and vanilla. There is no better place to get them than this old, touristy gift shop in the French Market. Aunt Sally's makes pralines all day long in a display kitchen, and they're irresistable: mellow and nutty, not devastatingly sweet. This shop also carries a fine collection of distinctly New Orleans food products at nonconfiscatory prices, plus one of the city's best collec-

tions of local cookbooks.
Open Mon.-Thurs. 8 a.m.-6 p.m., Fri.-Sun. 8 a.m.-8 p.m. Cards: AE, MC, V.

Café du Monde

800 Decatur St., French Market • 525-4544

New Orleans's coffee is one of the city's most distinctive and unforgettable gustatory thrills. It's an extremely rich, blue-black brew, fortified with roasted chicory root. Although it has less than half the caffeine of the typical American coffee, its flavor is so powerful that it's best to drink it as café au lait—half coffee, half milk. That's the cherished beverage served for a century and a half in the French Market along the riverfront. The Café du Monde is the classic French Market coffee stand, open 24 hours and a favorite last stop for Orleanians out on the town. The standard accompaniment to the coffee is a plate of beignets—square, dense, just-fried doughnuts dusted with powdered sugar. Warning: don't laugh or inhale while biting into one of these, or you'll end up with sugar-coated lungs. Café au lait and beignets for two cost about $3.50.
Open 24 hours daily. Closed Christmas Day. No cards.

BRACING BREW

No one can say the old Creoles didn't appreciate a decent cup o' java. To them, the perfect brew had to be *Noir comme le diable, fort comme la mort, doux comme l'amour et chaud comme l'enfer.* It simply wasn't coffee unless it was "black as the devil, strong as death, sweet as love and hot as hell."

Croissant d'Or

617 Ursulines St., French Quarter • 524-4663

La Marquise

625 Chartres St., French Quarter • 524-0420

These two small pâtisseries, owned by the same deft French baker, are both very pleasant stopping points on walks around the French Quarter. The display cases are replete with freshly baked pastries; particularly good are the fruity, custardy tarte maison, croissants and brioches. Espresso, cappuccino and other specialty coffees are well made, although, by New Orleans standards, the regular coffee is weak. Coffee and a sample tarte for two will cost about $4.
Open daily 7 a.m.-5 p.m. No cards.

La Madeleine French Bakery & Café

547 St. Ann St., French Quarter • 568-9950

In a corner of the historic Lower Pontalba building on Jackson Square, this French-owned bakery is a charming place for a Continental breakfast, dessert or a midafternoon snack. The pastries, particularly the puff pastries, are remarkable; the almond croissants beg for an encore. A wide assortment of breads is baked in a wood-burning stone oven; these are widely used in restaurants around town. The menu of light meals can be safely ignored. Coffee and a pastry for two will run about $4.
Open daily 7 a.m.-9 p.m. No cards.

HAMBURGERS

Camellia Grill
626 S. Carrollton Ave., Uptown
• 866-9573

How many diners have a maître d', linen napkins and waiters with snappy routines? The 50-year-old Camellia Grill's 29 counter stools are always full—particularly when Tulane and Loyola universities are in session. The offerings are extremely basic, but uniformly well-made from first-class ingredients. The hamburger is custom ground, hand-formed, grilled to a delightful crustiness—good enough to require no dressings. The omelets are also famous, although they're whipped into a rather dry froth. Deli-style sandwiches fill out the rest of the menu of good local pot-cooking specials at dinner. The pecan pie, pecan waffles and cheesecake are all the best of their kind locally. A couple having burgers here would spend about $8.
Open Sun.-Wed. 8 a.m.-1 a.m., Thurs. 8 a.m.-2 a.m., Fri.-Sat. 8 a.m.-3 a.m. No cards.

Port of Call
838 Esplanade Ave., French Quarter
• 523-0120

Snug Harbor
626 Frenchmen St., Faubourg Marigny
• 949-0696

These two hangouts on the eastern fringe of the French Quarter serve the same nonpareil hamburger: half a pound of freshly ground two-way chuck, grilled over coals to a lovely light char, served on a toasted bun and accompanied by a nearly perfect baked potato. Both places also have decent steaks and a few other things, but the burger is what most people get. The Snug Harbor is a bit more atmospheric, with a few extra seafood entrées and a fine program of live jazz in the lounge. Burgers and baked potatoes costs about $12.
Open Sun.-Thurs. 11 a.m.-1 a.m., Fri.-Sat. 11 a.m.-5 a.m. Cards: AE (Port of Call); AE, MC, V (Snug Harbor).

MEXICAN & CENTRAL AMERICAN

Café Florida
1228 Jefferson Hwy., Jefferson
• 838-9574

A friendly Cuban family cooks up dirt-cheap, enormous platters of the specialties of their homeland. Start off with hearty, spicy black-bean soup or a light, almost fluffy, Cuban tamale. Then it's on to some magnificent marinated, grilled meats—Cuban round steak that overlaps most of the plate, crusty chicken with rice and beans, and grilled pork. The squid with rice and the shrimp with rice

are as delicious as they are filling. Flights of fancy, such as round steak stuffed with shrimp, are better than you would ever expect. At lunch, they make crusty grilled Cuban sandwiches. Exotic juices, soft drinks and frozen drinks made with Caribbean fruits round out the fascinating fare. Lunch for two costs about $20.
Open Mon.-Sat. 11 a.m.-11 p.m. Cards: MC, V.

Castillo's

620 Conti St., French Quarter • 525-7467

Castillo's occupies an old French Quarter building filled—especially at lunch and late at night—with customers who have been eating there for decades. The menu makes the strong point that this is not Tex-Mex food, but real Mexican cuisine—and, indeed, you find sauces and herbs from deep in Mexico, particularly the Yucatan. Most of the food is familiar, however. Enchiladas de res, filled with a singular spicy beef, are superb by any standard. Castillo's makes a great chocolate-based, peppery mole sauce and slathers it to fine effect on chicken. Chilmole de puerco has a light, oily sauce, fragrant with roasted peppers over tender pork slices. Chicken soup with cilantro starts things off well, and the Mexican champurrada (hot chocolate) finishes the meal distinctively. Service is slow, but the place is pleasant. Two will spend about $20 for dinner.
Open Mon.-Thurs. 11:30 a.m.-2 p.m & 5 p.m.-10:30 p.m., Fri. 11:30 a.m.-2 p.m. & 5 p.m.-midnight, Sat. 5 p.m.-midnight. Cards: AE, MC, V.

Taqueria Corona

5932 Magazine St., Uptown • 897-3974

Somehow, a few dozen square feet of Central America have been moved to Uptown New Orleans. The premises are minimally appointed; the main action is at the counter, behind which is a grill used to char—with tall flames and rapid action—slices of beef, pork, tongue, chicken and a few other things. These are wrapped in toasted flour tortillas with the piquantly herbal, aromatic pico de gallo relish, and deposited onto a red-hot plate with a pool of sizzling black beans. Then the waiter-cook turns around and plops this great food in front of you. It's lusty, exotic eating, very popular with the adventuresome diners of the city. Dinner for two runs around $18.
Open daily 11:30 a.m.-2 p.m. & 5 p.m.-9:30 p.m. No cards.

Tula's Kitchen

3828 Hessmer, Metairie • 885-5661

This is a Nicaraguan restaurant. The owner and chef, Tula Lacayo, was a local consul of that country until the Sandinista revolution. Then, at the urging of the many Nicaraguans she'd entertained in that capacity, she

opened this pleasant café. Start with the fritanga, the Nicaraguan national dish of fried, marinated pork with an assortment of relishes, plantains and fried cheese, and it's irresistible. Entrée essays of note are the filet mignon (imported from Honduras) with a creamy jalapeño sauce, the whole fried drumfish with a slightly minty herb sauce and the pork loin, moistened with an intense sauce of tomatoes and red wine. For dessert, there's an incredible, custardy cake called tres leches, and Nicaraguan-style café con leche. Dinner for two should run about $24.
Open Tues.-Fri. noon-2 p.m. & 6 p.m.-10 p.m., Sat. 6 p.m.-10 p.m. Cards: MC, V.

MIDDLE EASTERN

Jerusalem Grocery and Restaurant
4641 S. Carrollton Ave.
• 488-1450

For Middle Eastern dishes and canned goods in Mid-City, this Palestinian restaurant serves as the only downtown outlet. They serve fresh tabouli, hummus, baklava and other delicacies to eat in or take out. This friendly shop is also a center for Palestinians in the city; Arabic is spoken here more frequently than is English.
Open daily 10 a.m.-9 p.m.

POOR BOYS & MUFFULETTAS

Café Maspero
601 Decatur St., French Quarter
• 523-6250

It's a mystery how hundreds of visitors to the city find this sandwich shop and get in line here, but they could do a lot worse. Maspero's makes wonderful, well-stuffed sandwiches of ham, pastrami, corned beef and fried seafood, served on crusty rolls of New Orleans–style French bread. They also grill hamburgers, but these are to be avoided. In recent times, Maspero's has added a line of surprisingly good platters of grilled fish. All of this is presented at gratifyingly low prices, which may explain the aforementioned mystery. Be ready to wait a while to eat here, but the delay is worthwhile. Two people having lunch should spend around $10.
Open Sun.-Thurs. 11 a.m.-11 p.m., Fri.-Sat. 11 a.m.-midnight. No cards.

Central Grocery Co.

923 Decatur St.,
French Quarter
• 523-1620

This is a grocery store full of imported (mostly Italian) food specialties, many of which are sold not by the jar, but by the scoopful. Its beginnings date back to the large influx of Sicilians at the turn of the century, and for that market a unique sandwich was created: the muffuletta. It's named for the bread, a ten-inch-diameter, four-inch-thick seeded loaf, onto which are layered ham, salami, provolone, mozzarella and a distinctive relish of olives, garlic, marinated vegetables and olive oil. One of these is enough for two. You can eat in, but a better idea on a nice day is to walk across the street to the riverfront and claim a bench. A muffuletta for two should cost about $10.
Open Mon.-Sat. 8 a.m.-5:30 p.m., Sun. 9 a.m.-5:30 p.m. No cards.

Martin Wine Cellar

3827 Baronne St.,
Uptown
• 899-7411

714 Elmeer (at Veterans),
Metairie
• 896-7300

Attached to the area's premier wine store is a deli that comes as close to New York style as we'll probably ever get in New Orleans. The meats, cheeses, breads, mustards and dressings are top of the line; they're assembled into a couple dozen oddball combinations, as well as more traditional sandwiches. This is one of the few places on earth where you can get both a roast beef po' boy and a bagel with lox in the same order—and both will be pretty good. Wines by the bottle or glass can be had; occasionally, there are tastings. Sandwiches for two cost $8.
Open Mon.-Sat. 9 a.m.-7 p.m., Sun. 10 a.m.-1 p.m. Cards: MC, V.

Mother's

401 Poydras St.,
Central Business District
• 523-9656

The joy of eating at Mother's centers on the enormous, lightly smoky, tender hams they bake here. The ham itself goes into a classic po' boy, the official sandwich of New Orleans. A po' boy looks like a sub or a hoagie, but the bread is much crustier and the flavor is different. A po' boy is supposed to be the length of your forearm; since that's far too big to eat comfortably, Mother's lets you order half a sandwich. Mother's also makes po' boys from roast beef, "debris" (the drippings and leftovers of the previous day's beef), turkey (roasted whole on the premises) and fried oysters and shrimp. The steam table is full of red beans and rice, jambalaya, gumbo and some of the homiest casseroles imaginable—all delicious and cheap. Breakfast is especially good here, because the eggs are cooked with a touch of rendered ham fat (the secret ingredient of much of Mother's cooking). Po' boys for two should run around $7.
Open Mon.-Sat. 5 a.m.-10 p.m., Sun. 7 a.m.-10 p.m. No cards.

Napoleon House

500 ChartresSt.,
French Quarter
• 524-9752

One of New Orleans's favorite crumbling ruins, the Napoleon House is an ancient bar with classical music, colorful old waiters, extremely low drink prices and a menu of very good sandwiches. Leading the list is the city's best muffuletta. Crusty Italian bread is piled high with three meats and three cheeses; the olive salad scattered across the whole has a fine, lightly garlicky flavor. They toast the bread to an aromatic crustiness, and the result is good enough that you might be able to eat more than the usual limit of half a sandwich per person. Muffuletta for two should cost about $9.

Open Mon.-Thurs. 11 a.m.-midnight, Fri.-Sat. 11 a.m.-2 a.m., Sun. 11 a.m.-6 p.m. Cards: AE, MC, V.

R&O's

210 Hammond Hwy.,
Bucktown
• 831-1248

Bucktown is a small fishing village that has kept its character despite having long ago been swallowed up by suburbia. The best restaurant in Bucktown is R&O's, which started as a pizza parlor but then evolved into a first-class purveyor of po' boy sandwiches. The bread here is unique: light, almost airy, and very crusty. A substantial length of it is filled with ham, roast beef dripping with gravy, meatballs, Italian sausage, fried seafood or combinations of the above. The muffuletta is also top-drawer. The menu goes on to include some better-than-decent fried seafood platters and Italian food, all very inexpensive. Dinner for two here should cost about $10.

Open Mon.-Thurs. 11 a.m.-10 p.m., Fri.-Sat. 11 a.m.-midnight, Sun. 5 p.m.-10 p.m. No cards.

Streetcar Sandwiches

1434 S. Carrollton Ave.,
Uptown
• 866-1146

The people who own the Streetcar came from Wisconsin but did a great deal of in-depth research to unlock the secrets of making poor boy sandwiches. The roast beef po' boy here has the classic neighborhood bar flavor (the ultimate accolade for the dish). That taste comes from the thick, natural gravy made from the drippings of the roast. Streetcar also takes the essential step—omitted by most po' boy vendors—of toasting the French bread. Some of the offbeat sandwiches here are marvelous—particularly the mesquite-grilled fish and barbecued ham po' boys. They also grill a delicious chicken and serve it with a pile of very good jambalaya, smoky and spicy. There are a few stools, but this is mostly a take-out place. Po' boys for two to go should cost about $7.

Open Sun.-Thurs. 10:30 a.m.-11 p.m., Fri.-Sat. 10:30 a.m.-midnight. No cards.

Uglesich's
1238 Baronne St., Central Business District • 523-8571

This crowded eatery may be the least handsome restaurant in New Orleans, located in a neighborhood that's distinctly on the way down. But it's worth seeking out for a look at, and a taste of, the oldest style of neighborhood eating around. The specialty here is fried seafood po' boys, and what makes them the best is the seafood, fried to order, with a crusty, cornmeal-coated exterior. The oysters are even shucked to order for your sandwich—which means you can also have a dozen raw on the half shell for an appetizer. A meal for two costs $8 to $16.
Open Mon.-Fri. 9:30 a.m.-4 p.m. No cards.

SEAFOOD

Acme
724 Iberville, French Quarter • 522-5973

The premier New Orleans seafood is the oyster. The bivalves are taken from the surrounding wetlands in enormous numbers, and they are in a league with the world's best. They're bigger than most, with a lightly salty, silvery flavor and a definite air of the sea. At oyster bars like the appropriately named Acme, Orleanians consume raw oysters by the dozen (the current solo one-sitting record is 21 dozen). The local style is to eat them with an oyster fork, used to dip the oyster into a self-made sauce made of ketchup, horseradish, lemon juice and hot sauce. You would do better, however, to eat them without the sauce. The ideal accompaniment is a cold beer. A dozen oysters (each) for two will run about $14.
Open Mon.-Sat. 11 a.m.-10 p.m., Sun. noon-7 p.m. Cards: AE, MC, V.

Barrow's
2714 Mistletoe (at Earhart Expy.), Uptown • 482-9427

Barrow's quietly served its middle-class, mostly black, neighborhood from 1943 until a couple of years ago, when an expressway cut through its block. Then the city at large found out that Barrow's fries what is, without question, the best catfish anywhere in the area. In fact, that's just about all they serve. The fish comes from natural bayous, not farms. It's fileted fresh every day on the premises, marinated in some secret stuff that makes it subtly spicy and fried to an incomparable lightness. You can eat this fish like popcorn. The plate also includes some fine homemade potato salad. On the few days Barrow's serves lunch, they cook up some great, cheap, old-style black Creole pot dishes. Dinner for two runs about $18.

Open Tues.-Wed. 5 p.m.-10 p.m., Thurs. 11:30 a.m.-10 p.m., Fri. 11:30 a.m.-midnight, Sat. noon-midnight. No cards.

Bozo's

3117 21st St., Metairie • 831-8666

This is a simple restaurant, as seafood places go—which may explain why it's so good. Start with the consistently fine, cold, deftly opened raw oysters at the bar. Then have a cup of the unique, light chicken-andouille gumbo, which builds steadily in deliciousness as you eat it. All the seafoods are fried or broiled to order here, and come out sizzling hot and free of oiliness. The fried catfish and oysters and the broiled shrimp are the best items. The stuffed crab, composed almost entirely of luscious claw crabmeat, makes a good side dish. In season, they serve crawfish tails, still in the shell, marinated in a spectacular oily, cold sauce made with artichokes, lemons, oil and crawfish fat: a mess to eat, but irresistible. The service is a little slow, and they don't fill the plate with frills, but the meticulousness of the cooking is unmistakable. "Bozo" is a Yugoslavian nickname for Christopher; Yugoslavs have dominated the southeastern Louisiana fishing industry for generations, all the way up to the restaurant level. Dinner for two will cost around $20, with beer.

Open Tues.-Thurs. 11 a.m.-3 p.m. & 5 p.m.-10 p.m., Fri.-Sat. 11 a.m.-11 p.m. Cards: MC, V.

THE CRAWFISH

New Orleans natives have been netting, boiling and eating crawfish for more than 200 years, and, for that matter, the French have been eating them since the Middle Ages. But it wasn't until around 1984 that the rest of the country suddenly caught on. Now the small, succulent, lobsterlike creature (known as the crayfish elsewhere) is shipped to markets all over the country. Commercial crawfish farming is a booming business for Louisiana, and production grows every year, to a current bounty of ten-million pounds annually. It's no wonder—there are 29 known species of the spiny crustacean living wild in Louisiana alone. This also makes for excellent sportfishing, immensely popular with both locals and visitors. Every spring, a solid chain of parked cars crowds the 80-mile stretch of Airline Highway from Baton Rouge to New Orleans, while their owners joust for a fishing spot. This creature has a few other names: crawdad, grasscrab, stonecrab or mudbug.

Bruning's

West End Park • 282-9395

West End Park is surrounded by restaurants built over the waters of Lake Pontchartrain, and Bruning's is the best of them. It's over 100 years old and has a colorful history. Nowadays, Bruning's has a comfortable shabbiness, as well as lots of windows for watching the sunset. The menu has three specialties. Either start with or make a meal of the spicy boiled crabs, shrimp or crawfish. These are served by the mound, with some disassembly required.

(Afterward, you wash your hands in a sink in the dining room—a bit of local color.) Ample fried seafood platters, light and grease-free, are the menu's second set of choices. The third specialty, and the best dish in the house, is the whole, very large broiled Gulf flounder—a great fish out of vogue these days—but still popular in antique seafood emporiums like this. The flounder can be had stuffed or not; both styles are delicious and fresh. Dinner for two here runs about $22.

Open Sun.-Thurs. 11 a.m.-9:30 p.m., Fri.-Sat. 11 a.m.-10:30 p.m. Cards: AE, MC, V.

Casamento's

4330 Magazine St., Uptown
• 895-9761

Two rooms of sparkling clean art-nouveau pastel tiles (the place resembles a large bathroom) are usually full of Uptowners, most of whom are indulging in oysters in some form. Both the cold, salty, raw bivalves on the half shell and the crackly, cornmeal-coated fried oysters make spectacular eating. The latter are made into an oyster loaf—a sandwich on big slabs of buttered, toasted bread. There is a smattering of other seafood and some forgettable Italian food, but most people stick with oysters. Enough so that Casamento's closes for the entire summer, when oysters are allegedly (but not really) out of season. Dinner for two here runs about $22.

Open Tues.-Sun. 11:30 p.m.-1:30 p.m. & 5:30 p.m.-9 p.m. Closed June-Aug. No cards.

Jaeger's Original Seafood Tavern

1701 Elysian Fields Ave., Downtown
• 947-0111

Boiled seafood is a New Orleans passion, particularly during the spring, when crawfish are fat and available in seemingly countless number. The boiling medium is heavily spiked with pepper and other seasonings that pervade the flavor of the seafood in question. Most restaurants, for reasons nobody quite understands, serve boiled seafood ice cold. Jaeger's is an exception. All its seafood comes to the table steaming hot, which enhances the flavor enormously. The waitresses are happy to demonstrate the technique of eating the stuff, which can be complicated—especially for boiled crabs. The rest of Jaeger's encyclopedic menu is merely adequate, but it's worth a visit just for the hot boiled stuff. Dinner for two runs around $20.

Open Tues.-Thurs. & Sun. 11 a.m.-10 p.m., Fri.-Sat. 11 a.m.-11 p.m. Cards: AE, MC, V.

HOTELS

INTRODUCTION

GRACIOUS ACCOMMODATIONS

Sleeping in New Orleans is a lot like eating in New Orleans. The choices are vast, and have a dash of the different. How many other city guides would have repeated entries of small hotels in nineteenth-century buildings? And mention patios more frequently than pools?

A few things you need to know right off: New Orleans has astronomical tax rates; by the time everything is added, there's an extra 11.5 percent on your bill. Also, rates at most hotels change throughout the year, depending upon the season—so much so that many don't have tariff sheets and are reluctant to quote prices unless you give a specific date. Summer and December are low season here for tourisists, so you can often find real bargains then. But if you're checking into town during Mardi Gras, the Jazz Festival, the Sugar Bowl or the Super Bowl, rates will be much higher than those listed here, in most cases, and there will be a minimum three- or four-night stay.

If you hit a time when hotels are packed, call the Central Reservation Service at (800) 548-3311. For Greater New Orleans, call the Hotel and Motel Association at 525-2264 or the Tourist and Convention Commission at 566-5068.

In case you're wondering where we'd stay, our top two choices would be the Soniat House, in the Quarter, and the Windsor Court; but if we couldn't get in either, we wouldn't be too disappointed. At least a dozen others would fit the bill just fine. New Orleans specializes in charm, and its hotels reflect that spirit.

SYMBOLS & ABBREVIATIONS

Our opinion of the comfort level and appeal of each hotel is expressed in the following ranking system:

Very luxurious

Luxurious

Very comfortable

Comfortable

Credit Cards

AE: American Express
D: Discover
DC: Diners Club
MC: MasterCard
V: Visa

FRENCH QUARTER

We focus mainly on the French Quarter because it's where most visitors will want to stay, in order to absorb the atmosphere of the city. This is the heart of the old city, also called the Vieux Carré (old square). It is seven blocks wide and thirteen blocks long, with Bourbon Street serving as a sort of dividing line. (Don't judge the Quarter by the jangling, tawdry first seven blocks of Bourbon.) Antique shops line Royal and Chartres streets; most residents live on the far side of Jackson Square, which is located between Chartres, Decatur, St. Peter and St. Ann streets. The most interesting spots for a walking tour are on the river side of Bourbon Street.

Surprisingly, there are three zip codes in this small part of the city: 70130 applies to the segment near the river, before St. Ann Street; 70116 is everything beyond St. Ann; 70112 is the far side of Bourbon Street, away from the river, before St. Ann.

Bourbon Orleans

717 Orleans St., 70116
• 523-2222; (800) 521-5338
Fax 525-8166

The Bourbon Orleans is chock-full of history. The pirate, Jean Lafitte, reportedly walked in its courtyard. And although the hotel brochures refer simply to the splendor of the "Orleans Ballroom," the local story is that in the early 1800s everyone knew it as the "Quadroon Ballroom," where beautiful, free young women of color (one-quarter black) met with wealthy white men, some of whom took the women as mistresses. Today, guests at this hotel, located behind St. Louis Cathedral, enter an elegant marble lobby with a comfortable seating area and the airy, peach-toned Lafayette restaurant to one side. Many of the 211 tastefully dcorated rooms have brick walls, pastel small-print wallpaper and reproduction Chippendale and Queen Anne furniture (many beds have wall canopies). There also are 50 two-level suites in which the bedroom is located in a loft. Baths are marble, each with a telephone and television set. While the hotel is well-kept in most places, a few room doors on the second and third floors display major scratches, which is a bit jolting when compared to the rest of the place.

Singles & doubles: $95-$150; suites: $160-$200. Packages available.

Bourgoyne Guest House

839 Bourbon St., 70116
• 524-3621, 525-3983
No fax

The wonderfully eccentric Englishman Quentin Crisp stayed in this 1830s townhouse when he lectured in New Orleans, and, indeed, Bourgoyne House appeals to the traveler looking for atmosphere without spending a fortune. The green suite on the third floor (it's a breathtaking—literally—walk up a curved cypress staircase) is a two-bedroom apartment with brass chandeliers, a huge gilded mirror dating from the 1800s and antique furniture; a bonus is a balcony overlooking what is the last semilively block of Bourbon. A first-floor suite opens to the patio, which has subtropical plants and cast-iron furniture. There are three small studio apartments in a three-story garçonnière (formerly a home for bachelor sons of those in the main house). Suites have televisions, but the studios do not. No room phone; you use pay phones in nearby businesses. There is no pool and no parking. Owners live on the premises; when they're not home, you check in at the laundromat next door.
Studio singles & doubles: $45-$49; suites: $60-$84 ($108 for four people).

Chateau Le Moyne

301 Dauphine St., 70112
• 581-1303, (800) HOLIDAY
Fax 523-5709

There are two Holiday Inns in the French Quarter; this is the one that doesn't feel like a Holiday Inn (except for somewhat garish advertisments in the elevators). Rooms tend to be standard hotel, but there is a pretty patio with a pool and some balconies off the 175 rooms. However, the long, narrow suites (about $150) in the renovated slave quarter building around the pool would be our rooms of choice.
Singles & doubles: $109-$136; suites: $136-$275.

Chateau Motor Hotel

1001 Chartres St., 70116
• 524-9636
No fax

This small hotel, a real find, with rooms around a patio and pool, is quiet and peaceful. Rooms are attractive; some have exposed beams and architectural details. The location is excellent, a couple of blocks past Jackson Square in a residential area. Free parking is a bonus.
Singles & doubles: $49-$89; suites: $89-$115.

The Cornstalk

915 Royal St., 70116
• 523-1515 , 523-1516
No fax

Once the home of Louisiana's first chief justice, the Cornstalk boasts that Harriet Beecher Stowe stopped here, and was so moved by nearby slave auctions that she was inspired to write *Uncle Tom's Cabin.* Whatever the history, the hotel is an old white Victorian home fronted by one of the city's several famous fences of ironwork, in

the shape of stalks of corn. There are crystal chandeliers, stained-glass windows, fireplaces and antique beds and furniture, although the one bedroom we were able to see was not quite the knockout we expected. Some beds have half-canopies. All rooms have televisions, telephones and private baths. A Continental breakfast is included. A long, central hall with antiques and green wall-to-wall carpeting leads to the registration desk. One disppointment is the lack of a parlor in which guests can gather, although they can eat breakfast on the gallery or patio. No pool.
Singles & doubles: $95-$135.

Dauphine Orleans

415 Dauphine St.,
70112
• 586-1800,
(800) 521-7111 (out of La.),
(800) 521-6111 (in La.)
Fax 586-1409

A renovated historic building (artist-naturalist John James Audubon completed his *Birds of America* series in one part of the hotel and prostitutes toiled in another section), the Dauphine Orleans has a more personal touch than some other hotels, and lots of extras. Guests in the 109 rooms receive a newspaper delivered to their door, Continental breakfast, welcome cocktail, hors d'oeuvres, bed turndown and a free windshield wipe after free parking. There's also a library (you can take a book home if you don't finish it), fitness facility and the "Dauphine Jitney," which transports guests around the Quarter and Central Business District. While rooms have modern or reproduction traditional furnishings, there are a few balconies, some wrought iron, and, of course, a patio and pool.
Singles & doubles: $90-$120 (patio rooms have the higher rates); suites: $155-$250.

Dauzat House

1000 Conti St.,
70112
• 524-2075
No fax

The owners (Richard Nicolais and Don Dauzat) of this quirky place like to boast that they provide New York efficiency with New Orleans hospitality. Dauzat House is different, that's for sure. Voodoo Queen Marie Laveau reportedly lived here, and now an inflatable dragon floats in the patio pool. The five suites have stuffed animals on the beds, homemade amaretto in decanters and fresh flowers. If management feels like cooking, guests may receive cookies or pies. Suites have woodburning fireplaces and kitchenettes (although we were told the management isn't too eager for guests to use them extensively). A Bentley is available for guests' use.
Suites: $150-$475.

De la Poste

316 Chartres St.,
70130
• 581-1200,
(800) 448-4927
No fax

One singer with the Metropolitan Opera won't stay anyplace else when he visits New Orleans. This small hotel with a landscaped patio and pool is located near the front of the French Quarter, surrounded by small doll and antique shops. Its restaurant is the only branch location of Chez Hélène (see Restaurants, page 32), inspiration for the *Frank's Place* television series, and specializes in fried chicken, corn bread and soul food. Rooms look as if they recently have been refurbished, and are decorated in good taste with hotel florals. One inconvenience: there's no real lobby, just a registration area with a sofa and some chairs.
Singles: $84; doubles: $95-$110; suites: $135 up.

The French Market Inn

501 Decatur St.,
70130
• 561-5621,
(800) 827-5621
Fax 566-0160

Rooms vary widely at this little hotel, built in the 1700s for a local philanthropist, Baron Joseph Xavier de Pontalba, and which later served as housing for Swiss troops and lodging for a governor. The hotel has been renovated and many rooms are furnished in good taste, though many are rather compact. Some feature brick walls and exposed beams as well as brass or four-poster beds. Ask for a third-floor room with a view of the river. There is no pool, no parking on premises (there's a parking lot aross the street). Those with teenagers might be interested to know that the Hard Rock Café is across the street.
Singles & doubles: $88 to $128.

French Quarter Maisonettes

1130 Chartres St.,
70116
• 524-9918
No fax

This is one of those places adventurous and independent travelers yearn to discover; it has charm at a good location in the residential, rear part of the French Quarter and a budget price. Guests enter the two-story brick building (1825) through iron gates and walk a few steps through a carriageway to a typical old fashioned French Quarter patio complete with fountain. Rooms open onto the patio; some have brick walls and gas-burning fireplaces, even a crystal chandelier, although furnishings are basic 1950s-style vinyl chairs and, frankly, could use a bit of sprucing up. Some rooms have small kitchens. The porter has been welcoming guests for 35 years, and the owner, Mrs. Junius Underwood, who calls herself the *chatelaine,* is legendary, an old-school grand dame, with lots of advice. A wonderful French bakery, Croissant d'Or (see Quick Bites, page 91), is around the corner and perfect for breakfast. All rooms have private baths and televisions, but no telephones and no pool. Closed July. No children under 12. No parking on premises.
Rooms: $39-$65. Reservations taken only between 10 a.m. and 6 p.m.

Grenoble House

329 Dauphine St., 70112 • 522-1331 No fax

There are seventeen suites in this discreet little apartment hotel that really does feel like home, as many like to claim. It's an ideal spot for those who want to stay a while, since twelve units are rented only by the week, with maid service every day but Sunday. Each has a kitchen and a Continental breakfast is provided, along with a morning newspaper. Stylish apartments are decorated individually and eclectically. Some have exposed brick walls and fireplaces (sorry, they don't work). Neutrogena is the "house soap." There's a small pool with a whirlpool area.
Suites: $105-$195; weekly rates: singles: $560-$695, doubles: $840-$910.

Lafitte Guest House

1003 Bourbon St., 70116 • 581-2678, (800) 331-7971 No fax

We're partial to this fourteen-room guest home with management that serves wine and cheese every evening in the parlor. Antiques abound (with some modern sofas in a few rooms), yet it's a livable place with books to read and working gas fireplaces. Honeymooners might like Room 22 or 32, with a balcony overlooking St. Philip Street, although one of the most popular rooms is No. 5, a cozy former slave's quarters with a loft bedroom. Several rooms have canopied beds; some can be joined into a large suite. This part of Bourbon Street is residential, though the delightfully atmospheric and cozy Lafitte's Blacksmith Shop, a pub, is across the street. Telephones in rooms; TV on request; no pool. Some free parking on premises. Continental breakfast and daily newspaper are included.
Singles & doubles: $55-$115.

Lamothe House

621 Esplanade Ave., 70116 • 947-1161, (800) 367-5858 No fax

Located on a divided street, with a grassy median that serves as the rear boundry of the French Quarter, Lamothe House is the epitome of a high Victorian townhouse hotel, with antiques and reproductions in its nine suites and eleven rooms. Guests gather around a large antique dining table for a Continental breakfast. Several rooms feature canopied beds; the most popular is room 208, with furniture by Mallard, a distinguished New Orleans furniture maker. Some patio rooms are quite small, but suites are large. Last year, the hotel decided to keep prices down by dropping some amenities, such as the decanter of port, bed turn-down service and shampoos that guests used to receive. There is no pool, but there is free parking.
Singles & doubles: $65-$105; suites: $125-$205.

Landmark Bourbon Street (Best Western)

541 Bourbon St., 70130
• 524-7611, (800) 535-7891
Fax 568-9427

The Landmark is one of two hotels right in the heart of the Bourbon Street action (Royal Sonesta is the other), which is great if you want to party, death if you're a light sleeper (although the poolside rooms may pass muster for relative quiet). The 186-room hotel recently was renovated. Several suites have balconies overlooking Bourbon; guests have access to other balconies. There is a cafeteria-style restaurant as well as a couple of lounges, one with a sing-along piano bar.

Singles & doubles: $100-$150; suites: $150 (balcony rooms)-$350 (hospitality suites).

Maison de Ville

727 Toulouse St., 70130
• 561-5858, (800) 634-1600
No fax

One of the country's original, small, charming hotels, Maison de Ville has received numerous accolades and has been favored by celebrities. There are only sixteen rooms in the main hotel, some quite small, but each tastefully furnished and most facing the patio that is just over a brick wall from the patio of the Court of Two Sisters Restaurant. Antiques are everywhere. Tennessee Williams stayed in Room 9 while he wrote part of *A Streetcar Named Desire.* There is no pool at the main hotel, which is located half a block from the heart of Bourbon Street activity (you have to ring the doorbell to enter the peaceful sanctuary of a homey lobby, exquisitely decorated). However, there is a pool at the Audubon Cottages, two blocks away in the 500 block of Dauphine Street. The cottages, once home to naturalist-painter John James Audubon, are favorites of repeat guests and have kitchens. Continental breakfast is included. The Bistro Restaurant in the main hotel is tiny and Parisian in flavor, popular with locals (see Restaurants, page 25). There is no parking on the premises, but valet parking is available. No children under 12 and no pets.

Singles & doubles: $105-$195; cottages: $295-$350 (and up).

Maison Dupuy

1001 Toulouse St., 70112
• 586-8000, (800) 535-9177 (outside La.), (800) 854-4581 (in La.)
Fax 525-5334

Owned by the Delta Queen Steamboat Co., the Maison Dupuy is a five-story hotel, converted from seven townhouses; it has 195 rooms and suites, many of them decorated in pastel colors and subdued florals, and many overlooking the patio, which has lush greenery, a fountain and a pool. Some rooms have balconies. There is a workout room across from the lobby and a restaurant with New Orleans cooking (as well as sandwiches, soup and salad).

Singles & doubles: $100-$150; suites: $200-$500 (3 bedrooms).

The Melrose

937 Esplanade Ave.,
70116
• 944-2255

Opened in January 1990, The Melrose had, as its first quest, Lady Bird Johnson. This eight-bedroom inn has some of the most expensive rooms in town. The owners are touting it as a luxury "home," with a butler, afternoon tea, Champagne and wine in the room refrigerator, fresh flowers, Godiva chocolates by the bed, English soaps, and breakfast, all included in the tariff. A limo will be available for use. Rooms are pretty, with quality furniture and designer fabrics. Four have whirlpool baths; there is a pool, but prices still remain shocking to us.
Rooms & suites: $250-$450.

Monteleone Hotel

214 Royal St.,
70130
• 523-3341,
(800) 535-9595
Fax 528-1019

To people all over the South, the Monteleone is the place to stay in New Orleans. It has been here since 1886 without a name change and is still owned by descendents of the original Mr. Monteleone. Pleasant rooms look as if they have been recently refurbished, mainly with vinyl textured walls done in patterns of bamboo and thrushes and such. See if you can get one overlooking the river. This rambling, 600-room hotel (it's been expanded several times and you can get a little lost among the hallways and elevators) has a health club, a rooftop pool and three restaurants, as well as a business center with a fax machine, photocopier and typists. Its location is tops, a few steps from the city's finest antique shops.
Singles & doubles: $105-$190; suites: $225-$625.

Olivier House Hotel

828 Toulouse St.,
70112
• 525-8456

The Olivier House is not for everyone; to be honest, it needs a bit of freshening here and there among its hallways and 40 rooms. Its appeal should be to those who like European guesthouses and family informality. The owners (the Danner family) and staff are very helpful and friendly, and there's a parrot in the courtyard. Rooms have TV and telephone (some have kitchenettes), and coffee and tea are available all day in the parlor, which has a real fireplace. Decor in the hotel, which has been expanded from an 1836 townhouse (built by one Madame Olivier), is mixed. Some rooms have a splashy Miami aura; there are a few antiques; most have basic furniture. Some room have gas-burning fireplaces. There is a small pool. Children and pets are welcome.
Singles & doubles: $55-$95; suites: $85-$150.

Omni Royal Orleans

621 St. Louis St., 70130
• 529-5333, (800) THE-OMNI
Fax 529-7089

One of the grand hotels of New Orleans, the Royal Orleans (or the Royal O, as everybody in the city calls it) was built in 1960, on the site of one of the grande dames of the 1800s, the St. Louis Hotel. The builders copied as much as they could of the Royal O's predecessor. Ironically, the one thing they couldn't replicate, because of building codes, was a huge rotunda; this was before Hyatt's atriums. Guests enter on St. Louis Street and walk up a flight of marble steps to the main lobby, with chandeliers, gilt mirrors and marble everywhere. The long, narrow lobby stretches from a ballroom backing onto Chartres Street to the Rib Room Restaurant, a dark, ornate, expensive restaurant that backs onto Royal Street (see Restaurants, page 73). In between is the Café Royale, actually a rather posh, pastel, little coffee-shop restaurant frequented by French Quarter residents who have figured out that a slightly smaller version of the Rib Room's prime rib costs several dollars less in the Café Royale. Next to the Café Royale is the lounge, where you can order dessert or have a drink while listening to the piano and sinking into deep chairs. Rooms at the Royal O are attractively done, although the "standard" rooms are only nine by twelve feet. The best rooms have balconies facing St. Louis. There's a rooftop pool with a lovely view of the city; there's also a snackbar as well as an exercise room.
Singles & doubles: $125-$205; suites: $290-$595.

Place d'Armes

625 St. Ann St., 70116
• 525-4531
No fax

Popular with tour groups, this 79-room hotel is located half a block from Jackson Square. Most rooms are done in motel style and overlook the extensive patio; a few have more personality and seem more recently decorated than others, not to mention some of the public areas. Some rooms open onto a balcony overlooking Chartres Street, which could be fun for guests who enjoy watching the daytime street entertainment in front of Jackson Square. A Continental breakfast is served in a patio room.
Singles & doubles: $79-$109.

Provincial

1024 Chartres St., 70116
• 581-4995, (800) 535-7922 (out of La.), (800) 621-5295 (in La.)
Fax 581-1018

This is yet another small hotel favored by New Orleanians who want to put up friends in the French Quarter. Rooms are all different and not a bit motelish. Some remind us of twin-bed rooms in our grandmother's home. A few have ceiling fans; some have canopied beds and overlook the river. Others overlook a pool. Room 223 is an often requested room, with a half-canopied bed and antiques. The restaurant has exposed beams and plaid wallpaper and looks as if it could be set in the French countryside. Free

on-site parking. There is no charge for children in the room.
Singles & doubles: $65-$125; suites: $115-$150.

Quarter Esplanade

719 Esplanade Ave., 70116
• 948-9328
No fax

A casual guest house with eight rooms in two Greek Revival townhouses, the Quarter Esplanade is decorated for the most part with modern, sometimes modular, comfortable furniture. Room 4, with a four-poster bed (not canopied), is the choice of honeymooners; the two-bedroom suite is a good choice for three or four traveling together, and also because of its balcony, which faces Esplanade. Most rooms have kitchens; all have telephones and TVs. Continental breakfast is included. No parking.
Singles & doubles: $65-$85; suite: $125.

Le Richelieu

1234 Chartres St., 70116
• 529-2494, (800) 535-9653
Fax 524-8179

Considered a "best buy" among savvy travelers, Le Richelieu's 88 rooms have mainly floral fabrics, ceiling fans and lots of mirrors, as well as refrigerators and ironing boards (ask for the iron). It's a friendly place, with owner Frank S. Rochefort, Jr., living on the premises. For $160, you can sleep in the Paul McCartney suite, where the singer spent two months. The lobby is full of brocade, and some boldly contrasting hallway wallpapers are, let us say, interesting. Ask for a room with a balcony. The hotel has a coffee shop and pool and free on-site parking.
Singles & doubles: $70-$95; suites: $110-$375 (three bedrooms).

Royal Sonesta Hotel

300 Bourbon St., 70140
• 586-0300, (800) SONESTA
Fax 586-0335

Located in the center of the frantic action of Bourbon Street, the Royal Sonesta is like a pink marble oasis. An artistic arrangement of exotic flowers welcomes guests to the amazingly quiet lobby. The patio is lush with fresh fruit trees. A narrow marble hallway, decorated with crystal chandeliers, crystal sconces and stone and mosaic wall fountains leads to Conti Street. For guests who want a lively atmosphere, there's the Desiré Oyster Bar, a well-executed re-creation of an old-style oyster bar that opens right onto Bourbon, as does a bar with the dubious name, Le Booze. A more luxurious lounge with sofas and comfortable chairs offers big screen sports television on weekend afternoons and piano and jazz at night. For real party-goers, there's the Can Can Cabaret with late-night entertainment on Bourbon. If you want to be part of the Bourbon Street hubbub, by all means request a room with a balcony overlooking the street. However, if sleeping is

something you occasionaly enjoy, insist on a room facing the patio. There are 500 rooms in this hotel, which takes up most of a city block. There's a pool, of course, an executive level, and fine dining in Begue's Restaurant, as well as a bountiful Sunday buffet that can be enjoyed in the bosky patio.
Singles & doubles: $115-$210 (Bourbon Street balcony $200); suites: $225-$800. Packages available.

Rue Royal Inn

1006 Royal St., 70116
• 524-3900, (800) 776-3901
Fax 525-6652

We almost passed this seventeen-room hotel, that was bought last year and reopened under another name (it was the Noble Arms), and we're glad we stopped in for a look. It's another good value hotel, in another nineteenth-century building. Owners Bob Feldman and Dick Mole work the front desk, aided by two Persian cats. Courtyard rooms in the former slave quarter are small, but rooms in the main building are enormous, if a little dark, and have refrigerators. Some have kitchens. Furniture is standard hotel-style, but there are some brick walls and balconies. Free coffee and tea are served, and on Sunday there is free Continental breakfast. No pool, no parking.
Rooms: $40-$75.

623 Ursulines, A Guest House

623 Ursulines St., 70116
• 529-5489
No fax

Owners Jim Weirich and Don Heil are former visitors to New Orleans who returned eleven years ago to open this budget guesthouse, next door to Croissant d'Or, the Quarter's best pastry shop (see Quick Bites, page 91). Accommodations are basic, just seven suites with private baths and televisions in an 1826 structure overlooking a patio. Guests receive a morning paper, but no breakfast ("With Croissant d'Or next door?" asked one owner). There is no on-site parking and no pool, and if you want a telephone, you have to use the pay phone in the hall.
Singles & doubles: $50-$60 (four people $70 to $80).

Soniat House

1133 Chartres St., 70116
• 522-0570, (800) 544-8808
Fax 522-7208

Our top personal choice among smaller French Quarter hotels, the Soniat House has been wonderfully decorated. It's also an immensely personal place. The sophisticated owner (Rodney Smith) helps guests, who include many famous literary names, with reservations and plans. Paul Newman stayed here when he filmed *Blaze*. Once the home of a plantation owner, the 1829 building has a stone carriageway, spiral staircases, galleries, and a wide central

hall. The most requested room is 32, a narrow bedroom with a sitting area, in a former slave's quarters; it has its own little porch overlooking the patio. Our favorites are the four rooms off the main hall, particulary 20 and 21, which open onto the front balcony, facing Chartres Street. Several rooms have Jacuzzis and several have canopied beds. There is an honor bar in the parlor. Continental breakfast is included. No pool and no parking on the premises; valet parking is available.
Singles & doubles: $100-$155; suites: $185-$395.

Ste. Hélène

508 Chartres St., 70130
• 522-5014
Fax 523-7140

A relatively new hotel with sixteen rooms, the Ste. Hélène offers traditionally decorated rooms and a Continental breakfast in the lobby. Balcony rooms facing Chartres Street will appeal to those who love street-scene watching, but they can be noisy. Instead, ask for a room overlooking the small patio and pool. The owner has opened a gospel club on Bourbon Street and guests will receive passes, according to the manager.
Rooms: $60-$226 (depending upon season).

The St. Louis

730 Bienville St., 70130
• 581-7300, (800) 535-9111
Fax 524-8925

The St. Louis has one of the most beautiful patios in the French Quarter, with almost all the rooms opening onto it. The little lobby is a jewel, so it is disappointing that many of the 69 rooms are rather bland by comparison. But it's an exceedingly friendly hotel, frequented by some high and mighty visitors. The Louis XVI restaurant is in the hotel (see Restaurants, page 62).
Singles & doubles: $95-$155; suites: $165-$410.

Villa Convento

616 Ursulines St., 70116
• 522-1793

Another small, European-style guesthouse owned by a family (the Campos), the Villa Convento has 24, mostly basic, rooms. Our choice would be those with balconies overlooking Ursulines Street (although the rooms are small) and the two newly renovated loft suites with fourth-floor views of the city. A Continental breakfast is included in the room rate. There is no on-site parking and no pool. No children under 8 are allowed.
Singles & doubles: $49-$69; suites: $75-$95.

CANAL STREET/ CENTRAL BUSINESS DISTRICT

Canal Street is the dividing line between the French Quarter and the Central Business District; many of the national chain hotels are located here. Parking generally is an additional $9 a night.

Doubletree New Orleans
300 Canal St., 70140
• 581-1300, (800) 528-0444
Fax 522-4100

This 363-room hotel, part of the small Doubletree chain, offers very good value; it looks far more elegant than its prices woud suggest. The marble lobby has a small, cozy sitting area with a French painting and tapestries; there's a friendly bar and restaurant, and bottles of wine are displayed behind glass in the hallway. All rooms are currently undergoing renovation; many have subdued floral fabrics and reproduction furniture. Guests find chocolate-chip cookies on their pillows upon arrival. There is a swimming pool and a game/exercise room. Ask for a higher floor if you want a river view. The hotel is across the street from the Rivergate convention center. *Singles & doubles: $96.90. Packages available.*

Fairmont Hotel
University Place, 70140
• 529-7111, (800) 527-4727
Fax 522-2303

One of the grand old hotels of New Orleans, the Fairmont was in previous lives the Grunewald, then the Roosevelt. It has a splendid, block-long, narrow lobby, and in the rooms such gilded amenities as down pillows and electric shoe buffers. There's an informal restaurant, open 24 hours, and the excellent Sazerac (see Restaurants, page 77) as well as a lively lounge, a pool and tennis courts. *Singles & doubles: $125-$195; suites: $315, $440 and up. Packages & weekend rates available.*

Holiday Inn Crowne Plaza
333 Poydras St., 70130
• 525-9444, (800) 522-6963
Fax 581-7179

Forget your preconceptions about the Holiday Inn part of the name; this is a first-rate, classy hotel with lots of glass, a streamlined lobby and 441 rooms. Top floors are devoted to concierge-level rooms, where the rates include complimentary hors d'oeuvres and buffet breakfast, as well as access to fax machines and photocopier services. There also are special rooms for women executives, a swimming pool and an exercise room. The hotel is a good bet for businesspeople with conventions at the Rivergate,

as the latter is just across the street.
Singles & doubles: $108-$146; suites: $250-$600. Riverview rooms $10 extra. Packages available.

Hyatt Regency

Poydras St. at Loyola Ave., 70140
• 561-1234, (800) 233-1234
Fax 587-4141

This is *the* place to stay if you're going to an event at the Louisiana Superdome. The hotel is attached to a new multistory shopping center that connects on the other side to the domed stadium, site of so many Super Bowls. This is one of the standard Hyatts—it has a vast atrium, two twenty-story windows (one with dangling metal mobiles), white balconies draped with vines, those familiar Hyatt glass elevators and millions of brown bricks that give the hotel a bleak, cold feeling no matter how hard they try to jazz things up. You enter through a block-long covered driveway; inside, the first things you see are fountains and escalators that lead to the main lobby on the third floor. The problem is that this shopping mall on the second floor serves an office tower, too, plus the entrance to the big mall that leads to the Superdome. It can be very confusing. There's a nifty "Children's Circus" toy store, as well as Woody Herman's Music Club and a Mrs. Field's cookie stand that never seems to be open when you want one most (at night). Lobby eating and drinking spots include the Sports Bar, Le Café Deli and the Courtyard Restaurant, that takes over most of the central part of the lobby. Be sure to zip up to the Top of the Dome revolving restaurant. Views are spectacular and there's a delightful innovation called the Chocoholic Bar, an all-you-can-eat buffet of spectacular chocolate desserts, surrounded by Hershey's kisses. A shuttle takes guests to the French Quarter. This is a vast hotel (1,196 rooms), but the staff is pleasant.
Singles & doubles: $139-$180; suites: $275-$550.

Inter-Continental New Orleans

444 St. Charles Ave., 70130
• 525-5566, (800) 332-4246
Fax 523-7310

The Intercontinental is known for its impressive collection of paintings and sculptures, created by New Orleans artists. The 494 rooms are attractively decorated with hotel florals and art and have minibars, hair dryers and tiny TV sets in the dressing room alcoves. There's a pool and health club on the top floor. A noted local chef, Willy Coln, took over direction of the restaurants last year. Pete's Pub is a gathering spot for local businesspeople in the Central Business District. One slight drawback is that the rest of the area shuts down at night.
Singles & doubles: $135-$250; suites: $300-$1,500.

Le Meridien New Orleans

614 Canal St., 70130
• 525-6500, (800) 543-4300
Fax 522-1456

Le Meridien is a superb, sleek hotel with a French flair. Walk-in guests enter from Canal Street and stroll through a long, narrow, high-arched marble hallway sided by the La Gauloise bistro (the Sunday buffet brunch is a feast; see Restaurants, page 49), a hairdresser, jeweler, gift shop and art gallery with very pricey old master paintings. This hallway ends with a rotunda that serves as a lounge and hot-spot jazz club with postmodern blond wood columns and rosy marble. Piped-in classical music plays when musicians aren't on stage. Then you continue through a short hall to the small main lobby, actually at the rear of the hotel, facing Common Street, entrance for guests arriving by car or taxi. It, too, is all marble, with a full-story sheet of waterfall, an antique tapestry and modernist crystal chandelier. Henri, one of the city's finest restaurants, is off the lobby (see Restaurants, page 52). Intimate, and done in dark green, it is supervised and visited twice a year by Marc Haeberlin, chef-owner of the fabulous L'Auberge de L'Ill in France. La Meridien has a business center and a health club with a sauna. The 497 rooms are done in soothing, monochromatic, pale shades of gray, tan and white and include toiletries from Hermès.
Singles & doubles: $130-$180; suites: $300-$1,400.

Le Pavillon Hotel

833 Poydras St., 70140
• 581-3111, (800) 535-9095
Fax 522-5543

One of the great bargains of New Orleans, Le Pavillon has been discovered by business people, who pack it during the week. Headquarters of the New Orleans Militia after the Civil War (they say a cannon on the front balcony kept order during the days of the carpetbaggers), it originally opened as a hotel in 1907, and has been completely overhauled in recent years, with a pseudo–Greek Revival facade and chandeliers and marble in the elegant lobby. The 200 rooms are currently being renovated (ask for one that's been finished) and are lovely. There's a rooftop swimming pool; business travelers can request photocopiers, typewriters and fax machines. This is another hotel in a business area that's fairly deserted at night.
Singles & doubles: $79; suites: $180.

New Orleans Hilton

Poydras St. at the Mississippi River, 70140
• 584-3999, 561-0500, (800) HILTONS

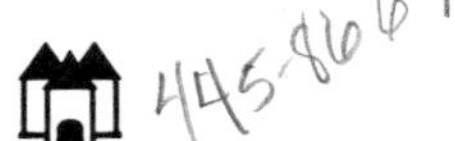

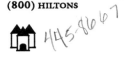

Big, huge, mammoth—every gargantuan adjective you can think of applies to this Hilton, with 1,602 rooms and 60 suites, making it one of the biggest hotels in the Gulf South. It's easy to get lost wandering from the main hotel to the riverside annex that tops the funky New Orleans Riverwalk shopping mall. The mall, incidentally, has everything from Abercrombie & Fitch and Sharper Image to fudge makers, who sing while they stir. In the hotel

itself there are five restaurants, six lounges (including Pete Fountain's; see Nightlife, page 133), two swimming pools, and a terrific health club with eleven tennis courts, a jogging track, squash and racquetball courts—even a newfangled indoor golf studio with video instruction, a putting green and a room in which to practice your swing. The rooms are usual Hilton fare. Ask for a river view.
Singles & doubles: $150-$205; suites: $300-$1,100. (Children stay free in parent's room.) Packages available.

New Orleans Marriott

Canal & Chartres Sts., 70140
• 581-1000, (800) 228-9290
Fax 523-6755

The Marriott is a humongous convention hotel, with 1,290 rooms in two towers. Its pseudo–New Orleans decor, however, distressed purists when it was built. This was the city's first skyscraper, and it infuriated a local architecture critic in its early days. Today, the sprawling, paneled lobby, almost always filled with milling tourists, looks merely uninspired, with a low ceiling and a raised central lounge with upholstered chairs and sofas, and big-screen television for sports events. Informal restaurants seem to sink into various side walls. The River View restaurant on the top floor is well named and has a noted Sunday brunch. The hotel decor is done in dustry rose, beige and celadon green. There's a health club with Nautilus equipment and exercycles next to the fifth-floor pool. Rooms are pleasant, but some face the opposite tower—ask for a high floor. If you're really splurging, the Mayor's Suite is something else, with two stories overlooking the Mississippi. As usual, the Mariott Hotel chain's service and friendliness cannot be faulted.
Singles & doubles: $160-$180; suites: $475-$525. Packages available.

Radisson Suite Hotel

315 Julia St., 70130
• 525-1993
Fax 525-1993 ext. 4109

Formerly the Sugar House, the Radisson offers 253 one-, two- and three-bedroom suites in the heart of the newly fashionable warehouse district, site of many of the city's finest art galleries and yuppie apartments; it's also only two blocks from the New Orleans Convention Center. (But if there's nothing on at the center and there are no gallery openings, the area is fairly desolate at night.) The lobby is a beautifully designed atrium with a skylight, a huge circular window and a geometric fountain. Each suite has a minibar and wet bar; many have balconies. Above the tenth floor, you're likely to have a city or river view. A couple of worthwhile bonuses of staying here are the free buffet breakfasts and happy hour cocktails. There's also a pool and jogging track.
Suites: $150-$500.

Sheraton New Orleans

500 Canal St., 70140
• 525-2500, (800) 325-3535
Fax 561-0178

There are 1,100 rooms in this 49-story skyscraper across Canal Street from the Marriott. Guests arrive in a block-long covered carriageway decorated with 1950s-style glass bricks and blue neon. Overlooking Canal Street is the lobby's Gazebo Lounge, an airy settling place with a two-story wall of windows, lots of greenery, sofas and comfortable chairs, and a bar that's topped by a gilded gazebo where muscians often entertain the tipplers with jazz. Also in the lobby is the Creole Tomato, a stylishly funky black-and-white-and-red cafeteria and snack bar with neon touches, where guests can have a luscious cinnamon roll and coffee for less than $3, and snack later in the day on New Orleans's famous po' boy sandwiches. Soft rock music plays in the Creole Tomato. Almost all of the bedrooms have a city or river view (for city views out to Lake Pontchartrain, ask for a room above the eighteenth floor). The top seven floors comprise the executive level, with all sorts of perks. Each of the tower suites on the top two floors has a wall of windows. The eighth-floor pool is being enclosed and a health club will be added by 1991. There's an extensive business center with computers and cellular phones for lease, as well as a secretarial service.
Singles & doubles: $109-$230; suites: $215-$1,100. Packages available.

Westin Canal Place

100 Iberville St., 70130
• 566-7006, (800) 228-3000
Fax 523-2549

Located atop the city's poshest shopping mall, Canal Place (Saks Fifth Avenue, Ralph Lauren, Laura Ashley, Guy Laroche), the Westin offers 438 rooms, most with sweeping views of the city or river, minibars, and Caswell & Massey toiletries. Guests soar to the eleventh-floor lobby, which has blond woods, comfortable sofas and chairs, antiques, tapestries and art purchased in local shops. There is a spectacular view of the French Quarter and river, and a rooftop pool. Guests can use racketball courts and a health club in the mall (which never seems to have any children in it), where there also is a first-rate four-screen movie theater. Afternoon tea is a delight in the hushed lobby of the hotel, and lavish Sunday buffet brunch is a favorite with sophisticated New Orleanians.
Singles & doubles: $165-$270; suites: $330-$1,200. (Price depends upon view.)

Windsor Court Hotel
300 Gravier St., 70140-1035
• 523-6000, (800) 262-2662
Fax 596-4513

We'll just go ahead and say it: this is the finest hotel in the city. Afternoon tea, complete with chamber music in Le Salon off the posh lobby, is a favorite escape of socially prominent New Orleanians, some of whom rank the scones and sweets better than any they've had in Britain. The hotel was developed by a local man (and partial owner, Jimmy Coleman, Jr.) who had roomed at Oxford University with the son of a former prime minister; he currently serves as honorary British consul in New Orleans. He spent a million dollars on eighteenth- and nineteenth-century British art before the hotel's opening a few years ago, and has hosted many members of the royal family here. The concierge staff wears tails, and there was a promotional exchange of executive chefs with Claridge's in London in early 1990, which will give you an idea of why New Orleans loves this world-class atmosphere so much. Many of the 323 spacious, traditionally decorated units are suites, most with English chintz and reproduction antique furniture, some with kitchen facilities, all with English soaps and numerous amenities. There is a pool and health club. The Grill Room restaurant is frequented by the city's decision makers (see Restaurants, page 51). The hotel is across the street from the Rivergate convention center. There is nothing so crass as a commercial shop or newsstand here—you simply ask for anything you might need.
Singles & doubles: $165-$185; suites: $210-$750.

UPTOWN

Avenue Plaza Hotel
2111 St. Charles Ave., 70130
• 566-1212, (800) 535-9575

Directly across a side street from that old favorite, the Pontchartrain Hotel, the Avenue Plaza is more family-oriented, a combination of timeshare units and hotel suites, with small kitchens in most rooms (ask for a studio to make sure that you're getting the standard junior suite; some have only wet bars and refrigerators). All units have coffee makers. Most rooms are decorated traditionally in beiges and burgundy. Request a room overlooking St. Charles Avenue, where you can catch the streetcar to the French Quarter. A major boon of staying here is the Euro-Vita Health Spa on the premises; it's one of the city's

best, and is free to guests. Splurge and get a massage while you're there (ask if Mike is on duty). There is a shuttle to downtown, a heated swimming pool in the patio, and a rooftop sundeck and whirlpool. The cozy restaurant (which offers room service) and lobby lounge with the ambience of an English library are much more inviting than the drab registration area.
Suites: $76-185.

The Columns

3811 St. Charles Ave., 70115
• 899-9308
No fax

The Columns has had its ups and downs (no pun intended). A onetime private residence, built in 1883 in the Italianate style, it has a faded grandeur. Its front porch is huge, and it has a dark, paneled Victorian entrance hallway and staircase. It would be an ideal set for a Gothic mystery, and, in fact, Brooke Shields made her acting debut when Louis Malle filmed *Pretty Baby* here in the 1970s. In past years, we were disappointed with the rooms we saw, but this year the one we were able to view was a big, pleasant room of the sort you'd see in a genteel home. We were told that some of the nineteen rooms still need work, so be specific about what you want if you stay here. The less expensive rooms share baths. There are telephones, and a TV in the lounge. A Continental breakfast is included in the rate. The Columns is in a fine location, right on the streetcar line. There is no parking or pool. (See also Nightlife, page 133.)
Singles & doubles: $55-$125.

The Josephine Guest House

1450 Josephine St., 70130
• 524-6361
No fax

A Greek Revival–Italianate home built in 1870, the Josephine is done in excellent taste and is filled with exquisite antiques, some of the finest we've seen in any place open to the public, outside museums and galleries, of course. There are six guest rooms (Dennis Quaid has stayed here) with televisions and books. The telephone is in the hall, but there are jacks in the room, so calls can be made in privacy. A Continental breakfast is beautifully served with sterling cutlery in the dining room or in guest rooms. The guesthouse is a block from the Pontchartrain Hotel, siding on Prytania Street. The posh Garden District is just a couple of blocks away from this quasi-commercial neighborhood undergoing renovation. There is no parking and no pool.
Rooms: $75-$135.

We're always interested to hear about your discoveries, and to receive your comments on ours. Please feel free to write to us, and do state clearly exactly what you liked or disliked.

Maison St. Charles (Quality Inn)

1319 St. Charles Ave., 70130
• 522-0187,
(800) 831-1783 (out of La.),
(800) 231-9685 (in La.)
Fax 522-0187

This upscale motel on St. Charles Avenue is good for those who have a car and want a central location. It was created with panache from five townhouses dating from the 1840s and contains Patout's restaurant, owned by relatives of Alex Patout, a name in Cajun cooking (see Restaurants, page 70). There is a swimming pool and a whirlpool.
Singles & doubles: $49-$189; suites: $199-$299.

Park View Guest House

7004 St. Charles Ave., 70118
• 861-7564
No fax

Frequented mostly by Europeans, students and parents of students at nearby Tulane and Loyola Universities, the Park View is in a great location, overlooking Audubon Park and the St. Charles Avenue streetcar line. While the downstairs parlor and breakfast room are comfortable and in good shape, the outside and some upstairs halls and rooms could use paint and attention. Some of the 25 rooms are plain; others have brass or wooden Victorian beds. Some rooms have balconies; some share baths. The public areas are not air-conditioned, although the bedrooms have window units. A Continental buffet breakfast is included in the rates, and tea, coffee and juice are available all day. No parking is available; there's no pool.
Rooms: $50-$75.

The Prytania Inn I

1415 Prytania St., 70130
• 566-1515
Fax 529-1404

The Prytania Inn II

2041 Prytania St., 70130
• 586-0858
No fax

We'd definitely go for the 22-room Prytania II, because it's in a better neighborhood and in a more architecturally noted building than the eighteen-room Prytania I. We are somewhat uneasy about this entry, because both places still needed some work early this year, but the co-owner, a former lawyer who is operating the guesthouses with his wife, assured us that it was progressing smoothly. However, they had just purchased yet another house, a once spectacular Greek Revival raised cottage unoccupied for years, and were planning to renovate it into guest quarters, too. Rooms that were finished were attractive, and painted mainly in shades of rose and blue. Both breakfast rooms were charming and inviting, with chintz cloths and lots of light. One problem was that guests in the 2041 address had to go to the other place for breakfast (a complete meal that visitors told us was excellent), since their guesthouse was not full. Some rooms have kitchenettes; TVs are available upon request. No room phones; no pool; limited parking.
Singles & doubles: $40-$55.

The Pontchartrain
2031 St. Charles Ave., 70140
• 524-0581, (800) 777-1700
Fax 529-1165

One of New Orleans's gracious old hotels, the Pontchartrain has retained its understated, elegant air through a change of ownership several years ago, and is undergoing a complete overhaul. You may be surprised at its minute lobby, barely more than a long hallway, but the observant will notice the elevator operators, the classical music in the hallways lined with bird prints and New Orleans art, and the subdued pastel ambience of old money. Every room in this small hotel is different; most are traditionally decorated, and many have silk flowers, even potpourri; all offer terry cloth robes and bottled water. Amenities in the small, old-fashioned tile bathrooms include Neutrogena products. Unfortunately, only the suites overlook St. Charles Avenue; ask for rooms on high floors with city views. The Caribbean Room is a grand restaurant (see Restaurants, page 31); the coffee shop is a favorite with local politicians, businesspeople and Uptown matrons. A great deal are the ten small pension rooms, where the rates include a Continental breakfast. There is no pool.
Singles & doubles: $70-$110; suites: $125-$500.

Terrell Guest House
1441 Magazine St., 70130
• 524-9859
No fax

Beautifully renovated Terrell Guest House (1858) provides a gracious experience for those seeking atmosphere. This nine-bedroom home, filled with antiques and chandeliers restored by the owner (restoration is a special interest of his), is, however, located in the midst of Operation Comeback, an area of renovation, and its block is not quite there yet. You would not want to walk in the area at night. No parking space is available, and there is no pool.
Rooms: $65-$100.

AIRPORT

Holiday Inn Holidome
2929 Williams Blvd. (at Interstate 10), Kenner 70062
• 467-5611, (800) HOLIDAY

The attraction here is the "holidome," a vast indoor swimming pool area with pool tables (really), lounge chairs and a garden restaurant. A few of the 303 rooms overlook the pool. There also is a workout center. This Holiday Inn was renovated in May 1989. Children stay free in their parents' room.
Singles & doubles: $59-$95.

New Orleans Airport Hilton & Conference Center
901 Airline Hwy.,
Kenner 70062
• 469-5000,
(800) HILTONS
Fax 466-5473

Done in an architectural style derived from Michael Graves (pediments with circular windows), this Hilton, which opened in January 1989, is mauve outside and blushed marble inside, sophisticated and posh for an airport hotel. We noticed nice touches, such as a pencil and notepad by each pay telephone in the lobby. The 315 rooms contain minibars; guests have a choice of daily newspapers. The Tower concierge rooms have robes and TV speakers in the bathrooms, as well as the usual freebie food and drink perks. The hotel has a restaurant and lounge, as well as a pool, tennis court, fitness center and business center. The hotel is located directly across the street from the airport.
Singles & doubles: $97-$139; suites: $275-$340.

Ramada Inn Airport
2610 Williams Blvd.,
Kenner 70062
• 466-1401,
(800) 228-2828
Fax 466-1401 ext. 570

With 195 rooms and suites, the Ramada offers standard services, a pool, lounge and restaurants, as well as 45 rooms on the concierge level. It's a short shuttle ride from the airport.
Singles & doubles: $60-$88.

Sheraton Hotel
2150 Veterans Memorial Blvd.
(at Interstate 10),
Kenner 70062
• (800) 325-3535

The Sheraton has 244 rooms and three suites as well as a lively nightclub and restaurant. It also has a pool and tennis court on the grounds.
Singles & doubles: $80-$116; suites: $150-$295.

BED & BREAKFAST

There's been a lot of controversy about the B & B industry in town lately, with usually genteel Garden District residents shouting that they don't want them in their ritzy neighborhood. Others who live in so-called prime areas have said the same. As of mid-1990, the situation still was fluid. However, Sarah-Margaret Brown at **New Orleans Bed & Breakfast** (Box 8163, New Orleans 70182; 838-0073, 838-0071) can book you a room at one of about sixty bed-and-breakfasts around town.

NIGHTLIFE

INTRODUCTION

STAYING UP LATE

New Orleans is a late town. Late dining, easy liquor laws and a love of spectacle are vestiges of the city's French and Spanish past. That past isn't just ***remembered***, it is ***relived*** daily in "the city that care forgot." From the calculated tawdriness of Bourbon Street to the frilly-mannered hotel enclaves, drinking and entertainment are considered necessities of daily life. Drinking on the sidewalks is legal, but not from glass containers. Bars are allowed to stay open 24 hours a day, though most do close by dawn. Every style of jazz and blues can be sampled on any given night, so a glance at the entertainment listings in the *New Orleans Times-Picayune*, *Wavelength*, *Offbeat* and *New Orleans* magazine can be helpful.

SWILLING WITH SPIRIT

One perfect measure of a city's character is to take a dip in its native drink, whether it be a deep Cabernet that tastes of the sun and earth, a bracing shot of chilled vodka or a tangy, festive margarita. In New Orleans, the drinks are long, strong and sweet or sweet-and-sour—full of the head-spinning glamour and gaiety of a Mardi Gras festival. Of course, in most of the rest of the country, cocktails are terribly passé, but you haven't visited this city until you've thrown back one or two of the following:

CAFÉ BRÛLOT - **A blazing brew of black coffee, brandy and curaçao, plus sugar, cinnamon, cloves and orange and lemon peel, heated and served in a brûlot bowl, or chafing dish. The ultimate Creole concoction.**

HURRICANE - **Invented at Pat O'Brien's, this fruity dark-rum punch truly resembles a cyclone in its size and effect.**

MILK PUNCH - **Bourbon or brandy, light cream, powdered sugar, a dash of vanilla and nutmeg; chilled.**

MINT JULEP - **Bourbon and simple syrup, poured over crushed ice and lavished with fresh sprigs of mint. A cooling breeze from the Gulf. Julep derives from the Arabic *julab*, or rosewater.**

PIRATE'S DREAM - **Four types of light and dark rum, plus grenadine, Angostura bitters, orange and lemon juice and heaps of fresh, crushed green mint; served on crushed ice. Sure to send you three sheets to the wind.**

RAMOS GIN FIZZ - **Named for 1880s bartender Henry Ramos; a frothy, blended gin drink with egg whites, cream, powdered sugar, orange flower water, lemon and lime juices and crushed ice. A morning favorite.**

SAZERAC - **Invented at Sazerac's bar; straight rye whiskey and absinthe, plus Angostura and Peychaud bitters, sugar and lemon peel. Not for the faint of stomach.**

BARS

Bayou Bar
Pontchartrain Hotel,
2301 St. Charles Ave.,
Uptown
• 524-0581

Nestled in the lobby of what many consider the city's finest traditional hotel, the Bayou Bar may seem to have an odd name. It's a piano bar of some vintage, but the pianists and other serenaders aren't always of the conversation-over-cocktails type. Fine service and muted, though convivial, surroundings add to the atmosphere. The music ranges from modern jazz to ragtime.
Open daily 11 a.m.-closing varies . All major cards.

Carousel Lounge
Monteleone Hotel,
214 Royal St.,
French Quarter
• 523-3341

In decades past, the Carousel Lounge was a mecca for politicos and showbiz figures, an elegant niche with eager service. Nowadays, it's a piano bar with echoes of the above, plus a cocktail-piano technician (Tuesdays through Saturdays) and a gently shifting clientele, many drawn from the conventions in town.
Open daily 5 p.m.-midnight. All major cards.

Cosimo's Bar
1201 Burgundy St.,
French Quarter
• 561-8110

The residential aspects of the French Quarter are reflected in this neighborhood bar, located in the area's northeastern corner. A lively jukebox complements a mix of regulars and cosmopolitan transients. Though Bourbon Street is just two blocks away, this isn't a tourist spot, and it shows.
Open daily 2 p.m.-3 a.m. Cards: AE.

Esplanade Lounge
Omni Royal Orleans Hotel,
621 St. Louis St.,
French Quarter
• 529-5333

Since it overlooks the lobby, and the plush chairs and piano are the focal points, this spot feels more like a large living room. French pastries are available from a cart, coffee is served as efficiently as anything else and the patrons are typically upscale.
Open daily 5 p.m.-1 a.m. All major cards.

The Half Moon
1125 St. Mary St.,
Uptown
• 523-8814

Located on the edge of the Irish Channel, the oddly shaped Half Moon echoes turn-of-the-century New Orleans, with a large, uncluttered bar that suits its image as a political hangout and former sports-crowd center. The walls are thick with photos spelling out the city's rich history as a boxing town, and local political movers still frequent it and the adjoining seafood restaurant.
Open Mon.-Sat. 8 a.m.-midnight. No cards.

Inter-Continental Lobby Lounge

Inter-Continental Hotel, 441 St. Charles Ave., Downtown • 525-5566

A conspicuously pleasant and well-appointed lounge with a centrally located piano, this spot can be a genuine afternoon delight. Sumptuous chairs and couches, attentive personnel and an onslaught of hors d'oeuvres welcome the nearby office-tower set as well as hotel guests.

Open daily 11 a.m.-midnight. All major cards.

Lafitte's Blacksmith Shop

941 Bourbon St., French Quarter • 523-0066

Located on the more subdued, residential stretch of Bourbon Street, this genuine eighteenth-century cottage is the stuff of New Orleans postcards. Inside is a vintage bar with a piano, and patrons who reflect the all-night habits of the neighborhood. Unfortunately for the bar, no historical evidence links the building with the pirate Jean Lafitte.

Open daily noon-closing varies. No cards.

Napoleon House

500 Chartres St., French Quarter • 524-9752

Built in 1814, the Napoleon House is said to have been the intended residence of Napoleon Bonaparte, some of whose local admirers plotted to rescue him and bring him to New Orleans. Today, the venerable bar and café serves as one of America's most picturesque establishments, a true, top-of-the-line bar that seems impervious to change. The house specialty is an excellent Sazerac, but a fine selection of imported beers and wines is available. The menu includes the muffuletta sandwich, fine soups and desserts that show the city's rich Italian influence. Unlike many other local bars, the air conditioning here is never used gratuitously, and the taped music is always classical. If you are able to visit only one bar in New Orleans, this should be it.

Open Mon.-Sat. 11 a.m.-2 a.m., Sun. 11 a.m.-7 p.m. Cards: AE, MC, V.

WHERE THE COCKTAILS ARE

Most sources (especially those farther south) agree that the word "cocktail"—and the drink itself—originated in New Orleans. In the 1790s, a wealthy Frenchman by the name of Antoine Amedee Peychaud arrived in New Orleans, one of many French plantation owners who fled to the city from an uprising in Santo Domingo, the Dominican Republic. Peychaud opened an apothecary and soon won applause for an alcoholic tonic he hawked as a cure for stomach disorders—its popularity probably boosted by the fact that it was taken with liberal amounts of brandy or cognac. The tonic itself persisted as a drink flavoring, and is still known as Peychaud bitters. And Peychaud's concoction, which was served in an egg cup the French call a "coquetier," soon graduated to coffeehouses and bars, where its merry imbibers mispronounced it as "cock-tay," and eventually "cocktail." Webster's dictionary traces its origin to 1806 and guesses that it's "prob. from cock [as in rooster] + tail"—but we know better!

Nick's

2400 Tulane Ave., Mid-City • 822-9407

Tucked away in a fading commercial area, the no-frills Nick's is not for the weak of stomach. Its unpretentious, shed-like exterior conceals a virtual boozer's Disneyland—multicolored, layered drinks such as the Flag and the Tangipahoa are the specialties here. Everything is potent, and the college crowd swells it up on the weekends. If you order scotch and water in this place, you're missing the point.

Open Sun.-Thurs. 2 p.m.-2 a.m., Fri.-Sat. 2 p.m.-4 a.m. Cards: MC, V.

Pat O'Brien's

718 St. Peter St., French Quarter • 525-4823

A tourist mecca held in almost as much esteem by locals, the centrally located Pat O'Brien's is the birthplace and home of the Hurricane—a skyscraper of a drink, guaranteed to fuel conversation and song among the pre- and postgame football carousers. Inhibitions are discouraged, the patio invites and souvenir-boxed Hurricane glasses are always on sale.

Open Sun.-Fri. 10 a.m.-4 a.m., Sat. 10 a.m.-5 a.m. No cards.

Port of Call

838 Esplanade Ave., French Quarter • 523-0120

A nautical motif, a well-stocked jukebox and a busy bar and kitchen mark this late-night hangout. Snugly off the tourist track, Port of Call has attracted bartenders and musicians among its neighborhood patrons. Dim lighting, ship's wheels and buoys aid the atmosphere, as does a late-night kitchen, renowned for its hamburgers and pizzas.

Open Sun.-Thurs. 11 a.m.-1 a.m., Fri.-Sat. 11 a.m.-5 a.m. Cards: AE.

Sazerac Bar

Fairmont Hotel, University Pl., Downtown • 529-7111

Almost hidden in the Fairmont's lobby mall, the Sazerac is an exactingly pleasant adjunct to the ultra-posh Sazerac restaurant. A long, streamlined bar is adorned by one of the city's largest indoor murals, depicting New Orleans of the 1930s. Governor Huey P. Long was a regular here, and it is said that the Sazerac was often an impromptu state capitol. They don't make them like the Sazerac anymore—it's a jewel of a bar that never gets overcrowded. The house specialty, the Ramos Gin Fizz, was invented here.

Open daily 11 a.m.-midnight. All major cards.

Tujague's

823 Decatur St., French Quarter • 525-8676

For more than a century, Tujague's has been a magnet, as much for its bar as for its renowned restaurant. Looking out on the intersection of Decatur and Madison, you get

a fine view of the pedestrian bustle, and looking in, a pleasant glimpse of the ninteenth century. A high bar and untouched woodwork please the eye; there are, alas, no spittoons, and a TV set lets you know that the twentieth century finally made it here.
Open daily 10 a.m.-11 p.m. All major cards.

CABARET & COMEDY

Slapstix
222 Clearview Pkwy., Metairie
• No phone

Some eight miles or so from the French Quarter, the suburban Slapstix is one of the city's few remaining comedy clubs. The performers range from ready-made for TV to the surprisingly polished. Service is adequate and laughs can be had.
Open Tues.-Sat. Shows Tues.-Sat. 8:30 p.m. & 10:45 p.m. Reservations recommended. Cards: AE, MC, V.

DANCE CLUBS

The Blue Crystal
1135 Decatur St., French Quarter
• 586-0339

A former neighborhood bar and seamen's dive, the Blue Crystal now caters to the ultra-contemporary rock crowd in the late hours. If progressive dance music and up-to-the-minute hairstyles are your cup of tea, this is the place for you.
Open nightly 10 p.m.-closing varies (usually 4 a.m.). Cover $2-$3. Cards: MC, V.

Déjà Vu
400 Dauphine St., French Quarter
• 523-1927

Perhaps appropriately, Déjà Vu never closes. Chic and ultramodern when it opened in 1972, it now serves as a dimly lit bastion of the red-eyes-and-bruised-ankle set. The disc jockey turns the volume up loud, blue hair is not uncommon, and the bar never quits.
Open daily 24 hours. No cover. All major cards.

The Max
601 Tchoupitoulas St., Downtown
• 525-6868

Regional trendies flock to this new high-intensity dance venue in the warehouse district. Local bands take over on weekends.
Open daily (times vary). Cover $5. No cards.

MUSIC CLUBS

Music clubs in New Orleans range from the tiny neighborhood bar with a jerry-built stage to the converted warehouse with a booming sound system. The city remains a hotbed of revived rhythm-and-blues stars, groundbreaking modern jazz performers and visiting artists. Starting times are always late—usually 10 p.m. or 11 p.m.—and the music continues until 3 a.m. or thereabouts. Cover charges vary from $2 or $3 in small clubs on weeknights to the upper ranges for ticketed events.

The Absinthe Bar
400 Bourbon St., French Quarter
• 525-8108

The Absinthe Bar is located in the thick of the Bourbon Street circus—and the prices reflect this. The crowd never thins. Local blues groups thrive here, on a tiny stage where bands play in shifts from afternoon to the wee hours. Built in 1806, the Absinthe Bar hasn't changed its original bar fountains, from which its absinthe frappé was dripped. Don't confuse this with its neighbor down the block, the Old Absinthe House.
Open daily noon-3 a.m. No cover. Cards: AE.

Absolute Bar & Grill
5300 Tchoupitoulas St., Uptown
• 899-7008

Essentially a restaurant of recent vintage, the Absolute is a well-appointed room where jazz and blues acts can be heard to good advantage on weekends. Seasoned pianists (such as Walter Lewis), bebop and rhythm-and-blues artists are common here.
Open Mon.-Thurs. 11 a.m.-10 p.m., Fri.-Sat. 11 a.m.-midnight, Sun. 10:30 a.m.-3 p.m. Music starts 9 p.m. Cover varies. Cards: MC, V.

Benny's Bar
938 Valence St., Uptown
• 895-9405

From the outside, Benny's looks more like a weathered tavern than anything else. It's a blues and rhythm-and-blues hangout, where a tiny stage can seem roomy compared to the bar and the (limited) seating area. Given that its shedlike features extend to the decor, Benny's is strictly for the blues and funk lover, not the comfort seeker. But prices and service are reasonable, and the Uptown college crowd can't seem to get enough of it.
Open nightly 6 p.m.-6 a.m. Music starts 11 p.m. No cover. No cards.

Bonaparte's Retreat

1007 Decatur St., French Quarter
• 561-9473

This section of Decatur has been part of the tourist circuit for only a decade or so, but Bonaparte's Retreat has been a neighborhood bar and a hippie hangout in the past. Now it's a calm afternoon and early-evening venue for traditional jazz groups.

Open daily 10 a.m.-2 a.m. No cover. Cards: AE, MC, V.

Borsodi's Coffeehouse

5104 Freret, Uptown
• 895-9292

Borsodi's is more of a pleasantly bohemian landmark than a music club. Musicians perform, yes, but often the program is poetry readings and plays. The decor can only be described as timelessly motley, and a fine selection of teas, coffees and pastries adds to its quiet, unpretentious charm.

Open Mon.-Sat. 7 p.m.-midnight. No cover. No cards.

The Bounty

1926 West End Park, Lakefront
• 282-9333

In years past, dance halls, dives and yachts packed the lakefront area. Many early jazz greats cut their teeth in this corner of town, which now houses seafood restaurants and places such as the Bounty, which showcases top-40 and oldies bands on weekends. The suburban-oldies crowd loves it, even when the disk jockey holds forth on weeknights.

Open nightly 8 p.m.-2 a.m. Cover varies (usually $3). All major cards.

Café Brasil

2100 Chartres St., Marigny
• 947-9386

Situated in the still-gentrifying Faubourg Marigny section, Café Brasil is an unabashedly eclectic place for a similarly inclined neighborhood. This former candy warehouse, two blocks outside the French Quarter, advertises its fare as "espresso, theater, art and music." Modern jazz takes the stage on weeknights, and the every-other-Sunday gospel show is a must.

Open daily 5 p.m.-2 a.m. Cover varies. No cards.

Cajun Cabin

501 Bourbon St., French Quarter
• 529-4256

Though Cajun and zydeco music originated in south-central Louisiana rather than in the New Orleans area, tourists expect it and someone supplies it. The relatively new Cajun Cabin packages it with a bayou decor and nightly music from a house band and special guests such as Allen Fontenot on weekends.

Open nightly 8 p.m.-closing varies (usually 12:30 p.m.) No cover; 2-drink minimum per music set. Cards: AE, MC, V.

Carrollton Station

8104 Willow St., Carrollton • 865-9190

Local rock and blues bands are the draw at Carrollton Station, a corner establishment where patrons have an excellent view of the streetcar barn across the street.
Open daily. Showtimes vary (usually 10 p.m.) Cover $3-$4. Cards: AE, MC, V.

Chris Owens

502 Bourbon St., French Quarter • 523-6400

The main attraction here is proprietor Chris Owens herself, a singer and dancer who harks back to the days when nightclub fare satisfied with suggestion more than explicitness. Owens is not a stripper, just a seasoned purveyor of bouncy song and dance.
Open Mon.-Sat. Shows 10 p.m. & midnight. Seating starts 9 p.m. All major cards.

The Columns

3811 St. Charles Ave., Uptown • 899-9308

A mansion turned hotel, the Columns's elegant setting easily explains why the film, *Pretty Baby,* was shot here. Its bar today more closely resembles a sprawling nineteenth-century parlor than a music club. On Wednesday, Thursday and Friday nights, the cream of the city's modern-jazz set, such as saxophonist Tony Dagradi and guitarist Steve Masakowski, play from 8 p.m. to midnight.
Open daily 3 p.m.-late. Cover varies (usually $5). Cards: AE, MC, V.

The Dream Palace

534 Frenchmen St., Marigny • No phone

From the street, the Dream Palace doesn't advertise itself well. Its windows are boarded up more for soundproofing than for secrecy, however. Local blues and rock acts have been a staple here since 1977, when this place opened as the first of the neighborhood's clubs before gentrification. Monday's Blues Night features red beans and no cover.
Open daily (hours vary). Music starts 10 p.m. Cover varies. No cards.

The Famous Door

339 Bourbon St., French Quarter • 522-7626

The Famous Door lists the names of celebrities who have patronized this jazz club over the decades. The enormous list frames the Dixieland groups playing inside, where the state of commercial Dixieland is defined. Rhythm-and-blues groups also play in the patio.
Open daily 1 p.m.-dawn. Cover varies. Cards: AE, MC, V.

Pete Fountain's

Hilton Hotel, 2 Poydras St., Downtown • 523-8939

The city's best-known clarinetist still swings impeccably four nights a week in his own club, which has seen capacity crowds almost every night since it opened. If you don't get reservations, you'll be sorry.
Open Tues.-Fri. & Sat. Show Tues. 10 p.m. Cards: AE.

Fritzel's

733 Bourbon St.,
French Quarter
• 561-0432

Fritzel's may be evidence that the farther down Bourbon Street you go, the less hurried the musical presentations can be. A relatively subdued bar (for Bourbon), Fritzel's can be a haven from the shrillness of the Strip. Traditional jazz groups, usually trios or quartets, play on weekends.
Open daily 1 p.m.-2 a.m. No cover; 1-drink minimum. Cards: AE, MC, V.

The Glass House

2519 Saratoga,
Uptown
• 895-9279

This otherwise undistinguished, low-ceilinged neighborhood bar built its reputation on being a home base for some of the city's young brass bands—groups not averse to blending bebop with the vaunted brass-band tradition. On Thursday nights, the Dirty Dozen Brass Band and the young Rebirth Brass Band still call this home.
Open nightly 5 p.m.-closing varies. Music Thurs. 11 p.m. Cover $3 Thurs. No cards.

Le Jazz Meridien

Le Meridien New Orleans,
614 Canal St.,
Downtown
• 525-6500

The rotunda of the plush Meridien holds one of the city's best-kept secrets in Le Jazz Meridien, which features perhaps the most authentic-sounding traditional jazz in town. Jacques Gauthe's Yerba Buena Creole Rice Jazz Band is heard on weekends. If you're interested in how New Orleans jazz sounded prior to 1930, this will give you a good idea.
Open Mon.-Fri. 7 a.m.-midnight, Sat. 4:30 p.m.-12:30 a.m., Sun. 3 p.m.-12:30 a.m. Music Mon.-Sat. starts 9 p.m., Sun. starts 3 p.m. No cover. All major cards.

Jimmy's

8200 Willow St.,
Carrollton
• 861-8200

Blues, new-wave and reggae acts have all trod the boards at Jimmy's. In recent years, the policy has been oriented more toward mainstream rock. When a popular local band plays on weekends, Jimmy's makes a sardine can seem roomy.
Open Mon.-Sat. 8 p.m.-late. Showtimes vary (usually 10 p.m.) Cover varies. All major cards.

Lulu White's Mahogany Hall

309 Bourbon St.,
French Quarter
• 525-5595

Lulu White was a Storyville madam, which is another story, since her only connection to this club is the use of her name. Traditional jazz is the fare here, and it is often of the highest quality found on Bourbon. The Dukes of Dixieland use this as a home base, as does Steve Pistorious' Mahogany Hall Stompers.
Open daily noon-1 a.m. Music 3 p.m. Cover $12.60 after 8:30 p.m. Cards: DC, MC, V.

Maison Bourbon
641 Bourbon St.,
French Quarter
• 522-8818

A cafélike setting and almost nonstop New Orleans traditional jazz pull in the crowds here. Bob French's Original Tuxedo Jazz Band works in the afternoons, while Wallace Davenport handles the night crowds. Good service and friendly musicians make this a tourist staple.
Open daily 2:15 p.m.-12:30 a.m. Music Mon.-Thurs. 2:30 p.m., Fri.-Sat. 11 a.m. No cover. No cards.

The Maple Leaf
8316 Oak St.,
Carrollton
• 866-9359

With its long, narrow music room and bar, and pressed-tin ceiling, the Maple Leaf looks almost untouched by twentieth-century hands. Blues and Cajun music are the attractions. Virtually every Cajun band in the region plays here, along with rhythm-and-blues and reggae groups. Collegiates and the shards of Uptown bohemia form the clientele. With its adjoining Laundromat, it may be the only place in the world where you can have a beer, sample a Cajun band and wash your clothes all at once.
Open daily. Music Mon.-Thurs. 9 p.m., Fri.-Sat. 10 p.m. Cover varies. No cards.

Michaul's
701 Magazine St.,
Business District
• 522-5517

Spanish moss and palmetto fans decorate Michaul's. the latest of the Cajun music venues. Cajun bands of every stripe are busy here, as is the kitchen.
Open Mon.-Thurs. & Sun. 6 p.m.-11:30 p.m., Fri.-Sat. 8 p.m.-midnight. Music Thurs.-Sat. 6 p.m.-11:30 p.m. Cover varies. Cards: MC, V.

The Mint
524 Esplanade Ave.,
French Quarter
• 522-5517

The Mint holds down one corner of the stately intersection of Decatur Street and Esplanade Avenue, across the street from its namesake, the old U.S. Mint building. Thursdays through Saturdays, this Mint features jazz, blues and folk music, sometimes combined by such groups as the Born Divas.
Open Thurs.-Sat. Showtimes vary. Cover varies. Cards: AE, D, V.

Muddy Water's
8301 Oak St.,
Carrollton
• 866-7174

A blues and rock club with a brief but busy past, Muddy Water's (formerly Jed's) packs them in with veteran rhythm-and-blues performers like Ernie K-Doe and the occasional Cajun band or out-of-town act.
Open daily. Showtimes vary (usually 10 p.m.) Cover varies. All major cards.

New Orleans Music Hall
907 S. Peters St., Warehouse District • 524-1722

More of a concert venue than a nightclub, the just-opened New Orleans Music Hall has a 1,000-plus capacity and big plans. Pink-and-black decor and an enormous bar complement a good sound system and touring rock bands on weekends.
Call for specific show dates, times & prices. No cards.

Palm Court
1204 Decatur St., French Quarter • 525-0200

The specialty at Palm Court is traditional New Orleans jazz in pleasant, cafélike surroundings. The fare is always high grade, such as banjoist-raconteur Danny Barker and His Jazz Hounds. A good kitchen awaits, and the music starts early.
Open Wed.-Fri. 6 p.m.-11 p.m., Sat.-Sun. noon-midnight. Music 7 p.m. No cover. Cards: AE, MC, V.

Preservation Hall
726 St. Peter St., French Quarter • 523-8939

Every jazz fan in the world eventually visits Preservation Hall. Some of the groups on the roster here are led by octogenarians, who still have their musical chops. Kid Sheik and the Humphrey Brothers (who are about the same age as this century) are a must for any visitor. The building, untouched by renovators, includes decor about as austere as any you'll ever find. But even on weeknights, you'll have to stand in line to get in. Expect no creature comforts, just the New Orleans sound.
Open nightly. Show nightly 8:30 p.m. Cover $3. No cards.

Snug Harbor
626 Frenchmen St., Faubourg Marigny • 949-0696

Carved out of an 1840s building, Snug Harbor is the city's best-known jazz and blues club. For seven nights a week, the club runs the gamut from stellar modernists, such as pianist Ellis Marsalis, to the up-and-coming singer Charmaine Neville. A fine restaurant and a nautical-motif bar (separate from the cozy music room) add to its no-pressure attractiveness.
Open nightly 6 p.m.-2 a.m. Show nightly 10 p.m. Cover varies. Cards: AE, MC, V.

Storyville Jazz Hall
1104 Decatur St., French Quarter • 525-8199

More of a musical lazy Susan than a true jazz hall, Storyville features local and national artists of blues, jazz and rock persuasions. Seating is adequate, and two bars beckon.
Call for specific show dates, times & prices. Cover varies. Cards AE, MC, V.

Tipitina's

501 Napoleon Ave., Uptown • 897-3943

The huge banner above the stage of this celebrated club honors the seminal pianist, Professor Longhair, who called Tipitina's home in his later years. The club, named after one of Longhair's songs, features a bit of everything—including national acts that simply want to say that they actually performed here.

Open daily. Shows weeknights 9 p.m., weekends 10 p.m. Cover varies. No cards.

Tricou House

711 Bourbon St., French Quarter • 525-8379

A mixed-bag musical policy marks Tricou House, where you may find traditional blues and jazz pianist Walter Lewis one night and multiple synthesizer wizard Randy Hebert the next.

Call for specific show dates, times & prices. Cards: AE, MC, V.

Tyler's

5234 Magazine St., Uptown • No phone

The oldest of Uptown jazz clubs, Tyler's includes an oyster bar, late-night sets and the saxophonist James Rivers, with the longest continuosly running jazz gig in town.

Open Wed.-Sat. Show 10 p.m. Cover. Cards: MC, V.

SHOPS

INTRODUCTION

SEARCHING OUT THE SPECIAL

Local color and a relaxed atmosphere are key words for shopping in New Orleans. The whole French Quarter is like an intimate European market with lots of small shops, boutiques, galleries and cafes. Where else in the world can you hear a soulful saxophone played in the street, watch a juggler or mime, sip rich chickory-laced coffee, and admire ornate iron-trimmed balconies all in the course of a shopping trip?

New Orleans was founded in 1718 around a market, a strip along the Mississippi that served as an early trading post where tribes from the Gulf area exchanged their wares. Today little remains of the herbs, spices, blankets and pelts of the Indians, but the city continues as a thriving marketplace with the famous French Market occupying the same land that the trading post once did.

What makes shopping such an exciting experience here is the great variety of small shops, local craftspeople and colorful regional items available. This variety, coupled with a friendly chat in a slightly accented voice of the salesperson, tends to bring the shopper back again and again. It has become almost de rigueur for visitors to take home a Mardi Gras mask, some beignet mix to try making those wonderful square French donuts at home, the Neville Brothers's latest album, or at least a brightly colored poster of the annual **Jazz and Heritage Festival** as a memento of a very alluring city and the good times spent there. If these don't make the greatest gift items, then perhaps some vetivert or magnolia fragrance, an alligator charm in silver by famed jewelry designer Mignon Faget, or an authentic crawfish polo shirt will.

The main shopping areas are all conveniently close to one another; the **French Quarter**, with **Jackson Brewery** and **Canal Place**, and the downtown **Central Business District**, with the **Riverwalk**, are neighbors that share the bustling boulevard of Canal Street. Public buses and streetcars shuttle people back and forth when distances become too far to walk. Within a short taxi ride range is the **New Orleans Centre**, a posh new metro mall beside the Superdome, and for the more adventuresome shopper there is **Magazine Street**, with its dozens of antique, curio and collectibles shops; understandably it has been called the Street of Dreams. Chic, modern fashions from the best national and international designers debut in an elegant milieu in two premier downtown shopping centers, Canal Place and New Orleans Centre, at the likes of **Macy's**, **Saks Fifth Avenue**, **Brooks Brothers**, **Lord & Taylor** and **Bally**. Other parts of the metropolitan New Orleans area sport clusters of venerable stores and specialty shops that often rival the quality and selection of larger downtown enterprises: the **Rink** on Prytania Street in the **Garden District**; **St. Charles Avenue**, between Lee Circle and Louisiana Avenue; the **Riverbend**, where St. Charles Avenue merges into Carrollton Avenue; and **Uptown Square**, whose name speaks for itself.

The climate, too, is conducive to leisurely browsing and shopping. Generally the weather is sunny and warm, though an umbrella is recommended for waiting out the almost daily flash showers in the summertime. And there is always a charming café, bistro or small restaurant nearby for a bite to eat and some air-conditioned comfort. Fine food and gourmet items are a natural part of shopping in a city that so loves to eat.

While New Orleans has not enjoyed a reputation as a great national shopping destination since the 1850s, astonishing changes in the past decade are now putting this city in direct competition with Houston, Atlanta and Miami. Haute couture; nationally recognized artists and craftspeople exhibiting in fine galleries; Cajun, Creole and French foods in shops and cooking schools; and a selection of antiques to rival the best in the world are now attracting national and international visitors. Together with the distinctive culture and traditions of New Orleans and natural Southern hospitality, all this makes for a truly memorable experience.

The selection of shops, galleries and centers that follows gives an overview of what is available in the French Quarter and downtown area with some recommendations in other parts of the city. Because it is a limited listing, don't be surprised if you discover treasures we may have overlooked. In New Orleans there is a word for that unexpected little extra—*lagniappe.*

ANTIQUES

The antique shopping scene in New Orleans centers around the lower French Quarter downtown and along Magazine Street as it passes through the Garden District to Uptown. There are dozens of curio shops that can double as antique outlets. This suggested listing gives you an idea of the range of antiques available.

Accent Antiques

2855 Magazine St.
• 897-9466

This shop imports fine European antiques directly and displays them in a spacious showroom. They also have a large selection of light fixtures and etchings, as well as bric-a-brac.
Open Mon.-Sat. 10 a.m.-5 p.m.

Bep's Antiques

2051 Magazine St.
• 525-7726

A recommended place to go for old bottles, so popular among local collectors, as well as crockery and glassware. This is a lovely shop filled with hand selected treasures.
Open Mon.-Sat. 9 a.m.-5 p.m.

Charbonnet and Charbonnet Antiques
2929 Magazine St.
• 891-9948

Large pieces of furniture, such as cupboards, chests and chifforobes are a specialty here. You'll find a lot of mid-nineteenth-century English and Irish pine. The brackets, cornices and stained glass make unusual touches for decorating.
Open Mon.-Sat. 9 a.m.-5:30 p.m.

Collector Antiques
3123 Magazine St.
• 897-0904

This is the place to find lovely antique linens and lace, sewing items, picture frames and books. Vintage bedspreads, quilts and table cloths round out the collection.
Open Mon.-Sat. 10 a.m.-5 p.m.

Charles Cooper Antiques
834 Chartres St.
• 523-4718

This is a shop to take you back in time to the baroque and Renaissance periods. There is a large selection of art and tapestries: you'll want to take some home to your castle.
Open Mon.-Sat. 10 a.m.-5 p.m. and by appointment.

James H. Cohen & Sons, Inc.
437 Royal St.
• 522-3305

This is a shop for gun and coin collectors. Now in its fourth generation of the Cohen family, it handles hundreds of antique weapons, all dating before 1898. The staff are experienced in all phases of the business and can justly advertise having one of the largest collections in the South.
Open daily 9:30 a.m.-5:30 p.m.

Jon Antiques
4605 Magazine St.
• 899-4482

For a fine selection of eighteenth- and nineteenth-century English furniture and porcelain, this is the place to look. Jon Strauss, owner, imports directly from England; her knowledge of antiques extends to giving slide lectures with Macon Riddle on English furniture and conducting tours of local antique shops. Getting acquainted with her is a good reason to visit this spacious shop.
Open Tues.-Fri. 10:30 a.m.-4:45 p.m., Sat. 11 a.m.-4 p.m. and by appointment.

J. Raymond Samuel Ltd.
The Rink, at Washington & Prytania Sts.
• 891-9061

Mr. Samuel is a New Orleans native and has been collecting historical art works and rare books and paintings for many years. A visit to his shop invariably includes an educational chat about the history of New Orleans and its environs. The shop is located in the Garden District; in fact, you'll want to pick up a copy of Samuel's book on the District before touring that lovely area of the city.
Open Mon.-Sat. 10 a.m.-4 :30 p.m.

Lucullus
610 Chartres St.
• 528-9620

The owners here are long-time collectors of fine Continental and English furniture from the seventeenth to nineteenth centuries. You'll find a good selection of art and cookware from this period as well.
Open Mon.-Fri. 9 a.m.-5 p.m., Sat. 10 a.m.-5 p.m., Sun. by appointment only.

Manheim Galleries
403-409 Royal St.
• 568-1901

The largest collection in New Orleans of antique English, Continental and Asian furnishings (in four buildings) awaits the antique shopper here. The porcelains, paintings, silver and jade are all of good quality and style. Manheim is the local agent for the famous Boehm Birds.
Open Mon.-Sat. 10 a.m.-6 p.m.

Mcbride-Whisnant Galleries
22 Chartres St.
• 524-9766

Ever seen a shop that defies a name for its contents? This is one of those places whose stock is impossible to label as antiques, art, or that catch-all term, "collectibles." You can spend hours here poking through the antique jewelry, African sculptures, clocks and other unusual items, so plan to take your time. We have never left disappointed.
Open Mon.-Sat. 9:30 a.m.-5:30 p.m., sometimes Sun. (call ahead for Sun.)

Moss Antiques
411 Royal St.
• 522-3981

The large selection of antique and estate jewels makes this shop unique. They also feature fine French and English furnishings, including paintings.
Open Mon.-Sat. 9 a.m.-5 p.m.

Morton Goldberg's Auction Galleries
3000 Magazine St.
• 891-8421

Magazine Street has dozens of antique shops; situated in the middle is this enormous king of them all. Goldberg's building fills a city block and contains sixteen rooms of antiques from local estates and from all over the world. It has truly one of the South's largest antique selections. The shop does a brisk wholesale and auction business, but retail shoppers are also welcome. Shipments arranged anywhere.
Open Mon.-Sat. 9 a.m.-5 p.m.

19th Century Antiques
4838 Magazine St.
• 891-4845

For rare and unusual clocks from around the world, this shop can't be beat. You'll also find the antique display cases that line the walls here crammed with cut glass, china, bisque, and bric-a-brac of all sorts. The owners, with over twenty years at this shop, are experts in the antique miscellany business.
Open Mon.-Sat. 10 a.m.-5 p.m.

Rothschild's Antiques
241 Royal St.
• 523-5816

321 Royal St.
• 321-2281

These long-established shops give Royal Street its name in fine antiques. The eclectic nature of the two shops makes browsing a pleasurable pastime; furniture, mantelpieces, silver, jewelry, and clocks from the eighteenth century to the twentieth century are all displayed with imagination, and the staff is good about explaining the wares.
Both branches open Mon.-Sat. 9:30 a.m.-5:30 p.m.

Royal Antiques
307-309 Royal St.
• 524-7033

Sharing Royal Street's reputation for fine antiques is this store, which accurately claims to have the largest stock of French and English country antiques in town. They even have a warehouse several blocks away. This is a good place to begin an antiques tour of the French Quarter.
Open Mon.-Sat. 9:30 a.m.-5:30 p.m.

Waldhorn Company
343 Royal St.
• 581-6379

Established in 1881, this is the oldest antique shop in town. The experienced staff will show you English and French period furniture, the good collection of Victorian and early American jewelry, antique English porcelain and Georgian silver.
Open Mon.-Sat. 9 a.m.-4:30 p.m.

ART & POSTERS

Bergen Galleries
730 Royal St.
• 523-7882,
(800) 621-6179

Designing and collecting posters is big business in New Orleans. Posters are created to celebrate almost any occasion, from the Crescent City Classic running race to Mardi Gras. Bergen is a good place to check out the latest and best of the current season's crop as well as browse through some timeless classics. Prices are usually very competitive, especially in the French Quarter. Among the artists featured in posters and limited graphics are Erté, McKnight, Patti Bannister, Nagel, and Muhai. Bergen will ship your poster anywhere in the world.
Open daily 9 a.m.-7 p.m.

The Black Art Collection
738 Royal St.
• 529-3080

This is one of few commercial galleries in town dedicated to contemporary African-American art. It carries a good selection of works by local luminaries, such as Bruce Brice and John Scott, plus those of many nationally acclaimed artists. We have always found some of the better posters

here, and the antique African artifacts are in themselves worth a visit. There are also jazz images in all media.
Open daily 10 a.m.-7 p.m.

Circle Gallery
316 Royal St.
• 523-1350

Internationally known artists are the specialty here, with many limited-edition graphics and paintings by Frank Gallo, Agam and Lebadang, Peter Max, Chuck Jones and Firz Freleng. You'll enjoy jewelry by Erté and animation art by Disney Studios; many works aren't found elsewhere in New Orleans. Convenient hours.
Open Mon.-Thurs. 10 a.m.-6 p.m., Fri.-Sat. 10 a.m.-10 p.m., Sun. 10 a.m.-5 p.m.

Davis Gallery
3964 Magazine St.
• 897-0780

The owners of this shop travel often and widely to replenish their stock of authentic African tribal art. You'll find quality jewelry, costuming, sculpture, baskets and weapons, and the staff really know their business.
Open Mon.-Fri. 10 a.m.-5 p.m.

Dumaine Corner Gallery
501-505 Dumaine St.
• 529-5950

Every afternoon Almarie Pittman Little comes to this gallery and works on her Black Heritage primitive paintings, which depict early life along the Mississippi and the bayou country of Louisiana. The elderly artist is represented in collections in many countries; she proudly displays her dozens of letters of satisfaction from famous and not so famous buyers. She also paints plantation homes and French Quarter scenes.
Open daily 10 a.m.-6 p.m. Artist in daily 3 p.m.-closing.

Dynasen Gallery
433 Royal St.
• 523-2902

An innovative and exciting gallery, this is where the exhibit of John Lennon's drawings was housed when it came to New Orleans. A specialty is a collection of bronze sculptures and lithographs and serigraphs by Erté, and also the premier collection of jazz artists in bronze by Paul Wegner. You'll find original paintings and limited-edition graphics by the likes of Zandra Rhodes, Michael Young, Ji Cheng, Gantner, Weglin and others. Convenient hours.
Open daily 10 a.m.-10 p.m., Fri.-Sat. 10 a.m.-11 p.m.

Gallerie Simonne Stern
518 Julia St.
• 529-1118

One of the better-known art collectors in New Orleans is Stern, with her gallery full of contemporary paintings, sculptures and master prints. She was one of the first collectors to relocate to the now fashionable Historic Warehouse District.
Open Mon.-Fri. 10 a.m.-5 p.m., Sat. 11 a.m.-4 p.m.

Gallery For Fine Photography

313 Royal St.
• 899-3001

Joshua Pailet, New Orleans photographer, has made a name for himself through his large collection by photographic greats such as Ansel Adams, Alfred Stieglitz, Henri Cartier-Bresson and Diane Arbus. He also specializes in rare photographs and images from the nineteenth century.
Open Mon.-Sat. 10 a.m.-6 p.m., Sun. noon-4 p.m.

Hanson Galleries

229 Royal St.
• 566-0816

For the art collector interested in investment-quality graphics, sculpture and work in other unique mediums, this gallery represents Peter Max, local artist Adriann Deckbar, Neiman, Kent, Ross, Tapies and Zjawinska, among others. It is one of the better-known and longer-established galleries in town.
Open Mon.-Sat. 10 a.m.-7 p.m., Sun. 11 a.m.-5 p.m.

Merrill B. Domas American Indian Art

824 Chartres St.
• 586-0479

One of few places in the city to stock authentic Native American art, this adobe-lined gallery also knows how to display the art to its best advantage. We enjoyed a brightly colored primitive wooden horse and some unusual weavings and sculptures during a recent visit. The shop carries a selection of Native North American baskets both antique and contemporary, along with jewelry and beadwork. Merrill Domas has rotating shows that focus on various aspects of this art.
Open Tues.-Sat. 11 a.m.-5 p.m.

Res Nova

440 Julia St.
• 586-1115

A contemporary art space in the Warehouse District, this gallery is known for its paintings, sculpture, drawings and photography. Artists represented here include locals Lynda Benglis, Casey Williams and Anne and Patrick Poirier. Much of the work is on the cutting edge of the art scene.
Open Wed.-Sat. 10 a.m.-6 p.m. and by appointment.

Still-Zinsel Contemporary Fine Art Gallery

328 Julia St.
• 588-9999

This is one of the most consistently up to date galleries in town. Located in the Warehouse District, it handles new as well as better-known artists in a broad cross-section of contemporary fine art. You'll find landscapes here beside figurative and abstract pieces. There's a good mix.
Open Tues.-Sat. 10 a.m.-5 p.m.

BEAUTY & HEALTH

BEAUTY & HAIR SALONS

Belladonna
1720 St. Charles Ave.
• 581-6759

When you enter this unique combination of boutique and body salon it feels like a private home. You can have a facial, manicure or massage while deciding which of the dresses or casual outfits to try on, or whether some of the ethnic jewelry displayed is to your liking. The clothing and accessories include many in-house designs, all for the discriminating shopper. Service is relaxed and friendly.
Open Mon.-Sat. 10 a.m.-6 p.m.

John Jay Beauty Salon
7600 St. Charles Ave.
• 866-2782

Local stylist and beauty consultant John Jay has won various national awards for his skill. His eight salons in the metro area have a reputation for quality hair care, skin care, beauty products and manicures. Jay is available personally by appointment. You can reach his uptown shop by taking a ride on the streetcar, which stops almost in front of the salon.
Open Mon.-Sat. 9 a.m.-5:30 p.m., Tues. & Thurs. 9 a.m.-7 p.m.

Lulu Buras Hair, Skin, Nail & Body Care
Canal Place,
365 Canal St.
• 523-5858

Another local hair and beauty expert is Lulu Buras, with three shops in town. She specializes in European skin care and has a full-service hair salon for men and women. As the name of her shop implies, she also offers massage and manicures.
Open Mon.-Thurs. 9 a.m.-6 p.m., Fri.-Sat. 8:30 a.m.-6 p.m.

Saks Fifth Avenue
Canal Place,
301 Canal St.
• 524-2124

Along with upscale fashions and accessories, this clothing store offers a very reputable hair and beauty salon in the downtown area. Facials, manicures, hair coloring and perms are available. It's advisable to call for an appointment at least a day in advance.
Open Fri.-Wed. 10 a.m.-6 p.m., Thurs. 10 a.m.-8 p.m.

Salonsenoj
101 Aris Ave.
(at Metairie Rd.)
• 835-5500

You can pamper yourself with a facial or massage in the plush surroundings of this new salon. You'll be greeted with champagne, coffee, fresh biscuits and muffins, and the service is superb. There is a full range of specialty

services: facials, manicures, pedicures, massage, makeup and hair. The serene country setting is conducive to your spending a truly relaxing morning or afternoon.
Open Mon.-Sat. 9 a.m.-6 p.m. Last appointment made at 5:30 p.m.

FITNESS

Most of the finer hotels have an in-house exercise and workout area. Offering more extensive equipment and services, the following clubs and salons welcome short-term and long-term visitors.

Euro Vita Health Club, Spa & Salon

Avenue Plaza Hotel,
2111 St. Charles Ave.
• 525-6899

Deluxe treatment with personal supervision is what sets this institution apart. The little touches make the difference: fluffy terry robes, a telephone, free lockers, a sitting area with TV. Universal and Paramount exercise machines are available for men and women, plus Precor treadmills, Stairmasters, Lifecycles, Air Dyne bicycles, and free weights. In the salon you can have a body massage, herbal wrap, or a "loofah salt glo." Lounge in the hot tubs, individual whirlpools, saunas, steambaths or Swiss showers. You'll feel like a million!
Open Mon.-Sat. 9 a.m.-5 p.m., Sun. 7 a.m.-9 p.m.

New Orleans Athletic Club

222 N. Rampart St.
• 525-2375

This historic French Quarter institution has only recently admitted women members. It is the third-oldest athletic club in the nation. You can enjoy the heated indoor pool and running track, four handball/raquetball courts, free weights, and the rooftop sun deck. There are also a Nautilus circuit, aerobics exercise classes, and computerized bikes and treadmills. A dining room, a bar and a barbershop round out this full-service club.
Open Mon.-Fri. 5:30 a.m.-10 p.m., Sat.-Sun. 7 a.m.-8 p.m.

Racquetball One Fitness Center

Canal Place,
380 Canal St.
• 525-2956

One Shell Square
• 522-2956

Two downtown locations make this facility convenient for out-of-town visitors. Owners Cliff Bergeron and Paul Bruno are generally on hand to greet members personally. Membership in the International Raquetball Sports Association in other cities is honored here. You'll find Nautilus equipment, free weights, Lifecycles, Stairclimbers and rowing machines to work out on, and Jacuzzis, saunas, steambaths and therapeutic massages for relaxation. Aerobic classes and personal trainers are available, along with, of course, several raquetball courts. Separate wet areas for

men and women.
One Canal Place: open Mon.-Fri. 6 a.m.-9 p.m., Sat.-Sun. 9 a.m.-6 p.m. One Shell Square: open Mon.-Fri. 6 a.m.-10 p.m., Sat.-Sun. 9 a.m.-6 p.m.

Rivercenter Racquet & Health Club

Hilton Hotel,
Poydras St. at the river
• 587-7242

Two outdoor pools are the center of this hotel club, with separate saunas, Jacuzzis and whirlpools for men and women. You can also participate in aerobics and yoga classes, have a massage, facial or herbal wrap, or grab a snack at the juice and sandwich bar. For the sports-minded, there are eight indoor and three outdoor tennis courts, two squash courts, five racquetball courts, a jogging track, a basketball court, an indoor golf driving range and a weight room with equipment by Universal Gym, Lifecycles and Stairmasters. This is a popular downtown club for locals and tourists alike.
Open Mon.-Thurs. 6:30 a.m.-10:30 p.m., Fri. 6:30 a.m.-9 p.m., Sat.-Sun. 8 a.m.-7 p.m.

PERFUMERIES

La Belle Epoque Parfumerie

Jackson Brewery
• 522-1650

For the special woman in your life a private-label fragrance could be the perfect gift. The staff here helps design the fragrance itself and the bottle and box to package it. With a laboratory on the premises, the possibilities of such design fragrances are unlimited. You'll also enjoy the shop's extensive selection of perfume bottles, one of the largest in the United States.
Open Mon.-Sat. 10 a.m.-9 p.m., Sun. 10 a.m.-10 p.m.

Bourbon French Parfums

525 St. Ann St.,
Jackson Square
• 522-0448

For your own signature perfume, this shop on Jackson Square can advise you and mix a fragrance to your taste. It also carries a large selection of its own perfumes and flasks. A New Orleans fragrance can make an original memento of your time spent there.
Open Mon.-Wed. 9 a.m.-6 p.m., Thurs.-Sat. 9 a.m.-7 p.m., Sun. 10 a.m.-6 p.m.

Hove Parfumeur

824 Royal St.
• 525-7827

Perfume shops have long been a tradition in New Orleans. This is the last of such small family-owned shops in the French Quarter, and it has been in the Hove family for three generations. Of special interest here is the vetivert fragrance, sachet, and fans used since the time of the early Creoles. Other local perfumes include sweet olive and

magnolia. Hove sells its fragrances around the country, to such stores as Lord & Taylor and Macy's.
Open Mon.-Sat. 10 a.m.-5 p.m.

BOOKS & STATIONERY

Beckham's Book Shop

228 Decatur St.
• 522-9875

Carey Beckham is the city's largest dealer in secondhand books and classical records. His three shops in the French Quarter (this one, Librairie Book Shop and Old Books) all feature used, out-of-print and rare books on topics of local and Southern interest. In addition, Beckham's specializes in classical records, the Librairie in old prints, and Old Books in antique postcards. The staff in all three stores consists of locals who enjoy talking about their hard-to-find stock.
Open daily 10 a.m.-6 p.m.

Bookstar

414 N. Peters St.
• 523-6411

This national-chain bookstore has one of the largest selections of current titles anywhere in the city, and both its location in the French Quarter and its long hours are a convenience. The newsstand is well stocked. We find the collection of local books, especially cookbooks and city guides, to be fairly good. And with such vast stock, you're sure to find a calendar, date book, or other accessory you might be looking for.
Open daily 9 a.m.-midnight.

Community Book Center

1200 Ursuline St.,
• 561-0036

For African-American literature, gifts, prints, and all-occasion greeting cards, this small shop, operated by community activist Vera Warren, is a good bet. She also carries a variety of books and publications about the local Black community and its role in New Orleans history.
Open Mon.-Sat. noon-7 p.m.

Deville Books & Prints

Jackson Brewery
• 525-4508

Riverwalk
• 595-8916

One Shell Square
• 525-1846

Deville is another independent bookstore group that specializes in Southern and regional books and is fun to explore. Along with current titles in the three Deville shops, you'll find rare books and lots of posters, greeting cards and postcards. The location of these shops in the major shopping complexes is another plus.
Jackson Brewery & Riverwalk: open Mon.-Thurs. 10 a.m.-9 p.m., Fri.-Sat. 10 a.m.-10 p.m. One Shell Square: open Mon.-Fri. 9:30 a.m.-5:30 p.m., Sat. 10 a.m.-4 p.m.

George Herget Books

3109 Magazine St.
• 891-5595

Located about midway along the winding stretch of antique and specialty shops of Magazine Street is this collector's bookshop, crowded not only with more than 20,000 used and old books but with old postcards, records and Civil War items as well. The book-collector can find lots of possibilities here. Herget, incidentally, knows his New Orleans and Southern history; a chat with him is likely to last hours.
Open Mon.-Sat. 10 a.m.-5:30 p.m., sometimes Sun. (call ahead).

The Little Professor Book Center

1000 S. Carrollton Ave.
• 866-7646

Personal service is a hallmark of this locally owned comprehensive bookstore, which serves the university community. We find their selection of cookbooks and self-help books very good, and there is no problem having a special order placed on a hard-to-find book. The staff is familiar with local authors.
Open Mon.-Sat. 9 a.m.-6 p.m.

Maple Street Book Shop

7523 Maple St.
• 866-4916

The Rink,
2727 Prytania St.
• 895-2266

200 Broadway,
Uptown Square
• 865-8310

As owner of one of the oldest bookstores in the city, New Orleans native Rhoda Faust strongly supports Southern writers and frequently hosts book-signing affairs. Her stores carry large selections of local books and periodicals. The Maple Street Children's Book Shop fills a house next to the shop on Maple Street, which makes an ideal shopping situation for the whole family. Anne Rice, author of the celebrated vampire books, lives in the Garden District just a short walk from the Maple Street Book Shop in the Rink.
Open Mon.-Sat. 10 a.m.-6 p.m.

The Mystic Moon

7808 Maple St.
• 865-9465

Billed as a feminist bookstore, this shop is one of the only places in town that stock a comprehensive collection of women's literature and music. As its name implies, there is an emphasis here on crystals and other healing stones, as well as "earth magic supplies." Check the bulletin board and the staff for information on activities in the local women's community.
Open Tues.-Fri. 10 a.m.-6 p.m., Sat. 10 a.m.-5 p.m.

CHILDREN

BOOKS

Maple Street Children's Book Shop

7529 Maple St.
• 861-2105

Although many bookstores around town have well-stocked children's sections, this is the only store that is just for children. Located in what was once a private Uptown home, the store has a homey and comfortable atmosphere, ideal for making young readers feel welcome; and the inventory is large. While the kids browse here, Mom and Dad can find their own reading material next door at the Maple Street Book Shop.
Open Mon.-Sat. 10 a.m.-6 p.m.

CLOTHES

Ballin's Ltd.

New Orleans Centre, Level 3
• 561-1100

721 Dante St.
• 866-4367

It isn't often that a designer clothing store caters equally to women and their children. This clothes shop, known for its many trunk sales during the year, specializes in dresses from sizes two to fourteen, with a range of preteen sizes from six to fourteen. Frequently mothers find gowns and dresses for themselves, with matching or similar designs for their daughters. There is also a good selection of clothing for boys. Favorite fabrics for gowns are taffeta, moiré and bengalin, and the signature of the shop is tiered ruffles and an abundance of bows.
N. O. Centre: open Fri.-Wed. 10 a.m.-6 p.m., Thurs. 10 a.m.-8 p.m. Dante St.: open Mon.-Sat. 10 a.m.-9 p.m., Sun. 10 a.m.-6 p.m.

Chocolate Soup

2026 Metairie Rd.
• 837-8314

All the designs in this shop were made exclusively for the Chocolate Soup label, a full line of all-occasion, durable children's wear from newborn to boys size seven and girls size fourteen. Feel free to bring the whole family when you shop; the atmosphere is friendly and very casual; and there is always a sale going on. Because of the large stock, it's easy to find identical designs in various sizes. Chocolate Soup clothes often have appliqués and are always machine washable. Special orders are welcome. You'll find lots of Oshkosh here, plus bibs, backpacks and other

accessories for the little ones. The store is a distance from downtown.
Open Mon.-Sat. 9:30 a.m.-5 p.m.

The Gap Kids Store
Riverwalk,
One Poydras St.
• 522-5828

A few doors down in the Riverwalk from the big people's Gap store is the kids' store, with the same styles and quality of clothing, but in sizes from toddler to boy's and girl's fourteen. You'll find designer clothes in durable fabrics, lots of tennis shoes and accessories for the fashion conscious tyke.
Open Mon.-Thurs. 9:30 a.m.-9 p.m., Fri.-Sat. 9:30 a.m.-10 p.m., Sun. 11 a.m.-7 p.m.

Laura Ashley
Canal Place,
333 Canal St.
• 586-8652

The English country look for mothers and their children permeates all the well-made clothing in this shop. Lots of bows and lace for little girls, and floral and country prints from this classic label. There are also china, lamps and figurines that make nice gift items.
Open Fri.-Wed. 10 a.m.-6 p.m., Thurs. 10 a.m.-8 p.m.

Nannie's
Riverwalk,
One Poydras St.
• 524-7067

Children's clothes found here are made with loving care and an emphasis on European styles and craftsmanship. Special orders are welcome. Sizes range from infants to size six-X for boys and girls.
Open Mon.-Thurs. 9:30 a.m.-9 p.m., Fri.-Sat. 9:30 a.m.-10 p.m., Sun. 11 a.m.-7 p.m.

FURNITURE

Doerr Furniture, Inc.
914 Elysian Fields Ave.
• 947-0606

This well-established, family-owned furniture store has a large selection of baby cribs and children's furniture and rockers. Many classic pieces by Child Craft and Bassett are built to last for generations. Just outside the French Quarter.
Open Mon.-Wed. & Fri.-Sat. 9:30 a.m.-5:30 p.m., Thurs. 10 a.m.-8 p.m.

TOYS

Hello Dolly
815 Royal St.
• 522-9948

This is the last word in dolls, though most are decorative and made of ceramics—not dolls to play with. You'll find a good selection of the popular Gambina dolls made in New Orleans, as well as Madam Alexander and other

national lines. The owner is a doll collector and can answer almost any question you may have about the subject.
Open daily 9:30 a.m.-5:30 p.m.

The Idea Factory
838 Chartres St.
• 524-5195

The name says it all for this inventive shop in the heart of the French Quarter. Many of the whimsical wooden toys and mechanical mobiles are made by the owners in the shop, so you have a chance to talk with them and discover how each unique piece functions. Children of all ages can have a good time here.
Open Mon.-Sat. 10 a.m.-6 p.m., Sun. noon-5 p.m.

Kaleido Shop
Riverwalk,
One Poydras St.
• 523-4769

This shop has to be the very last word in kaleidoscopes, for it is stocked with every imaginable type of the toy ranging from simple ones for $2.75 to $2,000 collector's items. The shop represents 70 artists from all over the country. Most kaleidoscopes are handcrafted and signed by their creator. We also love the crystal jewelry and array of marbles.
Open Mon.-Thurs. 10 a.m.-9 p.m., Fri.-Sat. 10 a.m.-10 p.m., Sun. 11 a.m.-7 p.m.

The Kite Shop
542 St. Peter St.,
Jackson Square
• 524-0028

In a city with as many open spaces and windy days as New Orleans, a kite store is a natural. The variety here is endless; everything from very simple mylar and nylon kites to elaborate Chinese dragons hang from the shelves and ceiling in a breathtaking array of colors and designs to please everyone from the youngest child up. Prices start at $12. A tip: Try one of the kites as decoration.
Open Sun.-Fri. 10 a.m.-6 p.m., Sat. 10 a.m.-9 p.m.

Little Toy Shoppe
900 Decatur St.
• 522-6588

Little Toy Shoppe Too!
513 St. Ann St.,
Jackson Square
• 523-1770

For the kinds of toys that children dream of, these two shops in the French Quarter offer top lines. Their Heroes trains and building blocks from West Germany are popular. The Madam Alexander dolls and those made locally by Gambina are fashioned to please the heart of any young girl. Black figurines by Martha Originals make a good collection. In the Jackson Square shop we are especially partial to Blue Zoo, unique Chilean blue ceramics by Pablo Zobal. You'll find a wide selection of coloring books, mechanical toys and educational playthings.
Decatur St.: open Mon.-Fri. 9 a.m.- 5:30 p.m., Sat.-Sun. 9 a.m.-9 p.m. Jackson Square: open daily 9 a.m.-5:30 p.m.

Zoo Keeper
Riverwalk,
One Poydras St.
• 522-6852

This zoo specializes in tame animals, the cuddly, stuffed toy variety. Naturally you'd expect to find a bevy of teddy bears here, and you won't be disappointed by the large selection of Gunn and Dakin bears. There are also dozens of other types of stuffed toys from Applause, Bravo, North American, and the West German Steiff brand. This is a good place to pick up a baby toy or a game for a young child.
Open Mon.-Thurs. 10 a.m.-9 p.m., Fri. & Sat. 11 a.m.-10 p.m., Sun. 11 a.m. -7 p.m.

CLOTHES & JEWELRY

ACCESSORIES

Fiasco
7913 Maple St.
• 861-8761

Looking for accessories featured in *Vogue* or *Elle*? You'll find them here, in the most modern and up-to-date look. Choose from a large selection of French and Italian costume jewelry, Paola del Lungo handbags, Alain Mikli sunglasses, Eric Beaman crystals to wear, Gaetano Fazio jewelry, or matte gold jewelry by Natasha Stambouli. A treat are the hand-sewn, creative hats by the Material Girls, local designers Julie Little and Caroline Spangenberg Walker. They use lots of different fabrics and notions to create whimsical pill boxes, ovals, berets and triangles. The effect can put a chic finishing touch on a special outfit.
Open Mon.-Sat. 10 a.m.-6 p.m.

Hats in the Belfry
Jackson Brewery
• 523-5770

For the largest selection of men's and women's hats anywhere in the city, this shop is it. Hundreds of brands, including Stetson, Dobbs and Sony; lots of New York designers. They will even special order a single hat if not in stock.
Open Sun.-Thurs. 10 a.m.-9 p.m., Fri.-Sat. 10 a.m.-10 p.m.

Lugene Opticians
Canal Place,
333 Canal St.
• 529-7674

Going to an opera or symphony at the Orpheum or a concert at the Saenger? Then you'll want to pick up a pair of fine opera glasses, or perhaps a lorgnette for that superelegant look. This store specializes in upscale eyewear, with Cartier frames in buffalo horn, tortoise shell, or solid gold, and sunglasses by Armani, Persol,

Serengeti—all in the latest European accents. For an eye exam or repair of your current glasses, their full-service lab offers one to two day service. Lugene is on the edge of the French Quarter, convenient to guests of downtown hotels.
Open Mon.-Wed. & Fri.-Sat. 10 a.m.-6 p.m., Thurs. 10 a.m.-8 p.m., Sun. noon-6 p.m.

CASUAL

Abercrombie & Fitch
Riverwalk,
One Poydras St.
• 522-7156

A sweater from this store can complete an upscale wardrobe. Located at the Spanish Plaza entrance to the Riverwalk, Abercrombie & Fitch has a large selection of sports and casual wear for the discriminating buyer. You'll be fascinated by their variety of accessories and adult games, including a fine line of stuffed animals.
Open Mon.-Thurs. 10 a.m.-9 p.m., Fri.-Sat. 10 a.m.-10 p.m., Sun. 11 a.m.-7 p.m.

ACA Joe
Jackson Brewery
• 525-6119

For some of colorful and stylish sportswear, this shop rates high on the list. Their chinos, T-shirts and cotton jackets are popular. And the ACA Joe label is everywhere. Don't expect any local designs; this is a national store found in almost every city these days.
Open Sun.-Thurs. 10 a.m.-9 p.m., Fri.-Sat. 10 a.m.-10 p.m.

Banana Republic
Riverwalk,
One Poydras St.
• 523-6843

For a canoe trip into the swamps or hiking with the Louisiana Nature and Science Center this store, with its classic "safari clothes" for adults, can fit you with a comfortable, natural-fiber outfit. Known foremost through their imaginative catalogs, this shop, one of many across the country, has good wardrobes for the humid Southern climate. Occasional sales offer some real bargains here. You'll find the store at the entrance to the Riverwalk in the good company of Abercrombie & Fitch.
Open Mon.-Thurs. 10 a.m.-9 p.m., Fri.-Sat. 10 a.m.-10 p.m., Sun. 11 a.m.-7 p.m.

Benetton
Jackson Brewery
• 581-3020

Canal Place,
333 Canal St.
• 524-7656

The internationally known Italian casual-wear line is well displayed in the French Quarter and on Canal Street. The latest styles can be found here and often at sale prices. Many styles are unisex and have that effortlessly athletic look. Their sweaters and vests with Navajo patterns are popular. The colors of Benetton, especially in cotton pullovers and cardigan sweaters, are in full bloom here.

Jackson Brewery: open Sun.-Thurs. 10 a.m.-9 p.m., Fri.-Sat. 10 a.m.-10 p.m. Canal Place: open Mon.-Wed. & Fri.-Sun. 10 a.m.-6 p.m., Thurs. 10 a.m.-8 p.m.

Esprit
901 St. Charles Ave.
• 561-5050

A must for the rad kid, this is called the Esprit Superstore because it is the only factory outlet store for the ubiquitous teenwear in the metro area. Discounts start at 20 percent and range up to 50 percent on current Esprit styles. Located downtown along the streetcar route, the shop has a chic, modern interior and piped-in hard-rock music that makes one forget it is an outlet store. You'll find clothes here to fit children age 3 to adults size fourteen. Esprit is known for its stylized accessories—scarves, belts, bags.
Open Mon.-Sat. 11 a.m.-6 p.m., Sun. noon-5 p.m.

The Gap
Riverwalk
• 529-4962

923 Canal St.
• 524-5517

You'll find practical American-designed casual and sportswear here, and the prices are reasonable. Lots of cotton and denim—Levi's, T-shirts, comfortable jackets, chinos for youth and adults.
Riverwalk: open Mon.-Thurs. 9:30 a.m.-9 p.m., Sat.-Sun. 9:30 a.m.-10 p.m., Sun. 11 a.m.-7 p.m. Canal St.: open Fri.-Wed. 10 a.m.-6 p.m., Thurs. 10 a.m.-8 p.m.

DISCOUNT

Coleman's
4001 Earhart Blvd.
• 821-4000

This no-frills outlet for designer family fashions has some real bargains. Most items are between 10 percent and 35 percent off the original price. There's a good selection of Lee and other designer-label jeans, Duckhead pants, Arrow shirts: everything for sports, casual and office wear. The store is in Mid-City, off the beaten track, but the price-conscious shopper will want to seek it out.
Open Mon.-Sat. 9:30 a.m.-6 p.m.

JEWELRY

The Acorn
736 Royal St.
• 525-7110

This French Quarter shop is fun to browse through because of its varied and unique stock. We like the jewelry, which consists of lots of estate, contemporary and ele-

phant-hair pieces. They have many one-of-a-kind gift items as well.
Open Mon.-Sat. 10 a.m.-5 p.m.

Adler's

722 Canal St.
• 523-5292,
(800) 535-7912

This store has been locally owned and managed on Canal Street since 1898—which should inspire confidence. You'll find quality and design here in many items on a par with Tiffany's in New York. Quadrillion diamonds, gold, stones and pearls are mounted in elegant pieces. Adler's handles major watch brands: Rolex, Cartier, Baume and Mercier of Geneva.
Open Mon.-Sat. 10 a.m.-5:30 p.m.

Hausmann's-Bailey, Banks & Biddle

732 Canal St.
• 581-9581

Another jeweler that has served generations of New Orleanians is this store on Canal Street. They carry brand-name watches and giftware, Waterford crystal, and are a major diamond source. The U.S. government has commissioned them to make official medals and insignia.
Open Mon.-Sat. 10 a.m.-5:30 p.m.

Jewelry 636

636 St. Ann St.
• 581-2880

For distinctive handmade jewelry, stop in to visit with the two couples who own this shop and create their work here. You'll find innovative and wearable designs in sterling silver, 14K gold and natural gemstones, many of them one of a kind and limited editions. Each piece is signed and dated, giving it a personal touch.
Open Mon.-Tues. & Thurs.-Sun. 11 a.m-6 p.m.

Mignon Faget Ltd.

Canal Place,
333 Canal St.
• 524-2973

710 Dublin St.,
Uptown
• 865-1107

For the quintessential piece of New Orleans jewelry, Faget's gumbo necklace with silver shrimp, crawfish and crabs as charms resting on white beads that suggest a bed of rice fills the bill. Much of the jewelry of New Orleans native Mignon Faget is inspired by the Louisiana culture and environs. She works primarily in sterling silver, 14K gold and bronze d'oré. Nationally famous for her collections featuring rings, cuff links, pens, bracelets and wearable flower holders, Faget designs and finishes her pieces in the workshop on Dublin Street. Her work, although pricey, is collectible; a Faget charm bracelet of hot peppers in sterling, for example, is sure to become an heirloom.
Canal Place: open Fri.-Wed. 10 a.m.-6 p.m., Thurs. 10 a.m.-8 p.m. Dublin St.: open Mon.-Sat. 10 a.m.-5 p.m.

Rhino Gallery

Place St. Charles,
201 St. Charles Ave.
• 582-1173

Expect the unusual and exotic from this creative group of artists. You can have a piece of jewelry custom-crafted for you or choose from a collection of one-of-a-kind items. The specialty here is bejeweled papier-mâché costume jewelry. There is also some finely etched silver. Many pieces have a distinctive New Orleans touch.
Open Mon.-Sat. 11 a.m.-4 p.m.

Thomas Mann Designs

Gallery I/O
1810 Magazine St.
• 581-2113

Sculptor-jeweler Mann first showed his work at the Jazz and Heritage Festival in 1978, and he has been in New Orleans ever since. His jewelry is known for its layered images, which form a collage effect. "Techno-romantic" is his term for the contemporary designs that combine found objects of nostalgia with technical and mechanical pieces from the present. The gallery features Mann's imaginative furniture, tabletops, lighting and sculpture. Each is an original piece of art, exciting to see as well as use and wear.
Open Mon.-Sat. 11 a.m.-6 p.m.

MENSWEAR

Brooks Brothers

Canal Place,
365 Canal St.
• 522-4200

For classic American style, the menswear in this shop sets the standard. The New Orleans store has its own local touch with the Mardi Gras rugby shirt, popular in its gold, purple and green stripes. The natural-fiber clothes are especially well suited to the southern climate.
Open Fri.-Wed. 10 a.m.-6 p.m., Thurs. 10 a.m.-8 p.m.

Euromoda

Canal Place,
Level 2,
333 Canal St.
• 568-1400

Looking for European design and service in ready-to-wear and accessories for men? The Euromoda and Enrico labels are exclusives here. Everything is manufactured in Europe by the well-known houses. Other labels include Pancaldi, Missoni, Redi, Principe by Marzotto, Mondo, and Brioni. Shoes made in Italy are by Ennesi. The custom-clothing department does fittings in the office or hotel room, and same-day alterations are available for all ready-made designs.
Open Mon.-Sat. 10 a.m.-6 p.m.

Meyer the Hatter

120 St. Charles Ave.
• 525-1048,
(800) 822-HATS

This store has been in the same family and located on the same block in the Central Business District since 1894. No one disputes its claim to be the largest men's hat store in the South. From winter caps and felt hats to summer straws, if you can't find it here, it probably isn't available anywhere in New Orleans. Favorite lines include Stetson, Dobb's, Borsolino and London Fog, among others. The service and quality are top-rate; with over a century of experience, it's no wonder.
Open Mon.-Sat. 9:30 a.m.-5:30 p.m.

National Clothing Liquidators

135 Carondolet St.
• 525-0826

For the well-dressed gentleman with an eye for good prices, this store should be on the list. Top American and European labels are sold here at prices well below those in other stores. Inventory is selected from store and factory closeouts from around the country. There are suits in sizes 38 short to 48 extra-long, and slacks from 28 to 54. Also available are dress shirts, ties and accessories.
Open Mon.- Sat. 10 a.m.-5 p.m.

Perlis

6070 Magazine St.
• 895-8661

A New Orleans tradition since 1939, this men's shop is the creator of the popular cotton Crawfish Classic, a polo shirt in a variety of colors with a crawfish insignia on the pocket. The store here and the one in the Esplanade Shopping Center also stock designer lines such as Kenneth Gordon, Ralph Lauren, Hilton, Southwick, Tommy Hill, Levi and Duckhead. Since it is locally owned, Perlis offers a personalized, down-home service often missing in larger chain stores. They also do a brisk shipping business, especially with the crawfish polos. Ladies' and boys' casual fashions available. The crawfish polo is available at Cajun Polo in the Riverwalk as well.
Open Mon.-Sat. 9 a.m.-6 p.m.

Polo/Ralph Lauren Shop

Canal Place
• 561-8299

The classic American designer Ralph Lauren is well represented here, with his dress and casual lines in a variety of styles and fabrics. The sportswear is some of the most durable, and the suits, sports coats and shirts have a European look.
Open Mon.-Wed. & Fri.-Sun. 10 a.m.-6 p.m., Thurs. 10 a.m.-8 p.m.

Rubenstein Brothers

102 St. Charles Ave.
• 581-6666

This family-owned business has built a name for itself as one of the finest men's stores in the South, as shown by its winning the *Gentleman's Quarterly* magazine award and being named by *M* magazine as one of America's top

ten men's wear retailers. The large stock includes everything from designer European and American suits to footwear, accessories, coats and pajamas. Featured are their tailored pants and suits by Italian designers such as Zanella and Canali, and traditional suits by Polo, Burberry and King's Ridge. This is a store where women can feel comfortable about shopping for their men. The staff, attentive and knowledgeable, can accommodate travelers with one-day alterations. Rubenstein's also has famous brand-name suits and sports coats for big and tall men.
Open Mon.-Sat. 10 a.m.-5:45 p.m.

The Tie Rack

New Orleans Centre
• 566-0679

Riverwalk
• 523-5333

The last word in ties, these shops carry their own brands imported from England and Italy. They also carry American labels, such as Perry Ellis. Prices range from $15 to $27.
New Orleans Centre: open Fri.-Wed. 10 a.m.-6 p.m., Thurs. 10 a.m.-8 p.m. Riverwalk: open Mon.-Thurs. 10 a.m.-9 p.m., Fri.-Sat. 10 a.m.-10 p.m., Sun. 11 a.m.-7 p.m.

Large & Small Sizes

Rubenstein Brothers

102 St. Charles Ave.
• 581-6666

This award-winning men's clothing store offers top brand-name suits and sports coats for tall and big men in their Extra-Ordinary Man Shop. You'll find longer neckties, a variety of tuxedos, shirts up to size 54 (with 20-inch necklines and 38-inch sleeves) and shoes up to size 15 from Bally, Rockport and Timberland. These guys are proud of having outfitted the New Orleans Saints.
Open Mon.-Sat. 10 a.m.-5:45 p.m.

Jimmy Stewart's Tall & Big Men's Store

3020 Severn Ave., Metairie
• 454-0940

For lots of designer labels and brand-name fashions for tall and big men, this is the place to go. Besides offering the Jimmy Stewart line of Lynx, the store has Christian Dior, Pierre Cardin, Palm Beach, Levi Dockers, Duckhead, and many other brands. Suits are from sizes 46 to 60, pants from 38L to 50L and 40R to 60R. Although located in a New Orleans suburb, Jimmy Stewart's is worth the drive because of its large selection.
Open Mon-Wed. & Fri.-Sat. 10 a.m.-6 p.m., Thurs. 9 a.m.-8 p.m.

RECYCLED CLOTHING

Fred & Ethel's Fifty's Clothes

1215 Decatur St.
• 523-2942

The 1200 block of Decatur Street in the French Quarter has for years been lined with nostalgia and vintage clothing shops. An afternoon spent browsing here will turn up some remarkable items. Fred & Ethel's is a good place to start. The emphasis here is on the fifties, but some clothes cross period lines. We especially like the bowling shirts, bomber jackets and Ozzie's Harriet-type housedresses.
Open daily noon-6 p.m.

Jazzrags

1128 Decatur St.
• 566-7835

Moving up Decatur street and into a nearer decade, this shop handles mostly 1960s memorabilia. Owner Bernadette Klotz is a child of the sixties and opened her shop on the former site of the first vintage apparel shop, Matilda's. Klotz is an experienced thrift-store shopper and clothing recycler. Her many rows of bell-bottom jeans, miniskirts and paisley-print shirts give the shopper ample selection for size and quality. Peace signs, love beads and all those other faddish things so dear to the hearts of baby boomers are lovingly collected and displayed here.
Open daily noon-6 p.m.

Legarage Antiques & Clothing

1234 Decatur St.
• 522-6639

This converted garage is like a museum; everything in it is unique and timeworn. Movie directors frequently shop here for period clothing, and no wonder, because it has a large selection of items from different eras. Sharing the limelight with the clothes is an array of antique signs, jewelry, bric-a-brac, and military gear. Owner Marcus Frazer loves advising customers on what pieces go well with certain time periods.
Open daily noon-6 p.m.

SHOES

Bally of Switzerland

Canal Place,
Level 2,
333 Canal St.
• 522-6767

Known for its fine-quality footwear for women and men, Bally also has a large selection of leather goods, such as briefcases, belts, wallets and key cases. Make a fashion statement with one of their suede ties. The New Orleans store has more casual and walking footwear for men and women than do most Bally stores.
Open Mon.-Wed. & Fri.-Sat. 10 a.m.-6 p.m., Thurs. 10 a.m.-8 p.m., Sun. noon-6 p.m.

Bergeron's Fine Footwear
Canal Place
• 525-2195

This is where many New Orleans ladies shop for shoes. Locally owned and managed, this store offers a good selection of modern classics from Papagallo, Yves St. Laurent, J. Renee, Anne Klein, and others. Their evening shoes in metallic leather, satin, faille and beads are popular, but they carry lots of midheel and flat shoes for comfort as well. Don't miss the evening bags by Imp, J. Renee and S. G. D'or.
Open Mon.-Wed. & Fri.-Sun. 10 a.m.-6 p.m., Thurs. 10 a.m.-8 p.m.

G. H. Bass Shoes
Riverwalk
• 522-3918

One of the reasons to shop in the Riverwalk complex is this fine shoe store, with the full range of classic dress and casual shoes made under the Bass label. Sizes range for ladies from five to eleven, for men from seven to thirteen. You might just luck out and catch one of their occasional sales. There's another Bass store in the Esplanade shopping mall.
Open Mon.-Thurs. 10 a.m.-9 p.m., Fri.-Sat. 10 a.m.-10 p.m., Sun. 11 a.m.-7 p.m.

WOMENSWEAR

Bagatelle
Uptown Square
• 861-3341

English designers of elegant evening ballgowns are in the spotlight here: Murray Arbeid, Tomasz Starzweski, Jacques Azaqury, Lorcan Mullany, Terrence Noider, Salmon Greene and Anna Cloonan. Their work is predominantly in silk, taffeta and duchess satin. And to accentuate the gowns, there is a good collection of quality earrings and costume jewelry. The Lunch at the Ritz collection is especially interesting. This is the only shop that showcases the exclusive Anje label by two local designers of evening wear in linen, silk organza and Swiss faille. Anje also has hair accessories featuring their signature buttons and trim.
Open Mon.-Sat. 10 a.m.-6 p.m.

Ballin's Ltd.
New Orleans Centre, Level 3
• 561-1100

721 Dante St.
• 866-4367

A women's fashion store known for being innovative, this shop features a series of trunk sales throughout the year. They have a large selection of sophisticated designer dresses and gowns. The select line of designer fashions for children makes shopping here a family affair.
N.O. Centre: open Mon.-Wed. & Fri.-Sun. 10 a.m.-6 p.m., Thurs. 10 a.m.-8 p.m. Dante St.: open Mon.-Sat. 10 a.m.-9 p.m., Sun. 10 a.m.-6 p.m.

Brent David Boutique

222 City Park Ave.
• 488-2288

Acclaimed young couturier Brent David, who debuts his lines in Paris and London, has set up shop near City Park, a short ride from downtown. This is haute couture in a very personal style. David, whose designs are worn by some famous women, brings his reputation from accounts with Bergdorf's and Saks Fifth Avenue to this shop filled with evening gowns, cocktail dresses, suits, and custom and bridal dresses. Size two and up. We like his one-of-a-kind accessories, including the imaginative hats by local designers Material Girls.

Open Mon.-Fri. 10 a.m.-5 p.m., Sat. 10 a.m.-3 p.m., Sun. by appointment only.

House of Broel

2220 St. Charles Ave.
• 522-2220

One of the oldest and most popular formal dress shops in the city, this antebellum mansion on St. Charles Avenue evokes true Southern charm. Locally owned and staffed, the shop offers personalized service to everyone from the young woman seeking a prom dress or bridal gown to the mother of the bride. Broel is known for its selection of evening wear

Open Mon.-Wed. & Fri.-Sat. 10 a.m.-6 p.m., Thurs. noon-8 p.m.

Joan Vass New Orleans

1100 6th St.
• 891-4502,
(800) 338-4864

The American knitwear designer Joan Vass opened her first and largest outlet in the country in uptown New Orleans. You'll find her selection of luxurious classics for the nineties to be exciting and innovative. This store deals exclusively with Joan Vass creations, but next door is her shop Martha and Me, which features key pieces from top young designers of tailored wovens, including the Italian Max Mara and the French Phillipe Adec. They also handle lots of new and unusual accessories.

Open Mon.-Sat. 9:30 a.m.-5:30 p.m.

Saks Fifth Avenue

Canal Place,
301 Canal St.
• 524-2200

Like Macy's and Lord & Taylor, this New York–based clothing store is known for its fine European and American designer fashions and accessories. Saks has been in New Orleans considerably longer than the other two and contributes to the local social scene by hosting a series of fashion shows throughout the year to benefit various charities. Their hair salon is one of the best in the city. The store and salon staff take a personal interest in their customers; you'll feel truly welcome and comfortable.

Open Mon.-Wed. & Fri.-Sun. 10 a.m.-6 p.m., Thurs. 10 a.m.-8 p.m.

Yvonne La Fleur
Riverwalk
• 522-8222

8131 Hampson St., Uptown
• 866-9666

Local designer Yvonne LaFleur has a bent for expressing the romantic in her very feminine dresses, suits, lingerie and hats. She closely supervises the design and sewing of all her creations; her work is known for its ability to capture the New Orleans flavor. (See also page 167.)
Riverwalk: open Mon.- Thurs. 9:30 a.m.-9 p.m., Fri.-Sat. 9:30 a.m.-10 p.m., Sun. 11 a.m.-7 p.m. Hampson St.: open Mon.-Tues. & Fri.-Sat. 9:45 a.m.-6 p.m., Wed.-Thurs. 9:45 a.m.-8 p.m.

Large & Small Sizes

Catherine's
3822 Dublin St.
• 482-2383

The large-size woman is welcome here and can choose from a select group of designs in dresses, evening wear and sportswear. The store carries moderately priced lines such as Catherine Lindsey, People, S & L and Sherbet in sizes 16 to 52. They also have a good variety of matching accessories.
Open Mon.-Sat. 10 a.m.-8 p.m.

The Forgotten Woman
Canal Place, Level 3
• 561-8898

A store well known across the country for its designer fashions in large sizes only, this shop in the posh Canal Place mall is a good tip for the full-figured woman. Clothing range from sizes 14 to 24, and you'll find fabrics and designs that are local favorites. Ask about their other stores in such cities as Houston, Palm Springs, Washington and Beverly Hills.
Open Mon.-Wed. & Fri.-Sun. 10 a.m.-6 p.m., Thurs. 10 a.m.-8 p.m.

Petite Sophisticate
New Orleans Centre
• 525-7857

For petite women this shop offers its own exclusive label in sizes one to twelve. Styles are predominantly for business and dressy occasions, but there are also some casual and sportswear. Quality and style that match the price. Lots of accessories available. Convenient hours.
Open daily 10 a.m.-8 p.m.

Lingerie

Victoria's Secret
Riverwalk
• 525-6900

Part of a national chain with a large catalog-order business, this shop has a wide variety of undergarments, including cotton men's-styled briefs and T-shirts for women (and men). The French laces, satins and soft cottons are elegantly displayed. Their sachets and satin pillows make nice gifts. There is something here for many

different women's tastes.
Open Mon.-Thurs. 9:30 a.m.-9 p.m., Fri.-Sat. 9:30 a.m.-10 p.m., Sun. 11 a.m.-7 p.m.

Yvonne La Fleur

Riverwalk
• 522-8222

8131 Hampson St., Uptown
• 866-9666

Almost all the clothes in these locally owned shops are designed and produced by New Orleans native Yvonne LaFleur: fine lingerie—beautiful laces and teddies—lots of romantic, elegant styles. A third of the shops' customers are men, and LeFleur caters to them with her "Sugar Daddy" nights around Christmas when models display the large selection of lingerie and accessories. LeFleur is also well known for her collection of self-designed hats, as well as her signature perfume. Watch for this popular and very successful local shop to go national in the near future, though we hope the personal, intimate service now offered will not be lost in the expansion. (See also page 166.)
Riverwalk: open Mon.- Thurs. 9:30 a.m.-9 p.m., Fri.-Sat. 9:30 a.m.-10 p.m., Sun. 11 a.m.-7 p.m. Hampson St.: open Mon.-Tues. & Fri.-Sat. 9:45 a.m.-6 p.m., Wed.-Thurs. 9:45 a.m.-8 p.m.

COLLECTIBLES

The Bank

1814 Felicity St.
• 523-2702

1819 St. Andrew St.
• 523-6055

One kind of collectibles is antique architectural accents, popular among local renovators and builders. The Bank specializes in old, original cypress shutters, which are getting harder and harder to come by, plus beveled glass, antique doors and millwork. Many antique patterns have been reproduced and are available at more modest prices. You might be interested in cornices, figurines and other smaller details that evoke the Victorian and gingerbread quality of New Orleans architecture.
Open Tues.-Sat. 9 a.m.-5 p.m.

Community Flea Market

French Market Place
• 522-2621

In New Orleans there are lots of enterprises that tread the line between being junk outlets and bona-fide antique shops. They really are a mixture of both; it's up to the tenacious shopper to ferret out the difference in each piece. The local term for these shops is "collectibles," suggesting that a trained eye can find items that though practically worthless today will someday be valuable. The Community Flea Market grew out of the hippy period in

the 1960s and has managed to survive as a well-established institution in the historic French Market, which rambles along the riverfront in the French Quarter. On a fair-weather day this is one of the best places to search for collectibles. Vendors coming from all over the city vie for tables to display new and used items; you'll find everything from military memorabilia to old photos, magazines and records, to vintage clothes. This is an open-air market, so weather often dictates who will be out here and how long. The Flea Market is next door to the Farmer's Market where watermelons, mirlitons, and Creole tomatoes make a colorful and aromatic display.
Open daily 9 a.m.-5 p.m. weather permitting.

Deco Dense

1817 Magazine St.
• 525-4901

This is a good stop for art-deco enthusiasts. The eclectic contents fall generally under the description "vintage modern 1910 to 1950." We were impressed with the wide variety of items, from furniture, art and home furnishings to clothing, hats and jewelry, all reasonably priced and in good condition.
Open Mon.- Sat. 10 a.m.-5:30 p.m.

Endangered Species

619 Royal St.
• 568-9855

Since ivory is no longer being imported, the antique ivory carvings and jewelry at this shop are real treasures. You can choose from a variety of other unique items, in the large collection of tribal art and antiques personally selected by the owners on trips to Tibet, India, New Guinea and Indonesia. Their wildlife trophies and skin rugs are quite rare.
Open daily 10 a.m.-6 p.m.

Ricca's Architectural Sales

511 N. Solomon St.
• 488-5524

Besides the Bank, Peter Ricca's warehouse in Mid-City is a local institution for renovators and collectors with its stained glass, chandeliers, old signs, and original wooden and iron locks and doorknobs. The variety is almost breathtaking. Some items are originals, others are clearly marked reproductions, and priced accordingly. A restored original antique leaded-glass door goes for $3,500, whereas a copy with zinc instead of lead sells for $1,350. This is a place to encounter the unusual and unique for any conceivable home decorating or renovating project. It takes a short cab ride to get here, but browsing possibilities make it worthwhile.
Open Mon.- Fri. 8:30 a.m.-5 p.m., call ahead for Sat.

DEPARTMENT STORES

Dillard's

Uptown Square, 200 Broadway • 861-8141

When the venerable D. H. Holmes Department Store, which had dressed generations of upscale New Orleans families, closed in the late 1980s, it was bought by Dillard Department Stores and the home store on Canal Street was closed. Some locals have still not recovered from the loss of this dear tradition, but most of them are getting accustomed to a similar quality and price range offered by Dillard's. The closest one to downtown now is in the Uptown Square shopping center, with other stores in the Esplanade, Lakeside and Oakwood shopping malls. Like D. H. Holmes, this store has a bridal registry, fine furs, beautiful crystal and china, and a fine clothing and home furnishings selection. For women and juniors there are the labels of CosCob, Villager, Lady Carol, A. K. F., Gemini II, and Croquet Club; for men, Bill Blass, Austin Reed, Cricketeer and Raquet Club; and for toddlers, Buster Brown, Joggles and Oshkosh. Furniture is by Natuzzi, Henredon, Century, Berhnardt and Lane.

Open Mon.-Sat. 10 a.m.-6 p.m., Sun. noon-6 p.m.

Krauss

1201 Canal St. • 523-3311

Canal Street was once lined with locally owned department stores. Today only this one remains. A fixture on Canal Street since 1903, the Krauss family department store continues to offer quality clothes and home furnishings at modest prices. They have some of the best leathers and suedes in town. For women there are dresses by Leslie Fay, Argenti and Evanna, and New Orleans's largest selection of rhinestones and Cubric Zirconia jewelry; in the children's department, Oshkosh and Carter's sportswear; for men, Arrow shirts, Farah pants, and Nunn Bush and Eastland shoes. The sewing fabric department is known as one of the biggest and best in the South. Because the store is relatively small and the only one of its kind in the city, there is an intimacy not present in other department stores. Locals always watch out for the famous Krauss sales.

Open Mon.-Wed. & Fri.-Sun. 10 a.m.-6 p.m., Thurs. 10 a.m.-7 p.m.

Lord & Taylor

New Orleans Centre
• 581-5673

This elegant New York–based store graces the ground-floor entrance of the New Orleans Centre, between the Hyatt Regency Hotel and the Superdome, and is a landmark in local shopping. Known primarily for its fine fashions for women, Lord & Taylor is also a department store with large selections of distinguished designer clothing for juniors, men, and children. They have a large shoe department, and the accessories, jewelry, cosmetics, and handbags are all of premium quality and price. You'll find a fairly well stocked home furnishings section as well. Many locals watch for months for their major twice-a-year catalog sale .
Open Mon.-Wed. & Fri.-Sun. 10 a.m.-6 p.m., Thurs. 10 a.m.-8 p.m.

Macy's

New Orleans Centre
• 592-5985

For fine styles and labels, this is a posh store in an even more alluring setting. The N. O. Centre, with its atrium and well-designed shopping area between the Superdome and the Hyatt Regency Hotel, can be congested during major events, but normally it is a relaxing place to browse. Macy's has something for everyone; for women top name designers (their Geoffrey Hunter Sport Collection is of special interest), for men Christopher Hayes, Clubroom and Austin Grey labels, for toddlers the Mine Alone line. You'll find the top-of-the-line accessories here, such as Seiko and Bulova watches, Susan Reade handbags, and Evan Picone hosiery. From cosmetics to cooking ware, we are never disappointed with this store.
Open Mon.-Sat. 10 a.m.-8 p.m., Sun. noon-6 p.m.

Maison Blanche

901 Canal St.
• 566-1000

MB, as it is called, is one of few department stores left on Canal Street. It has large stores in the Clearview and Lake Forest Plaza shopping centers, but the main store on Canal Street is dear to the hearts of downtowners. Fine quality here is reliable. Brand names and fashion lines tend to be made in the USA. Among them are labels such as Liz Claiborne for women, Hart Schaffner & Marx and Jack Nicklaus for men. You'll find the cosmetics counter well stocked with Clinique, Lancôme, and Estée Lauder. And ladies, don't miss the millinery section, with its large seasonal collections. For New Orleans cookbooks and souvenirs, check out the regional gifts section. At Christmastime, Mr. Bingle, an elfin snowman character who has become a local tradition, rings in the holiday season. And to top it all off, MB charge accounts are interest-free year-round.
Open daily 10 a.m.-6 p.m.

Stein Mart
5300 Tchoupitoulas St.
• 891-6377

For anyone in search of a real bargain, this clothing department store, which caters to men, women and children, may be the answer. Their advertised savings of 25 percent to 60 percent on fine brand-name fashions are in effect year-round. The clothes and accessories are displayed in a festive atmosphere in this store located in the Riverside Shopping Market upriver from downtown New Orleans. A second Stein Mart is on Veterans Highway in suburban Kenner.
Open Mon.-Sat. 10 a.m.-9 p.m., Sun. 12:30 p.m.-5:30 p.m.

FLOWERS

French Quarter Florist
223 Dauphine St.
• 523-5476

True to its name, this shops offers the most comprehensive flower service in the Quarter. It even hosts entire parties, with balloons, wine, favors, centerpieces and gift baskets. You can rent plants, send flowers FTD or have a custom-made boquet delivered to your hotel room.
Open Mon.-Sat. 9 a.m.-6 p.m., Sun. 10 a.m.-noon. Orders taken 24 hours.

The French Quarter Flower Mart
1029 Chartres St.
• 522-6563

This is a smaller, more personal shop with fresh flowers exclusively. Their tropicals add a special look to flower arrangements. Delivery in the Quarter is available.
Open Tues.-Sun. 10 a.m.-7 p.m.

FOOD

BAKERIES

Dong Phuong Oriental Bakery
3006 Elysian Fields Ave.
• 949-0155

The Vietnamese and Chinese communities are well served by this bakery. Traditional cookies, breads and pastries are baked on the premises and distributed to Asian restaurants and markets.
Open Mon.-Thurs. 9 a.m.-5 p.m.

La Madeleine French Bakery & Café
547 St. Ann St.
• 568-9950

601 S. Carrollton Ave.
• 891-8661

What would a city as French as New Orleans be without several authentic French pastry shops? La Madeleine occupies a corner on Jackson Square where croissants, brioche and sourdough breads are baked fresh by French bakers each day in a wood-burning oven built into the shop. It's fun to watch the loaves being inserted and then retrieved from the oven on long wooden spatulas, as the aroma wafts out into the street. Other, fancier pastries and cakes are made here, too, to take out or eat in with café au lait at tables surrounding the counter and oven. The café does a good lunch and dinner business with soups, salads and several entrées. A branch of La Madeleine operates uptown in the Riverbend area.
Both branches open daily 7 a.m.-9 p.m.

Pâtisserie Francaise–La Marquise
625 Chartres St.
• 524-0420

Croissant d'Or
617 Ursulines St.
• 524-4663

The oldest French bakeries in town are these two sister establishments, situated at opposite ends of the French Quarter and boasting fine croissants, brioches, quiches and fancy pastries. Both serve coffee and tea with the food indoors or on a patio. Owner Henri Delachalle of France personally does all the baking for both shops in his kitchen at the Croissant d'Or, and the results are delicious. The Ursulines St. shop has light lunches of soup, quiche and sandwiches. Both shops have patios for outdoor dining as well.
Chartres St.: open daily 7 a.m.-5:30 p.m. Ursulines St.: open daily 7 a.m.-5 p.m.

Your Daily Bread
7457 St. Charles Ave.
• 861-4663

For a local favorite, spinach-cheese bread, there is nothing like the one baked here; the jalapeño-cheese bread comes in a close second in our opinion. Chocolate-lovers should try the Sachertorte; you'll swear you're in Vienna. The pastries and breads are all baked fresh daily on the premises. Sandwiches and salads are made as you wait in the deli section. Service is quick and friendly. This is strictly take-out; no tables on the premises.
Open daily 7 a.m.-9 p.m.

BOOKS

Coffee, Tea, Or . . .
530 St. Ann St.
• 522-0830

Although coffee, tea and spices are the focus of this French Quarter shop, owner Don Myers also carries a large selection of local cookbooks, an exceptional bargain at a 20-percent discount, year-round.
Open daily 9 a.m.-6 p.m.

Louisiana General Store
Jackson Brewery
• 525-2665

Since this shop is part of Joe Cahn's New Orleans School of Cooking, it stands to reason that it would be a good place to look for cookbooks about local foods and recipes. You will not be disappointed, because there are over 150 Louisiana cookbooks here, along with skillets, pots and cooking utensils used in preparing Cajun and Creole cuisine. And if you have any questions about a recipe, the staff is very helpful in explaining and even demonstrating the peculiarities of local dishes.
Open daily 9:30 a.m.-9:30 p.m.

CHEESE

Whole Foods Market
3135 Esplanade Ave.
• 943-1626

For one of the largest and most diverse selections of domestic and imported cheeses, try this natural-foods supermarket. You can choose from over 175 varieties and have them sliced to taste at the counter. The staff is helpful in explaining which cheese will go best with various foods.
Open daily 9 a.m.-8 p.m.

COFFEE

Café du Monde Store
813 Decatur St.
• 581-2914

Like the famous New Orleans coffeehouse nearby, Café du Monde, this shop sells a special blend of chickory and coffee, but only by the can. If you enjoy the beignets, square French donuts served at Café du Monde, the mix is available here so that you can have beignets anywhere and anytime. Gift items such as aprons, bags and mugs all with the coffeehouse's logo make nice souvenirs as well.
Open daily 9:30 a.m.-6 p.m.

Coffee, Tea, Or . . .
530 St. Ann St.
• 522-0830

The mixture of aromas in this shop is enough to make you want to spend hours here, and proprietor Don Myers knows his stock well enough to keep you entertained while you linger. His inventory includes 50 kinds of herbal and decaf teas, 60 kinds of regular teas, 65 varieties of coffees, and 350 spices and herbs. He also has a large selection of local cookbooks, with 20 percent off the price year-round. Next door is a café that serves several of Myers's coffees and teas, plus French pastries and quiches. Both are housed in the historic Elizabeth Werlein house

off Jackson Square. Myers, a preservationist, has renovated the building and is pleased to explain it to visitors.
Open daily 9 a.m.-6 p.m.; café open daily 8 a.m.-5:30 p.m.

Kaldi's Coffeehouse & Coffee-museum

941 Decatur St.
• 586-8989

What would a coffee-loving city like New Orleans be like without a museum about coffee? This relatively new coffee house on the block has been introducing more than a few new traditions. One is their sparkling ice café, a carbonated coffee drink in a variety of flavors; it's a delightful alternative to the standard iced tea most of us use to get through the humid summers. Another tradition allowing shoppers to select a coffee from an international selection and have the beans freshly ground and roasted on the spot. And of course there is almost any conceivable brand of coffee available by the cup, including cappucino and espresso. Live entertainment by local musicians on a rotating schedule provides a festive atmosphere. The coffeehouse, located in a former bank, includes a vast display of home and industrial coffee grinders and brewers, servers and cups, posters and photos of the history of coffee and the Port of New Orleans. A visit here is fun and educational.
Open daily 24 hours.

BRACING BREW

No one can say the old Creoles didn't appreciate a decent cup o' java. To them, the perfect brew had to be *Noir comme le diable, fort comme la mort, doux comme l'amour et chaud comme l'enfer.* It simply wasn't coffee unless it was "black as the devil, strong as death, sweet as love and hot as hell."

PJ's Coffee & Tea Co.

5432 Magazine St.
• 895-0273

7713 Maple St.
• 866-9963

One of the few companies to sell coffee and tea by the cup or pound retail and also by hundreds of pounds wholesale, this coffeehouse has a loyal local clientel. It's not unusual to see university students poring over textbooks here, or to hear some heated discussion being held over an espresso. The Maple Street address includes a retail shop where you can buy fresh coffee beans in a large variety by the pound. They also sell French drip pots and other coffee paraphernalia.
Both branches open Mon.-Fri. 7 a.m.-11 p.m., Sat.-Sun. 8 a.m.-11 p.m. Maple St. retail store: open daily 10 a.m.-6 p.m.

True Brew Coffee

200 Julia St.
• 524-8441

As the name suggests, this coffeehouse near the Convention Center is serious about its coffee. There is a good selection of coffees and teas by the cup or pound, and usually with a freshly baked cake or some cookies. Live music on Saturday nights livens the atmosphere. True Brew shares its warehouselike space with the appropriately

named Actors' Warehouse Theater, which generally presents several one-act plays on the weekends. It's a comfortable combination of coffee drinkers and theatergoers.
Open Sun.-Wed. 7 a.m.-7 p.m.; Thurs.-Sat. 7 a.m.-9 p.m.

CONFECTIONERIES

Aunt Sally's Original Creole Praline Shop
810 Decatur St.
• 524-5107

There's nothing more New Orleans than the cloyingly sweet pecan-and-brown-sugar candies made in cookielike shapes and wrapped individually in waxed paper. You'll find pralines everywhere, especially in French Quarter gift and candy shops. Several stores specialize in this and other local varieties of brownies, cookies and sweets made daily on the premises. Aunt Sally's in the French Market justifiably calls itself an original praline shop because it has been around a long time. Its pralines are made and packaged much like those in other shops. You can have the sweets shipped anywhere.
Open Mon.-Thurs. 8 a.m.-6 p.m., Fri.-Sun. 8 a.m.-8 p.m.

Creole Delicacies
533 St. Ann St.
• 525-9508

Riverwalk
• 523-6425

This is another praline and confection shop that makes local candies to be shipped across the country. It's a good, reliable name and has an assortment of pralines in various flavors: chocolate, mint and so on.
Open daily 9 a.m.-5:30 p.m.

Evans Creole Candy Co., Inc.
848 Decatur St.
• 522-7111,
(800) 637-6675

If you really want to know how that delicious New Orleans candy, the pecan praline, is made, here's the place to watch the cook mix up the cream, brown sugar and pecans and set each piece of spreading goodness out on waxed paper on the marble counter to harden before packing the candies into boxes. This is the way it's been done for several centuries. Gift baskets of pralines, assorted pecan rolls and sugared pecans are available and can be shipped anywhere. Evans also has a shop in Riverwalk.
Open Mon.-Fri. 9 a.m.-6 p.m., Sat. 9 a.m.-9 p.m., Sun. 9 a.m.-7 p.m.

Godiva Chocolatier, Inc.
Canal Place,
333 Canal St.
• 524-1175

The famous Belgian chocolate maker serves up luxurious sculpted pieces. Their small gold carton contains just the right size of chocolate brick to make a good gift. Their items are pricey but of comensurate quality and status.
Open Fri.-Wed. 10 a.m.-6 p.m., Thurs. 10 a.m.-8 p.m.

Old Town Praline Shop
627 Royal St.
• 525-1413

It's like turning back the clock half a century to walk into this variety store in the heart of the French Quarter. Several elderly women run the shop with the same loving care they have put into it for years. Behind a rustic counter that runs the length of the store they make pecan pralines every morning and put them out on the counter top to harden. Among the postcards and typical souvenir items you're likely to find porcelain figures and rare photographs; it's that sort of unpredictable place. And don't forget to check the portrait of Adelina Patti that hangs on the back left wall; she was a famous singer in the 1800s, and this building and the patio beyond were her home. The current proprietors will be happy to tell you more about her.
Open Mon.-Sat. 10 a.m.-5:30 p.m.

GOURMET

Bards of London, Ltd.
• 529-5169

For fine smoked salmon, these exclusive importing agents for Bards of London can fill your order. Local deliveries in one or two days. Calls only; no retail shop.
Open Mon.-Fri. 9 a.m.-6 p.m.

Gourmet Shoppe
Canal Place
• 568-9634

Louisiana cooking has its own vocabulary and ingredients, and here's a shop that specializes in translating them for visitors. You'l find all the Creole and Cajun spices and seasonings, mixes and canned items that go into the famous recipes touted by local restaurants and chefs. The staff is helpful in explaining what it all means.
Open daily 8 a.m.-7 p.m.

Langenstein's
1330 Arabella St.
• 899-9283

This historic Uptown supermarket epitomizes personal service and an oldtime, relaxed approach to gourmet shopping. The staff knows most of the customers on a first-name basis, and a question about food, its preparation or care rarely goes unanswered. What is most fascinating here is the way the commonplace blends with the exotic. For instance, you'll find international delicacies, such as raw or baked pigs and goats, Maine lobster stuffed with crabmeat, pepper blood sausage, and geese and ducklings, in the same cooler as such New Orleans specialties as daube glacé, stuffed artichokes and crawfish pies. A year-round favorite is the custom, gourmet baskets in food, fruit, or wines and beers. Though located on a side street uptown, Langenstein's is worth an extra trip.
Open Mon.-Sat. 8 a.m.-7 p.m.

Loretta's French Market Gourmet
1100 N. Peters St.
• 529-6170

This shop, attached to the old Farmer's Market in the French Market, handles the spices, herbs and seasonings you need to prepare the Creole tomatoes, mirlitons and eggplants sold next door in the market. They also have coffees, teas, jams, and mixes of favorite Louisiana products for sale. And you won't want to miss their pralines, bran muffins and sweet potato cookies. A box of selected items from this shop makes a delightful gift and can be shipped anywhere.
Open daily 8:30 a.m.-6 p.m.

HEALTH FOODS

All Natural Foods & Deli
5517 Magazine St.
• 891-2651

For a sprout salad or tofu burger, this store-deli combination provides take-out or eat-in possibilities. The atmosphere is relaxed and friendly. You'll ses the most unusual items in their large macrobiotic section and on the shelves of vitamins and herbal supplements.
Open Mon.-Fri. 10 a.m.-7 p.m., Sat. 9 a.m.-9 p.m., Sun. 10 a.m.-5 p.m.

Whole Foods Market
3135 Esplanade Ave.
• 943-1626

The largest variety of organically grown and natural foods in the city is available in this supermarket a short ride from downtown. Featured are naturally fed beef and poultry, plus a good salad bar. Products are high in price, but generally of commensurate quality. This is a meeting place for many activists, environmentalists, and so on; notices posted around the entrance reflect such esoteric want ads as this one: "home needed for a vegetarian cat that eats only natural foods."
Open daily 9 a.m.-8 p.m.

ICE CREAM

Hansen's Sno-Bliz Sweet Shop
4801 Tchoupitoulas St.
• 891-9788

Sno-balls made of finely shaven ice and a variety of fresh, sweet flavors are a much bigger hit than ice cream in the long hot New Orleans summers. Every neighborhood has its share of seasonal sno-ball shops that spring up like mushrooms when the temperatures soar. Hansen's is legendary in the city as the best sno-ball outlet; people stand patiently in line at this out-of-the-way place to get a taste of the fabulous icy sweets. Be sure to call ahead about their hours, because they vary according to season.
Open: hours variable according to season.

The Ice Cream Shop
Jackson Brewery
• 525-4360

Fresh, creamy ice cream in a variety of flavors is available at this stand in Jackson Brewery. This is a local company that makes its own ice cream and serves it up in cones. No hard packed or fancy cakes.
Open Mon.-Thurs. & Sun. 10 a.m.-9 p.m., Fri.-Sat. 10 a.m.-10 p.m.

Swensen's Ice Cream Factory
528 St. Peter St., Jackson Square
• 522-8692

There's nothing better on a hot day while touring the historic French Quarter than a stop in this shop on Jackson Square for one of their sugar cones filled with smooth pralines-and-cream ice cream. Swensen's makes all its own products fresh daily, and the results show; there's a large selection of ice-cream, sherbert and frozen-yogurt flavors, with floats and banana splits made to order. You can sit down at one of the tables to relax while taking in the passing scene of the old square.
Open daily 10 a.m.-5 p.m.

MARKETS

A&P Food Store
701 Royal St.
• 523-1353

The only supermarket in the French Quarter, this store is understandably always crowded. It's also a very small, intimate store, compared with most supermarkets, but the variety is surprising. You'll find all the fixings for a dinner party along the narrow aisles. The selection of domestic wines is ample. Staff and customers invariably stop to chat in this neighborhood meeting place. Prices are generally higher than outside the Quarter, but the atmosphere and convenience (they never close) obviously compensate for Quarterites.
Open daily 24 hours.

Central Grocery Co.
923 Decatur St.
• 523-1620

This oldtime Italian market is a French Quarter institution. The lunch counter is often crowded with people ordering the local favorites—a muffuletta or po' boy sandwich. The store stocks a wide variety of imported food items and gadgets. With staff that is third or fourth generation Italian, there is a camaraderie that rubs off on the customers.
Open Mon.-Sat. 8 a.m.-5:30 p.m., Sun. 9 a.m.-5:30 p.m.

Farmer's Market
French Market
• 596-3420

This is one of our favorite sites in the French Quarter, probably because this historic open-air walk-through market, with its mounds of pumpkins around Halloween

and watermelons all through the summer, evokes such great memories for children who grew up in the city. Open year-round and 24 hours a day, the Farmer's Market has trucks from all over the state unloading produce and fruit, garlic strings, all those colorful fruits of the harvest that are used in the city's best restaurants and homes. It's worth a trip just to see and smell the produce and chat with the aging men and women who staff the various stalls.
Open daily 24 hours.

Progress Grocery Co.
915 Decatur St.
• 525-6627

Along with Central Grocery, this is the last of the dozens of Italian grocery stores and markets that once dominated the French Market area. The Progress store specializes in fancy and exotic imported food items, not limited to Italy. This is truly an international food market. They also do a brisk business preparing muffuletta and po' boy sandwiches for the local lunch crowd.
Open Mon.-Sat. 8 a.m.-5:30 p.m.

Ethnic Markets

African Harvest
3212 Tulane Ave.
• 822-2200

Exotic oils, herbs and spices are the mainstay of this African-American enterprise. There is also some art by local black artists, and artifacts and literature from Africa and the Caribbean. Weekends the store's contents move out to the Community Flea Market in the French Quarter. The staff here is helpful and pleased to educate visitors about the extensive inventory.
Open Mon.-Fri. 9 a.m.-5 p.m., Sat.-Sun. at the Community Flea Market (hours vary).

Cajun Magic/K-Paul's Louisiana Enterprises
501 Elysian Fields Ave.
• 947-6712

Internationally known Cajun chef Paul Prudhomme retails and wholesales his line of seasonings called Cajun Magic from this store on the edge of the French Quarter. You'll want to pick up his catalog while you're there. Prudhomme's cookbooks are also available here and around town to explain how he uses his Cajun Magic.
Open Mon.-Fri. 8 a.m.-5 p.m.

Kosher Cajun Deli
3520 N. Hullen St., Metairie
• 888-2010

The very name of this establishment seems contradictory, but locals Joel and Natalie Brown wanted a place that would welcome everyone, not only Orthodox Jews. Eveything in this suburban deli is strictly kosher, from potato

chips to gourmet French cakes. This is one of the few places in the New Orleans area where full kosher meals are served. Sandwich breads, meats, chopped liver and lox are shipped in fresh, and foods like matzoh balls and fresh salads are made on the premises.
Open Mon.-Thurs. 10 a.m.-7 p.m., Fri. 10 a.m.-3 p.m., Sun. 10 a.m.-5 p.m.

Louisiana General Store

Jackson Brewery
• 525-2665

The spices and herbs on sale here are used in the cooking demonstrations in Joe Cahn's New Orleans School of Cooking in the back of the store. There are lots of zesty Creole mustards, hot and spicy Louisiana sauces and other exotic seasonings and spices. And the selection of 150 Louisiana cookbooks has certainly enough ideas of how to use each spice. You'll find the staff enthusiastic about the New Orleans cuisine.
Open daily 9:30 a.m.-9:30 p.m.

PASS THE SPICE, PLEASE!

What creates the highly distinctive flavor of Creole cooking? Most often, a jumble of these spices, in myriad combinations: allspice, anise, caraway, cardamom, cinnamon, cumin, ginger, mace, mustard, nutmeg, black and white pepper, saffron and turmeric. And don't forget filé—a major ingredient in gumbo, (depending on whom you talk to)—used to flavor and thicken the stew. It comes from the tender green leaves of the sassafras tree, which are dried and ground to a powder.

N'awlins Cajun & Creole Spice

1200 N. Peters St.
• 566-0361

If the craving for some cayenne pepper strikes in the early morning hours, this shop in the Farmer's Market section of the French Market can accommodate your need. They never close. Here's a good place to get those strings of garlic and peppers that are de rigueur for hanging in any respectable Creole kitchen. And their filé spice for making gumbo is always fresh. You'll find the locals who staff this open-air walk-through market to be as colorful and helpful as any in the city.
Open daily 24 hours.

Union Supermarket

4129 S. Carrollton Ave.
• 482-5390

Although New Orleans has a large and diverse Hispanic community, there are few places that serve as a focal point as this small market in Mid-City does. Mixed in with the tortillas and dulces are flyers on political opinions and musical extravaganzas advertised only on the local Spanish

radio station. Many people come here for the first-rate meat cut in the Latin American style. There is also a counter where you can order sandwiches and other food to go.
Open Mon.-Sat. 8 a.m.-7 p.m., Sun. 8 a.m.-2 p.m.

SEAFOOD

Bayou to Go, Inc.

New Orleans International Airport
• 468-8040,
(800) 541-6610

For fresh seafood to carry on a plane or ship anywhere in the United States, this store can fill the bill. Located at the airport with offices on two concourses, they package seafood and Cajun dishes to travel in airline approved containers for sixteen hours guaranteed. Prices for carry-on or shipping range from $3 to $8, depending on whether the seafood is in season. Prices include packaging and handling charges. Nothing is frozen; all foods are made in Louisiana from fresh ingredients.
Open daily 8:30 a.m.-7 p.m. Call for individual orders.

Jaeger's Take-Out Dept.

1715 Elysian Fields Ave.
• 947-1116

Many restaurants in New Orleans serve seafood, but few have a large take-out service. Jaeger's Seafood Restaurant is an oldtime family-owned business with a reputation for fresh, tasty and reasonably priced seafood dishes prepared in the traditional manner. If you call ahead, your soft-shell crabs and boiled crawfish will be ready the moment you arrive. They're located downtown, a short ride from the French Quarter.
Open Wed.-Thurs. & Sun. 11 a.m.-9:45 p.m., Fri.-Sat. 11 a.m.-10:45 p.m.

Christina's Seafood Market, Inc.

527 S. Carrollton Ave.
• 486-5301

If you want good seafood, trust an experienced retailer like this one, with 85 years of experience. Christina's supplies many restaurants in town, and their fresh seafood is available to retail customers as well. But you'll have to catch them during the week, because they are gone fishing on weekends.
Open Mon.-Fri. 6 a.m.-1 p.m.

WINE & SPIRITS

Compleat Wine Cellar & Deli

The Rink,
2727 Prytania
• 897-9463

The Garden District would not be complete without this wine shop and deli, where a variety of wines can be tasted along with pâtés, cheeses and sandwiches.
Open Mon.-Fri. 10 a.m.-9 p.m., Sat. 10 a.m.-10 p.m.

Martin Wine Cellar

3827 Baronne St.
• 899-7411

714 Elmeer (at Veterans)
• 896-7300

Uptown wine connoisseurs have long depended on this wine and cheese store known for its wine tastings and large selection of gift baskets and seasonal specialties. The staff is knowledgeable about their large stock of domestic and foreign wines.
Open Mon.-Sat. 9 a.m.-7 p.m., Sun. 10 a.m.-2 p.m.

Vieux Carre Wine & Spirits

422 Chartres St.
• 568-WINE

To have a bottle of your favorite wine delivered to your hotel, you might call this fine wine store. It has positively the French Quarter's largest selection of imported and domestic wines, liquor and beer. The staff here can also arrange gifts and party specialties for festive occasions, large or small.
Open Mon.-Sat. 10 a.m.-10 p.m., Sun. 10 a.m.-8 p.m.

GIFTS

Friends of the Cabildo Museum Shop

523 St. Ann St.,
Jackson Square
• 524-9118

Several artists in New Orleans design architectural postcards and note cards to celebrate the wonderful diversity of historic styles in the city. This shop has one of the best selections of such cards. As an auxiliary of the Louisiana State Museum, it also carries hard-to-find items such as early jazz recordings, baskets woven by the Coushatta and Houmas tribes, streetcars carved of cypress, and gold pins of the cupola on the Cabildo building. You'll enjoy their seven-volume New Orleans Architecture series. This is the only place in the city where fire marks—authentic reproductions of emblems on early American homes to indicate they were insured—are sold. A good gift idea for lovers of colonial folklore, these fire marks are made of cast iron and hand-painted in Wrightsville, Pennsylvania.
Open Tues.-Sun. 10 a.m.-4:30 p.m.

The Idea Factory

838 Chartres St.
• 524-5195

This unique shop, with its mechanical mobiles and wooden toys, its humorous inventions and games, is a natural place to look in the French Quarter for one-of-a-kind gifts. The owners make most of the items in their shop on the premises and are happy to explain the function and workings of each piece. You're guaranteed to be suprised and amused by this store.
Open Mon.-Sat. 10 a.m.-6 p.m., Sun. noon-5 p.m.

New Orleans Cat House

840 Royal St.
• 524-5939

Looking for something special for a cat or a cat lover in your life? This cute French Quarter shop has just the item. How about a bag of catnip with a New Orleans decal on it? Or a deluxe scratching post? Owners here are serious cat lovers. They can identify both the cats and their owners in the many photographs that decorate the walls of the shop. As if the shop's pun of a name weren't enough already!
Open daily 9:30 a.m.-6:30 p.m.

Old Craft Cottage, Inc.

816 Decatur St.
• 522-0835

For a unique jacket, try the hand-painted ones here or those that incorporate pieces of old and new quilts. You can also choose a quilted pillow case or one of the dozens of country quilts lining the walls. Everything in this French Quarter store is made by the fourth generation of a Louisiana family (some members now live in Mina, Arkansas). King-size handmade quilts go for a reasonable $450 to $600, because they are sold directly from the artist to you. You can order your own design and have it shipped to you once it is made.
Open daily 9 a.m.-6 p.m.

The Persian Cat

5513 Magazine St.
• 899-6050

Here's a shop for those nimble of finger in needlepoint, knitting, cross stitch or crochet fans. The staff is as avid about such things as their visitors are, and there is even a videotape to sit down and watch if you're not sure of the latest stitch. Lots of pattern books and a large selection of yarns and threads and supplies. In case making an afghan is not your thing, there are lots of antique and collectibles shops on the same street where you can buy one.
Open Mon.-Tues. & Thurs.-Sun.10 a.m.-5 p.m., Wed. 10 a.m.-7 p.m.

Rapp's Luggage & Gifts

604 Canal St.
• 568-1958

New Orleans Centre
• 566-0700

Gift items are a tradition at this well-known locally owned store in New Orleans since 1865. Today Rapp's has grown from Canal Street to stores in shopping centers around the city: New Orleans Centre, the Esplanade, Uptown Square and Oakwood. Luxurious luggage, business cases and wallets by Boyt, French, Hartmann, Tumi and Atlas are the main items here, but Mont Blanc pens, designer umbrellas, and a good selection of exclusive and unique gifts also attract attention. You'll be sure to find a tasteful souvenir for the sportsman, businessman or executive. True to their hometown tradition, the staff is made up of friendly and helpful New Orleans originals.
Canal St.: open Mon.-Sat. 9:30 a.m.-5:30 p.m. New Orleans Centre: open Mon.-Sat. 10 a.m.-9:30 p.m., Sun. noon-6 p.m.

Sigle's Historic New Orleans Metalcraft

935 Royal St.
• 522-7647

Gerhardt Sigle, a German craftsman, owns this unique French Quarter shop. His wall planters, which he makes from solid cast iron, are faithful to the designs of the original New Orleans balcony and porch iron trimmings and make a fine gift-souvenir combination. For less than $20 you can have a practical gift shipped anywhere in the country. His shop also carries items in brass, glass and china.
Open Mon.-Sat. 10 a.m.-6 p.m.

HOME

CHINA & CRYSTAL

Cynthia Sutton

429 Royal St.
• 523-3377

The Sutton family has several stores of china, crystal, linens and other fine imported home furnishings in New Orleans. This one has a large selection of Dresden china and some of the finest crystal you'll find anywhere. If they don't have what you're looking for, they can tell you where to find it.
Open Mon.-Sat. 9:30 a.m.-5 p.m.

Maison Blanche
901 Canal St.
• 566-1000

This department store has a large selection of fine crystal by names such as Lenox, Mikasa and Geneva and china by Mikasa, Johnson Brothers, Lenox, Wedgewood and Dansk. They offer a bridal registry and attentive staff. Maison Blanche has dressed New Orleans tables for generations.
Open daily 10 a.m.-6 p. m.

FABRIC

Krauss
1201 Canal St.
• 523-3311

It might be a surprise to find one of the largest and best sewing-fabric departments in the South tucked away in this family department store on Canal Street. Krauss has served the tailors and seamstresses of this city since 1903, and their staff is very competent. You'll find lots of variety in their prints, antique satins, and almost any other fabrics or sewing accessories you may need.
Open Mon.-Wed. & Fri.-Sun. 10 a.m.-6 p.m., Thurs. 10 a.m.-7 p.m.

Promenade Fine Fabrics
1330 St. Charles Ave.
• 522-1488

For fine natural-fiber fabrics, this is the place to go. The selection of silks, woolens, cottons and linens is outstanding, and Promenade is well known for their great variety of notions, buttons and ribbons. A bonus to shopping here is that you can ride the streetcar right to their door.
Open Mon.-Fri. 9:30 a.m.-5:30 p.m., Sat. 9 a.m.-5 p.m.

FURNISHINGS

The Bombay Company
One French Market Place
• 522-2838

As the name suggests, this shop in the French Quarter specializes in British imports, and in eighteenth- and nineteenth-century antique reproductions. This is the place to find that Chippendale console you've been looking for, or an English wine table. They also handle a variety of fire tool sets and screens. The company has stores in the Esplanade, Lakeside and Uptown shopping centers as well.
Open Mon.-Sat. 10 a.m.-6 p.m., Sun. 11 a.m.-6 p.m.

Expressions
1400 St. Charles Ave.
• 524-2511

A popular name in custom furniture in New Orleans is this locally owned business on fashionable St. Charles Avenue, where the streetcar passes outside the door.

Within 45 days the staff here can bring a couch or chair from design to delivery. With over 150 frames and 600 fabrics to choose from, the possibilities are endless. Personal consultants are knowledgeable and can help with anything to do with upholstery and interior decorating. There is a good selection of accessories: rugs, drapery fabrics, lamps and tables. For the latest in locally and nationally made furnishings, this is a good bet.
Open Mon.-Sat. 9:30 a.m.-6 p.m.

Halpern's Furnishings Store

1600 Prytania St.
• 566-1707

An unusual combination, this store has two floors of dressers, sofas and chairs, with a first-rate restaurant tucked away on the second floor. Shoppers in the know are fond of this Uptown family-owned store, where they can lunch on chicken salad with poppyseed dressing while they decide which wall hanging or end table to buy. Halpern's specializes in fine wood furniture and custom-made sofas with 150 different fabrics to choose from. They also have lots of unique wall decorations, lamps and shelving units.
Open Mon.-Sat. 10 a.m.-6 p.m.

Hurwitz-Mintz

211 Royal St.
• 568-9555

Units

227 Chartres St.
• 568-9555

These two shops have been supplying New Orleans homes with fine furniture for years. Located in the French Quarter, Hurwitz-Mintz is a more traditional furniture store, with collections by Drexel, Henredon and Heritage, while Units, a block away and owned by the same family, specializes in the latest and most innovative pieces, including a large stock of Hancock and Moore leather sofas and chairs. Along with sofas and bedroom and dining-room sets, both stores also have a large selection of accent pieces, entertainment centers, pictures and lamps. The show windows of Units are some of the most imaginative in the city.
Open Mon.-Wed. & Fri. 10 a.m.-6 p.m., Thurs. 10 a.m.-9 p.m., Sat. 10 a.m.-8 p.m., Sun. 10 a.m.-7 p.m.

Jacqueline Vance Oriental Rugs

3944 Magazine St.
• 891-3304

Vance has a large collection of fine antique and contemporary Oriental rugs, including a very large selection of vegetable-dyed rugs from Turkey. The thousands of items in her inventory are all handmade, with many exclusive designs. She offers a complete range of services: selling, purchasing, appraising, cleaning and repairing rugs.
Open Tues.-Sat. 10 a.m.-5 p.m.

Leitmotif
434 Julia St.
• 891-7777

For ultramodern and sophisticated lighting, furniture and objets d'art, this gallery in the historic warehouse district stands out. Leitmotif deals exclusively with the modern masters. Price notwithstanding, there is a special feeling in owning your very own Le Corbusier, Noguchi, Mies or Aalto.
Open Tues.-Sat. 10 a.m.-6 p.m.

Peel & Co.
2030 St. Charles Ave.
• 522-2448

This shop features needlepoint rugs, and is reported to have the largest selection in the South. You'll also find Persian, Kelim, Dhurrri, Chinese, and Turkish rugs here, along with a good selection of Portuguese linen. Take the St. Charles streetcar and get off almost at the door.
Open Mon.-Sat. 10 a.m.-5 p.m.

Pier 1 Imports
808 Metairie Rd.
• 833-7820

For unique and casual home decorating items, this is a good place to check out. The fragrances, bright colors and imaginative displays make it a shopping experience. There is always a good selection of rattan furniture, practical indoor-outdoor tables and chairs, and shelves and shelves of china, glassware, vases, place mats and almost any trinket imaginable, from countries all around the world. Throw rugs, wall hangings and matchstick blinds are popular here. Sales are frequent.
Open Mon.-Sat. 9:30 a.m.-9 p.m., Sun. noon-6 p.m.

HOUSEWARES & KITCHEN

As You Like It
3025 Magazine St.
• 897-6915

Thought you'd never find a match for that missing fork or spoon from your old silverware set? Don't leave New Orleans without checking out this antique shop on quaint Magazine Street. Well known for its heavy estate silver, it also has literally hundreds of active and inactive flatware patterns in stock. And if you can't find it here, they might have what you're looking for in their shop in Natchez, Mississippi. You'll enjoy the Holloware, jewelry and other items as well.
Open Mon.-Sat. 11 a.m.-4 p.m.(hours vary).

Butterfield's
Riverwalk
• 523-1711

Billed as "the gadget capital of the world," this store has everything imaginable for the kitchen: citrus peelers, champagne openers, butter spreaders, pineapple slicers, bread tiles, ceramic dishes, pepper mills, and Belgian

waffle makers—to name the items that come first to mind. You'll find a whimsical selection of gadgets with the N. O. Saints logo to take home as a useful souvenir. Prices start as low as $1.75.
Open Mon.-Thurs. 9:30 a.m.-9 p.m., Fri.-Sat. 9:30 a.m.-10 p.m., Sun. 11 a.m.-7 p.m.

Jelly Sandwich
Rhino Art Gallery,
Place St. Charles
• 582-1173

Canal Place
• 525-1955

Jill Sanders of New Orleans was commissioned by a local artist to design a new table service; the result is Dig-ins, a new concept in tableware, sure to become a collector's item. Spoons are scoop shaped, fork tines are graceful, and the butter/steak saw is two knives in one. All handles are simulated wood. The new table service in a limited first edition makes eating seem like a new experience.
Place St. Charles: open Mon.-Sat. 11 a.m.-4 p.m. Canal Place: open Mon-Wed. & Fri.-Sat. 10 a.m.-6 p.m., Thurs. 10 a.m.-8 p.m., Sun. noon-6 p.m.

Maison Blanche
901 Canal St.
• 566-1000

For a full range of kitchen utensils and housewares, this downtown department store is convenient and reasonably priced. They carry Magnalite and Revere cookware among others, and also top brands in small appliances. Check ahead for frequent sales.
Open daily 10 a.m.-6 p.m.

LINENS

Linens
Canal Place,
335 Canal St.
• 586-8148

This is a specialty shop where you can find good imported and domestic linen: bedding, comforters, towels, table cloths, and some children's clothes (infants and girls up to size six). Most items are handmade. The store will special-order items not in stock.
Open Mon.-Sat. 10 a.m.-6 p.m., Sun. noon-6 p.m.

Sutton's Linen Shop
Fairmont Hotel,
125 Baronne St.
• 529-7111

Imported linens from around the world make up the collection in this elegant shop. Battenburg, Alencon, Colonial and Quaker lace are featured, plus tablecloths, towels and pillowcases. You'll enjoy their large selection of Ladro porceleain, David Winter cottages and Sworovski crystal as well.
Open Mon.-Sat. 9:30 a.m.-5:30 p.m.

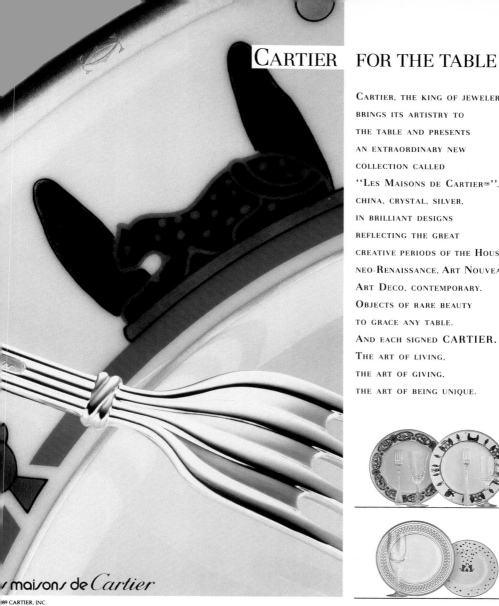

Cartier FOR THE TABLE

Cartier, the king of jewelers,
brings its artistry to
the table and presents
an extraordinary new
collection called
"Les Maisons de Cartier®".
China, crystal, silver,
in brilliant designs
reflecting the great
creative periods of the House:
neo-Renaissance, Art Nouveau,
Art Deco, contemporary.
Objects of rare beauty
to grace any table.
And each signed CARTIER.
The art of living,
the art of giving,
the art of being unique.

/ maisons de Cartier

Cartier

THE ART OF BEING UNIQUE

AT CLUB MED,
WE TAKE DINING SERIOUSLY.

Exquisite cuisine prepared by our specially-trained chefs, served to you in a sunny sea-side bistro, or under an evening sky blanketed by stars—that's dining, Club Med-style.

For breakfast, freshly-baked croissants, danish, and *pain au chocolat*. Eggs, any style, with sausage and bacon. Crepes and French toast. The ripest fruits.

For lunch, bottomless buffets. Dozens of salads, grilled meats and fish, savory local specialties, and the freshest vegetables and fruits.

For dinner, delicious appetizers from our salad buffets, and lavish main courses starring scrumptious fare from the four corners of the globe.

Did we mention the fresh-from-the-oven breads and rolls, baked right on the premises by our hand-picked *boulanger*? And the tempting assortment of pastries created daily by our own pastry chef? Or free-flowing wine and beer at lunch and dinner?

Between meals, there's every sport under the sun. From windsurfing and scuba diving to golf and tennis, complete with modern equipment and expert instruction. Laugh-out-loud games and activities like picnics, arts and crafts, boat rides, and classical music concerts on CD video discs. After dinner, there are Broadway-style extravaganzas, comedy shows, theme parties. In exotic, tropical settings as sumptuous as our cuisine.

Pre-paid and hassle-free. So you can enjoy your vacation, and your meals, without having to reach into your pockets.

If you now have a craving to sample a bit more of the Club Med vacation, simply call your travel agent or 1-800-CLUB MED.

CLUB MED®

The antidote for civilization.℠

IMAGE & SOUND

PHOTOGRAPHY

Alfredo's Cameras

805 Gravier St.
• 523-2421

Questions about cameras and how they work can be answered here by an experienced staff. They have the latest in filming equipment. No fast film developing or camera repairs.
Open Mon.-Fri. 8 a.m.-5 p.m.

K & B Camera Center

227 Dauphine St.
• 524-2266

This is the only camera store in the French Quarter. You'll find a knowledgeable staff who can help you with your camera and its accessories. They develop black-and-white film in the store, but color film is shipped out for developing.
Open Mon.-Fri. 8 a.m.-6 p.m., Sat. 8 a.m.-2 p.m.

Wolf Camera & Video

New Orleans Centre
• 581-6905

4332 St. Charles Ave.
• 891-6796

For last-minute camera repairs or film developing, this store has the experienced staff to do a fine job. They have several stores in the metro area, with a large selection of cameras, camcorders and video equipment. It feels good to have your favorite camera in the hands of an authorized service and repair center for brands like Nikon, Canon and Minolta.
N. O. Centre: open Mon.-Sat. 10 a.m.-8 p.m., Sun. noon-6 p.m. St. Charles Ave.: open Mon.-Sat. 10 a.m.-6 p. m.

RECORDED MUSIC

GHB Jazz Foundation

1204 Decatur St.
• 525-0200

This is a combination restaurant, music club and jazz store. The foundation operates eight jazz record labels and a listening and information facility inside the Palm Court Café, where local jazz bands perform live throughout the week and jazz aficionados meet to chat. The long hours every day couldn't be more convenient. Call the Palm Court for a schedule of live music.
Open daily noon-midnight, kitchen closes at 11 p.m.

Mel's Records & Tapes
626 St. Ann St.
• 525-8882

Louisiana music is easy to find in all major record stores around town, but this small shop in the French Quarter specializes in only Cajun, zydeco, Dixieland jazz, and rhythm-and-blues. The owners, brothers Dennis and Mel Fitts, are experts on the local music scene. If they don't stock a certain album or tape, they'll be sure to tell you where you can find it.
Open daily 10 a.m.-6 p.m.

Record Ron's
407 Decatur St.
• 525-2852

1129 Decatur St.
• 524-9444

Record Ron has been in the record business in New Orleans for a long time, and his stores attest to a wide range of interests; anything from hard-to-find oldies and collectibles to the newest of the new. If a record is not available in the store, a staff person will usually know how and where to find it. There is also a large selection of local music from famous as well as lesser-known artists.
Open daily 11 a.m.-7 p.m.

Smith's Record Center
2019 St. Charles Ave.
• 522-7969

In the Uptown–Garden District area this is one of few record and tape stores. It's been here for what seems like forever, and the service is neighborly.
Open Mon.-Fri. 10 a.m.-6 p.m., Sat. 10 a.m.-5 p.m.

STEREO & VIDEO

Alterman Audio
7323 Freret St.
• 866-3579

This modern shop Uptown is a knowledgeable and reliable source for the shopper interested in the latest equipment and the best buys. Frequent sales and helpful personnel are what keep locals coming back.
Open Mon.-Thurs. 10 a.m.-7 p.m., Fri.-Sat. 10 a.m.-6 p.m.

Tulane Stereo
1909 Tulane Ave.
• 524-2343

Shop where New Orleans's artists often go for their home audio, studio and stage equipment. One of the newest and most contemporary stereo outlets, this store is designed for the music connoisseur. Prices are competitive, and the staff is up on the latest technology. The location near the central business district is convenient.
Open Mon.-Fri. 8 a.m.-5 p.m., Sat. 11 a.m.-4 p.m.

Video Alternatives
4721 Magazine St.
• 891-5347

With videos being so popular these days, there are stores all over the city with rentals. This place has some of the best quality videos, as well as a large selection of classic, art, and out-of-the-mainstream videos.
Open daily 11 a.m.-8 p.m.

LEATHER

BBH Leather Goods
4221 Magazine St.
• 891-4992

For fine leather goods this shop on Magazine Street has a first-rate selection. Their boots and shoes are custom-made. BBH has its own line of belts, handbags and wallets, and they carry several other brands that combine silks and velvets with leathers and suedes. You'll have a hard time leaving here empty-handed.
Open Mon.-Thurs. 11 a.m.-6 p.m.

R-U-4 Eel?
Jackson Brewery (Millhouse)
• 529-7331

Everything that can be made from eelskin is to found here: purses, evening bags, belts, shoes, earrings and necklaces. There is a wide range of unique designs and colors; the soft and supple quality of the products is unique.
Open Sun.-Thurs. 10 a.m.-9 p.m., Fri.-Sat. 10 a.m.-10 p.m.

Wehmeier's Belt Shop
719 Toulouse St.
• 525-2758

Almost anything that can be made in leather is displayed in this shop. Their handbags, belts, wallets and shoes are all well crafted. Much of the work is custom-made. The shop also offers a leather repair service to reattach that broken strap on your handbag or fix a belt buckle that has worn through your belt.
Open daily 10 a.m.-6 p.m.

MARDI GRAS & MASKS

Accent Annex
1120 S. Jefferson Davis Pkwy.
• 821-8999

If you can't visit New Orleans during Mardi Gras, this is the next best thing. This store, informally called Mardi Gras Headquarters, is a supermarket of beads, throws, costume accessories and souvenirs. Virtually any of the posters, cups, doubloons and other accoutrements of the famous Carnival season can be found here, and the staff consists of oldtime Mardi Gras fans who delight in telling visitors all about the favorite local holiday. You can ship some Carnival madness to friends around the world. Accent Annex has five locations around the Gulf area; this one, ten minutes from downtown, is the closest to the city.
Open Mon.-Sat. 9 a.m.-5 p.m., Sun. 10 a.m.-5 p.m.

The French Market
Along Decatur St.
• 522-2621

For several weeks before Mardi Gras the open-air shops in the French Market have a good variety of masks, from the sedate to the most outrageous. Some 30 members of the New Orleans Mask Makers Guild tend these shops and can tell you all about their artistry. In most cases they take orders for custom-made work if given enough advance notice. It's a sure bet that you'll find a face covering to express your personality for the frivolity of Mardi Gras here—in Rio or even in Peoria. Masks make great wall decorations as well. Some individual mask makers display their work year-round in this area. Prices for handcrafted masks can vary a lot; here you'll find them priced from $5 to $5,000, depending on materials, style and originality.
Open daily 9 a.m.-5 p.m.

Mardi Gras Center
831 Chartres St.
• 524-4384

Join the locals in the French Quarter in their preparations for Carnival. This shop is for the serious masker; there are literally hundreds of masks, costumes, wigs, and accessories. Check out their animal face masks, which can turn the sweetest lamb into a cagey wolf. Prices are reasonable but can go quite high for the elaborate custom-made elaborate headpieces. The staff here is local and experienced.
Open Mon.-Sat. 10 a.m.-5 p.m.

Serendipitous
831 Decatur St.
• 522-9158

Here is another shop in the French Quarter that knows the mask business. No cheap imports here; everything is made by artists on the premises. The feathered headdresses and masks are pieces of art. Much of the work is custom-made.
Open daily 10 a.m.-7 p.m.

RENTALS & SERVICES

A BABYSITTER

Nannies
• 282-2200

If you need child care, check with the reception desk in your hotel. If no such care is available, Nannies is a reliable alternative. Within short notice (four to six hours), they can send a babysitter to your hotel room. The sitters are certified and experienced. Nannies charges a $30 minimum based on $5 an hour and parking fees for the sitter. *On call 24 hours daily.*

A CLEANERS

Alessi Cleaners
837 Gravier St.
• 586-9632

Most major hotels offer valet service for care of clothing. If you're on your own in this department, for reliable and professional dry cleaning this shop is convenient to visitors, but will not pick up or deliver. One-day service is available; if clothes are left before 9:30 a.m., they can be picked up that afternoon at 4 p.m. Alessi does not launder anything but shirts. Their rates are reasonable.
Open Mon.-Fri. 7 a.m.-5:30 p.m.

Washing Well Laundryteria
841 Bourbon St.
• 523-9955

This French Quarter washateria picks up laundry at local hotels and delivers it washed, dried and folded for $5 a machine load, which is a real bargain. Prompt and friendly service included.
Open Mon.-Fri. 7:30 a.m.-6 p.m., Sat. 7:30 a.m.-2 p.m.

A DRUGSTORE

Walgreen Drugstore
134 Royal St.
• 522-2736

This is a store for all seasons and people; besides a full pharmacy, it has lots of souvenirs and the usual shampoos, dental supplies, and cosmetics. Its location in the French Quarter just off Canal Street brings in an odd assortment of visitors.
Open Mon.-Sat. 8 a.m.-10 p.m., Sun. 9 a.m.-9 p.m.

A FIVE-AND-DIME

F. W. Woolworth & Co.
737 Canal St.
• 522-6426

"Woolsworth," as locals often call this Canal Street institution, has a full range of household, clothing and hardware items. And don't overlook their lunch counter; some of the best donuts, soups and cups of chicory coffee are served there. The assortment of types stopping off to chat makes for great people watching.
Open Mon.-Sat. 9 a.m.-7 p.m.

A FLORIST

French Quarter Florist
223 Dauphine St.
• 523-5476

To accommodate the round-the-clock parties this town is known for, this special shop can deliver flowers, balloons, plants, wine and champagne 24 hours a day. They specialize in European and exotic flower arrangements, but can also handle smaller favors.
Open daily 24 hours (phone service).

A FOOD-DELIVERY SERVICE

Déjà Vu
400 Dauphine St.
• 568-1771

Besides room service, for hotel guests in the French Quarter there is an alternative for in-room eating: delivery (on bicycles) by this 1950s-style grill, which is open 24 hours a day and known for its omelets, half-pound charbroiled burgers, overstuffed club sandwiches, and old-fashioned malts and shakes. Breakfast is served any time. The reasonable prices will surprise you, and the quality of food, including light diet items, is reliable.
Open daily 24 hours.

A HARDWARE STORE

Mary's True Value Hardware
908 Bourbon St.
• 525-6279

The only hardware store in the French Quarter, Mary's packs a lot of stock into a small space. You'll find the usual hardware items here with a few local things like oyster knives thrown in. Convenient hours and neighborly service are a plus here.
Open Mon.-Fri. 7:30 a.m.-7 p.m., Sat. 8:30 a.m.-7 p.m., Sun. 10 a.m.-5 p.m.

A LIMOUSINE

Carey-Bonomolo Limousines
1401 Lafitte Ave.
• 523-LIMO

A wide range of touring services is offered by this limo company. They will arrange to take you on swamp, plantation, city and industrial tours, or take you to and from the airport. Their vehicles are current models in Mercedes-Benzes, Lincolns and Cadillacs. Prices for limos begin at $40 an hour. Friendly, prompt service assured.
On call daily 24 hours.

London Livery, Ltd.
3037 Royal St.
• 944-1984

This is a top-of-the-line limousine service offering stretch limos, luxury sedans, Rolls-Royces, vans and mini–motor coaches. They will even accommodate you with a motor yacht. A fully stocked bar and telephone are standard features in their VIP motorcars. Prices start at $50 per hour, plus a 15-percent service charge.
On call daily 24 hours.

A MESSENGER

United Cab
1627 Polymnia St.
• 522-9771, 524-9606

One of the fastest and most efficient ways to send packages and letters within the city is to call a United cab. Drivers are courteous and reliable, and they work round the clock. A $5 minimum is charged; prices vary depending on service and distance.
On call daily 24 hours.

A NEWSSTAND

Sidney's Newsstands
917 Decatur St.
• 524-6872

Riverbend at 620 Carrollton Ave.
• 866-9898

1332 S. Carrollton Ave.
• 865-1780

If it can't be found at Sidney's, it can't be found. This is almost a local institution; especially at the Decatur Street newsstand in the French Quarter, there is a fascinating variety of stock and people hard to find anywhere else. You have over 2,000 magazine titles to choose from, some in French, German, Spanish and Italian. Picking up *The New York Times* here and heading off to a café is a Sunday ritual for lots of folks. There are also the *Washington Post, Houston Chronicle, Chicago Tribune* and *Miami Herald*, among others. Sidney's is known for its eclectic array of posters, post cards and bumper stickers, many of which are X-rated. This is the only shop to carry such esoteric journals as *Red Bass,* published in New Orleans but appealing to a national readership, and radical political publications on both sides of the spectrum. Cashiers tend to be colorful.
Decatur St.: open daily 9 a.m.-9 p.m. Riverbend: open Sun.-Thurs. 10 a.m.-10:30 p.m. Fri.-Sat. 10 a.m.-11 p.m. 1332 S. Carrollton Ave.: open Mon.-Sat. 9 a.m.-10 p.m., Sun. 8 a.m.-10 p.m.

A PET HOTEL

Begue Veterinary Hospital
1428 N. Rampart St.
• 944-6855

Pets are welcome to board here no matter what the size or length of stay. This experienced veterinary clinic provides a full range of services to pet owners. Prices vary according to circumstances. Tender loving care is assured.
Open Mon.-Fri. 8 a.m.-6 p.m., Sat. 8 a.m.-2 p.m.

A PHOTO LAB

Fox Foto
414 Canal St.
• 568-0198

This veteran photo-developing service can have your color film made into prints within an hour. They charge $11.96, plus tax, for a roll of 24 shots.
Open Mon.-Fri. 8 a.m.-6 p.m., Sat. 10 a.m.-5 p.m.

Photo World/Camera America
Riverwalk
• 523-5632

For photos developed while you wait, this camera shop can give you top-quality service. The good thing here is that you can browse through the many shops and eateries in the Riverwalk while waiting for your photos. Film and camera accessories are also available. Convenient hours.
Open daily 10 a.m.-10 p.m.

A SECRETARY

Workload Inc.
225 Baronne St.
• 522-7171

Professional secretaries from this office personnel agency are on call for on-site business and conference assignments. Fees range according to length of job and types of skills required.
Open Mon.-Fri. 8 a.m.-5 p.m., on call daily 24 hours.

A SHOE-REPAIR SHOP

Heel Quik
346 Baronne St.
• 566-0916

For that last-minute heel cap or shoe shine, this shop is indispensable. They guarantee shoe repairs while you wait. You can also have your luggage repaired here. Friendly service in the business district.
Open Mon.-Fri. 8 a.m.-5 p.m.

A TAILOR

Vu Tailors
330 Baronne St.
• 525-4026

If you need the services of a tailor, check first with the concierge at your hotel for referrals. Vu Tailors are available weekdays and competently handle the gamut of clothing repairs, alterations and fittings in the Central Business District. No pickup or delivery available.
Open Mon.-Fri. 8 a.m.-5:30 p.m.

A TRANSLATOR

Professional Translators and Interpreters Inc.
World Trade Center
• 581-3122

This well-established translation agency is ready to step in whenever interpreting or translating is needed. The staff will travel to hotel and convention sites. Services are available on a 24-hour basis.
On call daily 24 hours.

A TUXEDO

Gentlemen's Quarter
232 Royal St.
• 522-7139

Tuxedos in single-breasted and double-breasted styles, plus tails, are sold and rented from this French Quarter shop. Rentals start at $65, and accessories are extra.
Open Mon.-Sat. 9:30 a.m.-6 p.m., Sun. 11 a.m.-6 p.m.

A VETERINARIAN

Begue Veterinary Hospital
1428 N. Rampart St.
• 944-6855

Located just outside the French Quarter, this animal clinic provides a full range of services, including boarding of pets. No animal is too large or too small. Emergency service available.
Open Mon.-Fri. 8 a.m.-6 p.m., Sat. 8 a.m.-2 p.m. Emergency service on call 24 hours daily.

The Cat Practice
1823 Magazine St.
• 525-MEOW

This veterinarian handles nothing but felines and offers complete medical, spaying and grooming services. Boarding a cat costs between $6 and $8 per day.
Open Mon.-Fri. 7 a.m.-6 p.m., Sat. 8 a.m.-2 p.m.

SPORTING GOODS

Bicycle Michael's
618 Frenchmen St.
• 945-9505

This shop just outside the French Quarter is a convenient place to rent or buy a bicycle. Michael's sells, rents and repairs bicycles with prompt, helpful service and reasonable prices. You can also find almost any biking accessory here.
Open Mon.-Sat. 10 a.m.-7 p.m.

Joe's Bicycle Shop
2501 Tulane Ave.
• 821-2350

New Orleans is a great city for bicycle riding, and this store can answer most bikers' needs. It sells both new and used bikes, starting at $25 and going up to $1400. You'll find such brands as Cannon Dale, Peugeot, Murray, Mongoose and GT, with accessories to match. How about a folding bike to take along on your next sailing trip across the lake? If it's a new tire or pedal you need, Joe's has a repair shop on the premises. Located near downtown and next to Dixie Brewery.
Open Mon.-Fri. 8 a.m.- 5 p.m., Sat. 8 a.m.-3:30 p.m.

Oshman's Sporting Goods
5300 Tchoupitoulas St., Riverside
• 895-7791

A short cab ride from downtown is this department store of sports equipment and fashion. You'll find Reebok, Nike and Converse shoes, Speedo racing and swimsuit fashions, Insport, Hind, Spettro and Nike tights, and a large variety of accessories. For working out, there's a complete Weider collection. Oshman's has occasional sales; their regular prices are in the medium to expensive range. They have four other stores in the metro area.
Open Mon.-Sat. 10 a.m.-9 p.m., Sun. 12:30 p.m.-5:30 p.m.

Security Sporting Goods
3604 S. Carrollton Ave.
• 488-1381

This large sporting goods store has been dressing and outfitting the city's athletes for a good many years. Frequent sales and the latest sportswear and sports equipment make this a popular place. They also sell guns, as well as hunting and fishing equipment.
Open Mon.-Sat. 10 a.m.-8 p.m., Sun. noon-6 p.m.

TOBACCONISTS

The Epitome in Fine Tobacco
729 St. Louis St.
• 523-2844

From the moment you open the door of this shop, there's no mistaking the aromatic fragrances that mix in the air. A large selection of pipes and smoking accessories is available, plus lots of fine tobaccos and blends. Convenient hours and friendly service are a plus.
Open Mon.-Wed. 10:30 a.m.-6 p.m., Thurs.-Sat. 10:30 a.m.-10:30 p.m., Sun. 11 a.m.-5 p.m.

Ye Olde Pipe Shop
306 Chartres St.
• 522-1484

With 120 years in the tobacco store business, this French Quarter shop is a good bet for a range of pipes and tobacco blends. They have their own line of blends and are knowledgeable about smoking paraphernalia. This is a friendly, oldtime place, ideal for the devoted pipe smoker.
Open Mon.-Sat. 10 a.m.-5 p.m.

SIGHTS

FRENCH QUARTER & DOWNTOWN

The **French Quarter** is the historic and spiritual heart of New Orleans. It also is the top tourist spot, because of its restaurants and nightclubs and unparalleled assemblage of distinctly French- and Spanish-flavored buildings from the eighteenth and nineteenth centuries. The Quarter's 84 square blocks are so saturated with compatible and complementary structures that preservationists refer to the area's *tout ensemble*, or collective totality, and battle fiercely to protect it. It was one of the first government-protected historic districts in the United States, and any architechtural alterations are strictly regulated.

The French planned New Orleans from the outset as a great city, the port that would rule the mighty Mississippi River near its mouth and serve as the capital of the vast territory of Louisiana. When they founded it in 1718, they laid out the streets in a proper grid, stretching from a main square, although it would be years before the grid filled up. The main plaza, now called **Jackson Square**, remains the focal point of the Quarter, at least in the daytime.

ST. LOUIS CATHEDRAL

Dominating Jackson Square is St. Louis Cathedral, built in 1851 and remodeled since World War II. Relatively modest as far as cathedrals go, it is the mother church of the Roman Catholic archdiocese in a city that has always been overwhelmingly Roman Catholic, and it serves as the site of major civic-religious events, such as inauguration masses and funerals for former mayors. It is open daily from 7:30 a.m. to 7 p.m., with free guided tours every fifteen minutes from 9:30 a.m. to 4:45 p.m., except at lunchtime. For more information, call 525-9585.

Jackson Square is a marvelous public space, with people flooding its flagstones to critique the sidewalk artists, gaze at some of the city's most important historic buildings or hopscotch among the shops and cafés. In the middle of the square, surrounded by a high iron fence, is a well-maintained green park, centered on a flamboyant equestrian statue of Gen. Andrew Jackson, who beat the invading British in the Battle of New Orleans in 1815 and went on to become president.

In the left of the square, as one faces the **St. Louis Cathedral**, is the **Cabildo**, once the City Hall, and to the right is the Presbytere, once the archdiocesan headquarters. Both were begun in the late eighteenth century, after two devastating fires had wiped out most of the crude wooden buildings that made up the original French colonial city. That was during the nearly half century of Spanish rule in Louisiana (1763–1801), and it is the Spanish who gave the French Quarter its distinctive architectural character, with their predilection for ironwork balconies, stuccoed facades and houses shuttered to the sidewalk but open to cool courtyards within.

The United States purchased Louisiana in 1803, after its brief (and secret) return to French control, and the Americans added fashionable Mansard hipped roofs to the Cabildo and **Presbytere** before the Civil War. The Cabildo's roof and upper stories were severely damaged by fire in 1988, and the building has been closed while undergoing restoration; the Presbytere, part of the **Louisiana State Museum**, displays historic exhibits and artifacts Wednesday through Sunday from 10 a.m. to 5 p.m., with admission $3 for adults (568-6968).

Across **St. Peter Street** from the Cabildo, on the corner of Chartres, is **Le Petit Theater,** a community theater dating from 1922 and regarded as the first in the United States. The building is a reproduction of the eighteenth-century home of the last Spanish governor of Louisiana. The wrought-iron balconies are original.

Stretching along either side of the square are the red-brick **Pontalba** buildings, built in 1850 as apartments by a Spanish baroness who lingered after the Louisiana Purchase; her family names, Almonaster and Pontabla, are memorialized in the intertwined A and P of the iron balconies. One of the buildings is owned by the city and one by the state, and, as originally intended, the upper floors are private apartments and the ground floors house shops and cafés. The apartment at 523 St. Ann St. is part of the Louisiana State Museum, which calls it the **1850 House** and maintains it with furnishings of that era. The 1850 House is open Wednesday through Sunday from 10 a.m. to 5 p.m., with hourly guided tours for $3 (568-6968).

FOR A BREATHER . . .

Weary travelers on foot can stop for a satisfying treat, Creole-style, at Café du Monde, on the corner of Decatur and St. Ann streets in the French Market. Sit down to its renowned rich, dark café au lait and a few of those irresistible sugar-dusted fritters known as beignets, and you'll be prepared to brave the rest of the French Quarter *sans* complaint!

The riverward end of the square is bounded by **Decatur Street,** where horse-drawn carriages line up to take tourists on rides, with inventive narratives provided by the drivers. The carriages roll from 9 a.m. to midnight daily; fares are $8 for adults, $4 for children. Across Decatur at the corner of St. Peter is the **Jackson Brewery,** a former beer-making plant turned into one of those ubiquitous festival marketplaces. The string of buildings along Decatur Street is called the **French Market,** parts of which date to the War of 1812. The market once throbbed with the cries of fishmongers, butchers and vegetable vendors, but a 1970s renovation filled it with gift shops and their ilk.

Between the brewery and the café, the steps of the **Moonwalk,** named after former Mayor Moon Landrieu, surmount floodwalls and levees to reach a wooden riverside promenade affording a panoramic view of the **Mississippi River.** The port of New Orleans is the city's raison d'être, and the river bustles with tankers and freighters and tugboats. For most of the city's existence, the riverfront has been strictly functional, and warehouses and wharves cut it off from the public. The Moonwalk, built in the 1970s, was the first attempt to provide access to the river, and the idea of a recreational riverfront picked up steam in the 1980s. **Woldenberg Riverfront Park** opened in 1989, stretching from near Jackson Square to the site of a major aquarium, set to open in September 1990, and showcasing marine life of the Americas. A riverfront streetcar line, with vintage cars collected from around the world, opened as part of the city's transit system in 1988 (fare 60 cents, exact change). The city has announced ambitious plans to expand the riverfront park, aquarium and streetcar line in the coming years.

Turning back to dry land, the view of Jackson Square from the Decatur Street end of the Moonwalk presents the plaza at its most stately, symmetrical and well-proportioned. Ahead and to the left, reaching six blocks back to Rampart Street and six blocks over to Canal Street, is the Upper Quarter, location of most of the shops and bars and restaurants of the neighborhood. To the right, back to Rampart and six blocks to Esplanade Avenue, is the more residential Lower Quarter. Directly behind St. Louis Cathedral is **St. Anthony's Garden**, a tiny private park flanked by two narrow alleyways.

THE UPPER QUARTER

The commercial, touristy **Upper Quarter** includes the strip joints and T-shirt shops of **Bourbon Street**, which is thronged almost every night but, despite is fame, is more tacky than titillating. It also includes the upscale antique stores of Royal Street.

Historic highlights of the Upper Quarter include the **Napoleon House** at the corner of **Chartres** and **St. Louis** streets, an early nineteenth-century home (with a late eighteenth-century wing) that legend says was offered to Napoleon by some admirers as a house in exile; it contains a quiet bar on the ground floor today. The **Omni Royal Orleans Hotel**, across Chartres Street, is a modern interpretation of its vanished predecessor, the St. Louis Hotel, which was the unofficial headquarters of French Quarter Creole society from its construction in the 1840s. The Chartres Street facade incorporates a fragment of stone arcade from the original structure. Across St. Louis from the hotel is a turn-of-the-century state building, planned for renovation as a courthouse. Although rather grand and imposing, it is deplored by preservationists for its architectural intrusiveness and for the demolition of a square block of vintage buildings that its construction entailed.

The police station at 334 **Royal Street** occupies an 1826 building that formerly served as the **Bank of Louisiana** and the state capitol. **The Historic New Orleans Collection**, a private research institution, is housed in a 1792 building at 533 Royal Street that is one of the oldest in the French Quarter. Its ground floor displays changing exhibits of New Orleansiana at no charge; at the rear of its lovely inner courtyard is the **Williams Residence**, with a lush 1940s interior reflecting the taste of the collection's benefactor. Hours are 10 a.m. to 4:45 p.m., Wednesday through Saturday, with tours of the residence $2 per person (523-4662).

The 1831 **Hermann-Grima House** at 820 St. Louis showcases up-to-the-minute American construction techniques of its era, and its furnished rooms are open for tours Monday through Saturday from 10 a.m. to 3:30 p.m., with a $3 admission fee (525-5661).

THE LOWER QUARTER

The commercialism of the Upper Quarter ebbs in the blocks reaching across Orleans Street and stretching into the **Lower Quarter**. It is here, among the neoclassical town houses, Creole cottages and Victorian shotgun homes, that the genius of the nineteenth-century city neighborhood is revealed. It is unequivocally urban, with buildings crowded in cheek by jowl, and hardly a tree in site. But it is urban in a reassuringly human way, with low buildings of a modest scale, balconies to shield pedestrians from the sun and rain, and rich textures of wood, plaster and soft brick. It is a wonderful place for aimless strolling, with occasional stops to peer down dim passageways to shady hidden courtyards.

A rare wooden survivor of the devastating late-eighteenth-century fires that swept the French Quarter is the simple house at 632 Dumaine Street, known as **Madame John's Legacy**, so called after the title of a George Washington Cable short story featuring the home. It dates from about 1790. A few blocks away, at 1110 Chartres Street, is the substantial **Ursuline Convent**, which was built around 1750 and is the oldest building in New Orleans. Across the street, at 1113 Chartres, is **Beauregard House**, an 1826 residence occupied briefly by Confederate Gen. P.G.T. Beauregard after the Civil War. The house, which adjoins a trim formal garden, is open 10 a.m. to 3 p.m. Monday through Saturday, with hourly tours for $4 (523-7257).

IRONWORK BEAUTIES

Take note of the buildings at the corner of St. Ann and Royal streets—they sport a spectacular collection of oft-photographed ironwork balconies. Only a few French Quarter balconies are authentic wrought iron, made by the centuries-old technique of hammering unpainted metal into geometric shapes and curves. Most are cast iron, the product of a nineteenth-century technology that can mass-produce more elaborate patterns from molds, but which results in a more brittle metal that must be painted to prevent rust.

The most impressive house museum in the French Quarter is **Gallier House**, at 1119-32 Royal Street, built in the mid-1800s by prominent local architect **James Gallier Jr.** as his private residence. Painstakingly restored, it is state-of-the-art, 1850s style, and filled with handsome period furnishings. It is open from 10 a.m. to 4:30 p.m. Monday through Saturday, and selected Sundays from noon to 4:30 p.m.. The tours, which cost $4 for adults, may be capped off with a leisurely cup of coffee on the enchanting second-floor balcony overlooking the street (523-6722).

On the edge of the French Quarter, at 400 Esplanade Avenue, is the red stone **Old U.S. Mint**, which was built in the 1830s and which minted coins until 1909. Part of the **Louisiana State Museum**, it houses permanent exhibits on the history of jazz and Mardi Gras, and is open Wednesday through Sunday from 10 a.m. to 5 p.m., with a $3 admission charge for adults (569-6968).

DOWNTOWN

Esplanade Avenue once was the grand promenade for the Creoles of New Orleans, that segment of the city's population rooted in the French-Spanish colonial period. Many of the great mansions have fallen on hard times, but the street is redolent of faded grandeur as it stretches beneath the live oaks from the river to Bayou St. John. At the bayou end, two miles from the river, is **St. Louis Cemetery No. 3**, with its rows of whitewashed, New Orleans–style above-ground tombs forming the eerie dwellings of a city of the dead; it's open Monday through Saturday from 8 a.m. to 4:30 pm. and Sunday 8 a.m. to 4 p.m. (482-5065). Also along the bayou, a few blocks away at 1440 Moss Street, is **Pitot House**, a 1790s West Indian-style home built as a weekend retreat by a Spanish grandee who lived in the French Quarter. Pitot House is open Wednesday through Saturday from 10 a.m. to 3 p.m., with admission $3 for adults (482-0312).

Across Esplanade from the French Quarter is **Faubourg Marigny**, a quaint and colorful neighborhood of mostly nineteenth-century houses, that is less formal and compact than the Quarter. Another old neighborhood on the Quarter's fringe is **Treme**, across **North Rampart Street** between **St. Philip Street** and Esplanade. It is the historic home of *les gens de couleur libres*, the mostly mixed-race "free people of color," who, in the years before the Civil War, developed a culture of artistic and economic accomplishment. Treme today is rather rundown and should not be visited on foot, but it still contains hints of its prouder past and exudes a certain tattered charm.

THE CITY OF THE DEAD

New Orleans may be unique among American cities in the appeal of its cemeteries, which are bona-fide tourist attractions in their own right. Because of the city's swampy underpinnings, the departed generally are laid to rest above the surface in wall vaults or in masonry tombs decorated with columns, pediments, urns and cherubs. The oldest and most famed graveyard is St. Louis Cemetery No. 1, on Basin Street, between St. Louis and Conti streets. Established in 1789, it is a crowded warren of crumbling, fern-draped tombs and timeworn grave markers, a haunting evocation of the city's storied past. Celebrated residents include voodoo queen Marie Leveau, whose supposed tomb is covered with crosses marked in chalk by seekers of good luck; Etienne de Bore, the city's first mayor; and Paul Morphy, the chess genius of the nineteenth century. The cemetery has a marked foot path and a few explanatory markers to guide visitors, but explorations should be undertaken with considerable caution; the cemetery is not in the best part of town. A good way to see St. Louis No. 1 is on a National Park Service tour, conducted at 9:30 a.m. daily, beginning at the visitors center, 916-918 N. Peters Street (589-2636). The cemetery gates are open from 8 a.m. to 4:30 p.m. Monday through Saturday and 8 a.m. to 4 p.m. Sunday (482-5065).

UPTOWN & THE GARDEN DISTRICT

The **French Quarter, Faubourg Marigny** and **Treme** all belong to downtown New Orleans, the neighborhoods that spread along the river downstream of Canal Street. Downtown is the traditional preserve of the city's Franco-Spanish population, which viewed with contempt and dismay the "Americans" who poured into the city after the Louisiana Purchase in 1803. Spurned by the elegant Creoles, the Americans settled uptown, across **Canal Street**. Although they may have lacked the social graces of the Creoles, the rough-and-tumble newcomers soon displayed superior mercantile instincts. Their commercial enterprises boomed and formed the foundation for what today is the city's skyscraper-studded **Central Business District**, or CBD.

Canal Street is the traditional main drag of New Orleans, and although it has lost its retail preeminence to suburban shopping malls, it still includes its share of shops and stores—and a precious number of the street's flamboyant nineteenth-century cast-iron facades have escaped defacing by twentieth-century renovations. The massive granite **U.S. Customs House** at 423 Canal was built in stages in the mid-1800s and features a spectacular Greek Revival atrium inside. (Open Monday through Friday from 8:30 a.m. to 4 p.m., 589-2976). The skyscraper **World Trade Center** at 2 Canal Street, at the river's edge, includes a 31st-floor observation deck that affords a panoramic view of the city; open daily 9 a.m. to 5 p.m., the charge is $2 for adults, $1 for children 6 to 12 and free for children under 6 (581-4888).

ST. CHARLES STREETCAR

Canal Street is the jumping-off point for the St. Charles Avenue streetcar, a historic attraction in its own right, and one that also provides a great way to explore uptown New Orleans. A ticket costs 60 cents exact change, and reboarding is another 60 cents each time. The line is the oldest continuously operating streetcar system in the world, dating to 1832. It is more than a tourist attraction, providing transportation to and from CBD offices for uptown commuters. The 1920s-vintage cars are carefully preserved, with mahogany seats, cloth window shades—and no air conditioning.

What Esplanade Avenue was for Creole New Orleans, **St. Charles** was—and to a greater extent still is—for the more prosperous American section uptown. As it reaches out from the CBD under its own canopy of live oaks, it boasts dazzling mansions from the nineteenth and early twentieth centuries, the homes of many of the city's past and present business and social leaders. And it is flanked by comfortable, shady residential neighborhoods that make Uptown something of a synonym for established wealth and prestige (although, in a pattern typical of New Orleans, some of the wealthiest blocks are around the corner from the poorest).

The first few blocks of the city uptown of Canal Street make up the Central Business District, with the usual assemblage of bank buildings and office towers. A bit of nineteenth-century commerical New Orleans lingers in the balconied brick buildings in the 300 block of **Magazine Street**, which is parallel to St. Charles and two blocks closer to the river.

Poydras Street, which cuts across St. Charles and Magazine four blocks from Canal, is the city's high-rise highway, lined by Houston-style skyscrapers of recent vintage. Many of them were built for the oil industry; one of them, the 51-story **One Shell Square** building, at St. Charles and Poydras, is the city's tallest. Several blocks further away from the river on Poydras is the **Louisiana Superdome**, a vast domed stadium that is the home of the **New Orleans Saints** football team. (It was also the site of the 1988 Republican National Convention.)

A half-block uptown of Poydras, between St. Charles and **Camp Street**, is **Lafayette Square**, originally intended as the Americans' counterpart to Jackson Square. The jewel of the square is **Gallier Hall** on St. Charles. The psuedo-Greek temple, designed by noted local architect **James Gallier Sr.**, served as City Hall from 1853 until the 1950s. Now used for miscellaneous city purposes, it's open 9 a.m. to 5 p.m. Monday through Friday (524-5066).

Just up the street from the square, at 716 Camp St., is **St. Patrick's Cathedral**, a granite-looking plaster and wood church in the English Gothic Revival style, that appears much as it did when it was consecrated 150 years ago; it's open Monday through Friday from 11:30 a.m. to 12:30 p.m., Saturday from 3 p.m. to 5:45 p.m., Sunday from 8 a.m. to 1 p.m. (525-4413). A bit further uptown, on **Julia Street** between Camp and St. Charles, is a line of attached brick town houses, known as **Julia Row**, that made the block the swankiest address in town 150 years ago. After a long decline that turned the stretch into **Skid Row**, the buildings have been restored and now house artists' lofts and galleries, although some of the hoboes are still around.

A block and a half beyond Julia on St. Charles is **Lee Circle**, dominated by a statue of Confederate Gen. Robert E. Lee, atop a 100-foot column. Along the edge of the circle is the **K & B Plaza** and its contemporary headquarters building of a regional drugstore chain. An impressive collection of modern sculpture fills the marbled terrace around the building, and more contemporary art hangs in the lobby, open to the public Monday through Friday from 8 a.m. to 5 p.m. and Saturday from 8 a.m. to noon (586-1234).

ROOM WITH A DOME

A $200-million architechtural extravaganza, the Louisiana Superdome is a familiar sight to sports fans all over the world as the home of the Super Bowl (and New Orleans's less famous Sugar Bowl). The enormous white dome and its shimmering metallic enclosing wall house the largest "room" in the world: it can seat more than 72,000 cheering fans for a football game, and more than 95,000 people when used as an auditorium.

Guided 40-minute tours of the Superdome are offered at 10 a.m., noon, 2 p.m. and 4 p.m. daily; the fee is $4 for adults, $3 for seniors and children from 5 to 12. For more information, call 587-3310.

On the river side of Magazine, stretching from Poydras to the **Mississippi River** bridge approaches, is the New Orleans version of SoHo: the **Warehouse District.** Given a boost by the 1984 world's fair along the riverbank, the area of blocky, low-lying nineteenth- and twentieth-century warehouses has been transformed into an emerging trendy neighborhood of high-tech apartments for the singles set, with art galleries grouped along Julia Street and a scattering of hip bars, restaurants and coffee shops.

The crowning glory of uptown New Orleans is the **Garden District**, a paradisiacal enclave whose heart is bounded by St. Charles, Magazine and **Jackson** and **Washington** avenues. Between the 1830s and 1850s, New Orleans was a raging boomtown built on the flourishing river trade. Millionaires were minted by the bushel, and they staked out the turf on what was then the edge of the city to display their wealth in grandiose palaces. Mostly Anglo-American, they set their homes amid green lawns of the type the English called gardens.

The coming of railroads and civil war dimmed the luster of New Orleans's golden age, but the mansions of the cotton factors and tobacco magnates remain, their fluted columns and lofty parapets bespeaking the grandeur of days gone by. Many members of the city's aristocracy continue to live in the splendid houses, and the quiet streets, draped in luxuriant live oak, include some of the most desirable addresses in the city.

The homes are not open to the public, but no trip to New Orleans is complete without a stroll through the neighborhood. The **National Park Service** conducts tours of the Garden District, starting daily at 2:30 p.m. at St. Charles Avenue and First Street (589-2636).

The **Toby House** at 2340 Prytania Street, on the corner of First Street, is a fine example of a raised Greek Revival cottage, with front and side galleries. It is the oldest home in the district, dating from 1838.

First Street in the Garden District is one of the loveliest residential settings in New Orleans—or anywhere else. The house at **1331 First** is an examplar of grace and proportion, with slender cast-iron columns and filigree adorning the masonry facade. Down the black at **1315 First** is a larger version, little changed from its antebellum origins and including a charming carriage house in the rear. At **1239 First**, the two-story front gallery is supported by gleaming white wood columns in Doric, Ionic and Corinthian styles. Jefferson Davis, president of the Confederacy, died in the stately home with a lovely side garden at **1134 First**.

The house with outbuildings at **2605 Prytania** at Third Street is the only example of Gothic Revival in the neighborhood. A block away, at **1448 Fourth St.**, stands a rambling mansion on a large lot, surrounded by a distinctive cornstalk iron fence. In the 1400 block of Washington Avenue is **Lafayette Cemetery No. 1**, where ancient tombs and towering magnolias lend an air of melancholy mystery. The gates are open from 7:30 a.m. to 2 p.m. Monday through Friday and 7:30 a.m. to noon Saturday. Save Our Cemeteries, a private preservation group, conducts tours of the cemetery Mondays, Wednesdays and Fridays at 10:30 a.m. for a fee of $5 per person (589-2636).

The Garden District's predecessor, known as the **Lower Garden District**, is centered around **Coliseum Square** several blocks downtown of Jackson Avenue, between Coliseum and Camp streets. The Lower Garden District is less well preserved than its uptown brother, and some of its finest buildings were lost to bridge construction in the 1950s, but it has benefited from recent renovations, and expresses some of the nouveau riche strivings of the antebellum steamboat kings. The decaying mansion almost hidden behind a riot of vegetation at **1221 Orange St.**, near its intersection with **Felicity Street**, fairly drips with romance. It was featured as the home of the photogapher Ernest J. Bellocq in the movie *Pretty Baby*, which starred the young Brooke Shields as a fledgling prostitute.

Out beyond the Garden District, at 3811 St. Charles Avenue, is the remodeled 1883 home of a tobacco dealer that is now the **Columns Hotel**; its richly paneled lobby and bar served as the interiors for *Pretty Baby*. The house is one of many Gilded Age mansions that line the avenue for several miles. In the 6300 block of St. Charles is **Loyola University**, a private Jesuit school, and next to it is **Tulane University**, a private, nonsectarian school. Across St. Charles from them is **Audubon Park**, a sylvan retreat, with jogging paths and a golf course, as well as a first-class zoo, between Magazine Street and the river.

HISTORIC HOUSES & BUILDINGS

Beauregard House

1113 Chartres St., French Quarter • 523-7257

Built in 1823, the house was briefly the residence of Confederate Gen. P. G. T. Beauregard. It was carefully restored in the twentieth century by the late novelist Francis Parkinson Keyes (*Dinner at Antoine's*). The house includes nineteenth-century furnishings and the Keyes apartment and there is a nice formal garden, too.

Open Mon.-Sat. 10 a.m.-3 p.m. Admission $4.

Gallier Hall

545 St. Charles Ave., Central Business District • 524-5066

A striking Greek Revival temple at Lafayette Square that served as City Hall for a century, the building was designed by James Gallier, Sr., a noted local architect, and built in 1845–1850. It is now used for various municipal purposes.

Open Mon.-Fri. 9 a.m.-5 p.m.

Gallier House

1119-32 Royal St., French Quarter • 523-6722

This painstakingly restored midnineteenth-century home of prominent local architect James Gallier, Jr., features period furnishings and use of *faux* marble and *faux bois* techniques.

Open Mon.-Sat. 10 a.m.-4:30 p.m., occasionally Sun. noon-4:30 p.m. Adults $4, senior citizens & students $3, children 6-12 $2.25.

Hermann-Grima Historic House

820 St. Louis St., French Quarter • 525-5661

The house, built in 1831 by a wealthy merchant, includes period furnishings and changing historic exhibits.
Open Mon.-Sat. 10 a.m.-3:30 p.m. Admission $3.

Historic New Orleans Collection

533 Royal St., French Quarter • 523-4662

The collection, a posh private research center, offers changing exhibits of New Orleans artifacts in one of the oldest buildings in the French Quarter, as well as tours of its benefactor's 1940s residence.
Open Tues.-Sat. 10 a.m.-4:45 p.m. Gallery exhibits free; house tours $2.

Longue Vue House & Gardens

7 Bamboo Rd., Carrollton • 488-5488

This twentieth-century residence on the city's edge was laid out along the lines of an English country estate by a Sears, Roebuck, heiress. It includes extensive and elaborate gardens, antique furnishings and exhibits of modern and decorative art.
Open Tues.-Sat. 10 a.m.-4:30 p.m., Sun. 1 p.m.-5 p.m. Admission $5.

Old U.S. Mint

400 Esplanade Ave., French Quarter • 568-6968

Part of the Louisiana State Museum, it includes exhibits on the history of jazz and Mardi Gras in an 1830s building that minted coins until 1909.
Open Wed.-Sun. 10 a.m.-5 p.m. Adults $3, children 13-17 and senior citizens $1.50.

Pitot House

1440 Moss St., Bayou St. John • 482-0312

Pitot House is a late-eighteenth-century home, built on Bayou St. John as a weekend getaway by a wealthy Spanish resident of the French Quarter. Its wide galleries reflect Caribbean architectural influences.
Open Wed.-Sat. 10 a.m.-3 p.m. Adults $3, children under 12 $1.

St. Louis Cathedral

615 Père Antoine Alley, French Quarter • 525-9585

The cathedral is the queen church of the New Orleans archdiocese and the focal point of Jackson Square. It was built in 1851 and has been remodeled since World War II. Not at all grand, on the order of Notre Dame or Chartres, it is nonetheless forthright and solid.
Open daily 7:30 a.m.-7 p.m.; free guided tours every 15 minutes 9:30 a.m.-4:45 p.m., except at lunchtime.

St. Patrick's Church

724 Camp St., Central Business District • 525-4413

The church is a 150-year-old English Gothic Revival gem, with wood and plaster simulating stone vaulting.
Open Mon.-Fri. 11:30 a.m.-12:30 p.m., Sat. 3 p.m.-5:45 p.m. & Sun. 8 a.m.-1 p.m.

MUSEUMS & DISPLAYS

American-Italian Renaissance Foundation Museum
537 S. Peters St. (2nd floor), Central Business District
• 891-1904

The small musuem offers exhibits on the achievements of Italian-Americans.
Open by appointment. Admission free.

Amistad Research Center
Tilton Hall, Tulane University, 6823 St. Charles Ave., Uptown
• 865-5535

Primarily a scholarly archive of African-American history (and considered one of the best in the United States), the center houses documents, papers and some artwork.
Open Mon.-Sat. 8:30 a.m.-5:30 p.m. Admission free.

Blaine Kern's Mardi Gras World
233 Newton St., Algiers (west bank)
• 362-8211

The tour takes in the workshops of the city's leading builder of colorful Mardi Gras floats.
Open Mon.-Fri. 10 a.m.-4 p.m. Admission $2; guided tours $3.50 adults, $2 children under 12 (includes admission).

Confederate Museum
929 Camp St., Central Business District
• 523-4522

The museum holds one of the finest collections extant of Civil War uniforms, along with flags, weapons, maps and other items.
Open Mon.-Sat. 10 a.m.-4 p.m. Adults $3, students & senior citizens $2, children under 12 $1.

Contemporary Arts Center
900 Camp St., Central Business District
• 523-1216

Reopened in the fall of 1990 after renovation, the CAC is the hip response to the established museums, with changing exhibits of the latest work by local, regional and national artists, as well as plays and other performances.

K & B Plaza
1055 St. Charles Ave., Central Business District
• 586-1234

This modernistic headquarters of a regional drugstore chain hangs outstanding works by internationally known contemporary artists in its lobby and displays impressive modern sculptures on the surrounding plaza.
Open Mon.-Fri. 8 a.m.-5 p.m., Sat. 8 a.m.-noon. Admission free.

Louisiana Children's Museum

428 Julia St.,
Central Business District
• 586-0725

The museum features hands-on stuff for kids, including a miniature supermarket, port and coffee factory.
Open Tues.-Sun. 9:30 a.m.-4:30 p.m. Admission $3.

Louisiana Military History & State Weapons Museum

Jackson Barracks,
6400 St. Claude Ave.,
Lower Ninth Ward
• 278-6242

The museum includes weapons and other military memorabilia.
Open Mon.-Fri. 7:30 a.m.-3:30 p.m. Admission free.

Louisiana Nature & Science Center Joe Brown Park,

5600 block of Read Rd.,
Eastern New Orleans
• 246-5672

The center includes a wildlife preserve on 86 acres in suburban eastern New Orleans. Nature trails, a natural-history museum and a variety of programs for adults and children are among its offerings. Planetaruim shows are $1 extra.
Open Tues.-Fri. 9 a.m.-5 p.m., Sat.-Sun. noon-5 p.m. Weekdays adults $2, children 2-17, $1; weekends adults $3, children $2.

Louisiana State Museum

751 Chartres St.,
French Quarter
• 568-6968

Three buildings in Jackson Square: Cabildo (closed for repairs); Presbytere, flanking St. Louis Cathedral and 1850 House, 523 St. Ann Street. The Presbytere houses changing exhibits on state history and culture. The 1850 House is a restored residence of the antebellum era (last guided tour 3 p.m.). Also part of the museum, the Old U.S. Mint, housed in an 1830s building that minted coins until 1909, has exhibits on the history of jazz and Mardi Gras. (See also page 193).
Open Wed.-Sun. 10 a.m.-5 p.m. Adults $3 per building, students and senior citizens $1.50, children under 12 free; discounts for two or three buildings.

Louisiana Superdome

Sugar Bowl Dr.,
Central Business District
• 587-3810

This vast domed stadium is the home of the New Orleans Saints football team and was the site of the 1988 Republican National Convention.
Open daily for guided 40-minute tours at 10 a.m., noon, 2 p.m. & 4 p.m. Adults $5, senior citizens and children 5-12 $5.

Musée Conti Wax Museum

917 Conti St.,
French Quarter
• 525-2605

Displays include historic New Orleans figures and Mardi Gras exhibits.

Open daily 10 a.m.-5:30 p.m. Adults $4.95, children 4-17 $2.95.

New Orleans Historic Voodoo Museum & Gift Shop

724 Dumaine St.,
French Quarter
• 523-7685

This store displays and sells voodoo artifacts and offers walking tours, cemetery tours, swamp tours and special rituals (prices vary).

Open Sun.-Thurs. 10 a.m.-6 p.m. (10 a.m.-sundown in summer), Fri.-Sat. 10 a.m.-8 p.m. Adults $4, students and senior citizens $3, children 5-12 $2.

New Orleans Museum of Art

City Park
• 488-2631

NOMA is the city's mainstream art museum, centered in a 1912 neoclassical building, with the usual permanent collections surveying the history of art. It is strongest in photography, the decorative arts and non-Western art. It also displays traveling exhibits, including occasional blockbusters. A major expansion is planned.

Open Tues.-Sun. 8 a.m.-5 p.m. Admission $3.

Pharmacy Museum

514 Chartres St.,
French Quarter
• 524-9077

Located in an apothecary shop opened in 1823 by what is believed to have been America's first licensed pharmacist, the exhibits include phials, potions, elixirs and equipment of nineteenth-century pharmacies.

Open Tues.-Sun. 10 a.m.-5 p.m. Admission $1.

Ripley's Believe It or Not Museum

501 Bourbon St.,
French Quarter
• 529-5131

The New Orleans branch of this chain includes more than 400 oddities.

Open daily 10 a.m.-midnight. Adults $4.50, children 7-12 $2.75.

Rivertown

Williams Blvd.,
Kenner

Rivertown is a modest collection of museums and shops near the Mississippi River in suburban Kenner, about 25 minutes from the center of New Orleans. Museums include the Freeport McMoran Daily Living Science Center & Planetarium, 409 Williams Blvd. (468-7229). It is open Tuesdays through Saturdays from 9 a.m. to 5 p.m. and on Sundays from 1 p.m. to 5 p.m. Adults will pay $1.50, seniors $1, children 17 and under, 50 cents. Educational and participatory exhibits of a washing machine, vending machine and other everyday products are included, and sky shows are mounted in the planetarium.

BEACHES

The marshy Louisiana coast provides few accessible beaches. The closest beaches to New Orleans are about an hour east along the Gulf Coast of Mississippi, beginning at Pass Christian. They are not particularly appealing, having been made artificially from dredged sand, and the water is murky, flat and often shallow well offshore. Real beachgoers from New Orleans head farther east, to Gulf Shores in Alabama or points east of that on the Florida Panhandle. The drive is close to four hours, but the beaches are spectacular, with sugary white sand and clear blue-green water roiled by a moderate surf.

CEMETERIES

Cemeteries in New Orleans are tourist attractions in their own right. Because of the swampy soil, the departed generally are laid to rest above ground, often in elaborately decorated tombs and vaults. The resulting cities of the dead can be beautiful, haunting and evocative, as well as chronicling the long history of New Orleans. The native citizenry is not at all squeamish about cemeteries, which frequently coexist comfortably with homes in residential neighborhoods.

Lafayette Cemetery No. 1

Washington Ave. & Prytania St., Garden District

With lofty magnolias shading its tombs, the cemetery, established in the mid-1800s, fits in well in the leafy Garden District. Save Our Cemeteries, a private preservation group, conducts tours Mondays, Wednesdays and Fridays at 10:30 a.m. (589-2636). The fee is $5.

Open Mon.-Fri. 7:30 a.m.-2 p.m., Sat. 7:30 a.m.-noon.

St. Louis Cemetery No. 1

Basin St., between St. Louis and Conti Sts., Treme
• 482-5065

St. Louis No. 1 is the oldest cemetery in the city, dating to 1789. Its ancient brick walls are filled with burial vaults and its grounds are packed with fading, moss-covered tombs. It is said to include the tomb of voodoo queen Marie Leveau, marked with hand-drawn crosses by good-luck seekers. There's a marked footpath and descriptive plaques, but the cemetery is in a rundown neighborhood and the safest way to see it is on a National Park Service walking tour.

Open Mon.-Sat. 8 a.m.-4:30 p.m., Sun. 8 a.m.-4 p.m.

St. Louis Cemetery No. 3
Esplanade Ave. at Leda St., Bayou St. John
• 482-5065

A safer, spiffier version of St. Louis No. 1.
Open Mon.-Sat. 8 a.m.-4:30 p.m., Sun. 8 a.m.-4 p.m.

St. Roch Cemeteries
1725 St. Roch Ave., Gentilly
• 945-5961

In addition to the usual whitewashed tombs, St. Roch, which was established in 1874, includes a Gothic chapel (closed Sundays) dedicated to St. Roch and festooned with protheses associated with prayers for health.
Open Mon.-Sat. 8 a.m.-4:30 p.m., Sun. 8 a.m.-4 p.m.

PARKS & WILDLIFE EXHIBITS

Audubon Park
6500 Magazine St., Uptown
861-2537

Audubon Park, in an upscale neighborhood in uptown New Orleans, is a compact (385-acre) and well-tailored retreat. Its front section, between St. Charles Avenue and Magazine Street near Broadway, includes a 1.8 mile paved oval that rings lagoons, a golf course and picnic grounds and is popular with joggers and bicyclists. Its other half, between Magazine and the river, includes the zoo, a swimming pool, a riding stable, tennis courts, athletic fields and a riverside walkway offering a panoramic view of the Father of Waters.
Open daily 24 hours.

Audubon Zoological Garden
6500 Magazine St., Uptown
• 861-2537

Audubon is a world-class zoo, with 1,500 species of animals in spacious habitats on 55 acres. Exhibits include Grasslands of the World, with rhinoceros, antelope and other grazing animals, and the Asian Domain, featuring elephants and exotic cats. There's a hands-on natural history museum, a live-animal wildlife theater and a petting zoo for children. A prize feature is the Louisiana swampland exhibit, with abundant native flora and fauna. The Cotton Blossom riverboat (586-8777) makes round trips to the zoo from the foot of Canal Street. Fare is $7.75 for adults round trip, $5.25 one way (zoo admission extra). For an afternoon's adventure, a high-speed catamaran makes the trip back and forth from the zoo to the recently opened Aquarium of the Americas in the French Quarter (see page 218).
Open daily 9:30 a.m.-5 p.m. Adults $6.50, children under 12 $3.

City Park

City Park,
Gentilly
• 482-4888

With 1,500 acres, City Park is the largest in the city and the fifth-largest urban park in the country. Its farthest reaches are almost rustic. The New Orleans Museum of Art stands near its main entrance at the end of Esplanade Avenue. The park harbors extensive lagoons (some offering good bass fishing), a rose garden, picnic grounds and abundant vegetation. Recreational facilities include 39 tennis courts, four golf courses, a golf driving range, baseball, volleyball and soccer fields, rowboats and canoes for hire, and a small amusement park with a restored antique carousel and a miniature train.

Open 24 hours daily. New Orleans Botanical Garden: open daily 10 a.m.-4:30 p.m., admission $1.50, children under 12 free. Storyland (a children's play area filled with plaster Mother Goose characters): open Wed.-Sun. 10 a.m.-4:30 p.m., admission $1.50, children under 2 free. Live pony rides: open Sat.-Sun. 10:30 a.m.-4:30 p.m., charge 50 cents to $1. Amusement park: open Sat.-Sun. 11 a.m.-5:30 p.m., admission $2 (includes three 50-cent ride tickets).

Lake Pontchartrain

Lake Pontchartrain is a vast expanse of shallow brackish water that isn't actually a lake, but an enclosed bay, linked by narrow straits to the Gulf of Mexico. The water is too polluted for swimming, but the lake is popular with sailors, fishermen and windsurfers. A ribbon park extends for five miles along its southern shore in the city, with plenty of room to stroll or picnic while taking in the spectacular view. It's often crowded on sunny summer weekends with sunbathing teenagers.

Open daily 7 a.m.-10 p.m.

Louis Armstrong Park

901 N. Rampart St.,
Treme
• 522-0592

Named for the native son who become the international ambassador of jazz, Armstrong Park is an inner-city park of 31 acres adjoining the French Quarter. It includes walkways, bridges, lagoons and lawns. Congo Square, in the N. Rampart–St. Peter street corner, once was a spot where slaves gathered on Sunday afternoons to dance and play the music that historians believe contributed to the development of jazz. Considerable caution should be exercised in Armstrong Park, which is surrounded by poor neighborhoods.

Open daily 8 a.m.-10 p.m.

Woldenberg Riverfront Park & Aqwarium of the Americas
French Quarter
861-2537

Woldenberg Park opened in 1989 on fourteen acres of French Quarter riverfront between Toulouse and Bienville streets, adjoining the site of the lavish Aquarium of the Americas, opened in September 1990. The park includes walkways, benches, shrubbery beds, a bandstand and a sweeping view of the river.

The aquarium, which, with the park, cost about $42 million, showcases 7,000 animals of 750 species in four major exhibit areas at Bienville Street on the riverfront. The Amazon River Rain Forest Habitat recreates a slice of the Amazon Basin, complete with fish, trees, orchids, free-flying birds, butterflies, snakes and even sultry jungle air. The Caribbean Reef Environment features a transparent walk-through tunnel to give visitors a fish-eye view of the colorful undersea world of a tropical ocean. The Mississippi River Delta Habitat brings the South Louisiana environment inside, with alligators, catfish and fierce snapping turtles. And the Gulf of Mexico Exhibit displays the rich marine life that flourishes around the artifical reef of an oil rig. Other exhibits spotlight creatures of the U.S. mountains, Galapagos Islands and elsewhere. The building also houses a restaurant and a gift shop. The aquarium is operated by the same agency that runs the Audubon Zoo, and a high-speed catamaran ferries visitors the seven miles from one to another in less than twenty minutes.

SPORTS

BOATING

City Park rents paddle boats, rowboats and canoes for exploring the lagoons for $5 to $6.50 an hour. For details, phone 482-4888. **Sailboats South** rents sailboats of nine to 36 feet by the hour or day from a marina on Lake Pontchartrain. Reservations required; call 288-7245.

FISHING

Louisiana is a fisherman's paradise. In south Louisiana, the vast saltwater marshes teem with redfish and speckled trout, while the deep waters of the Gulf of Mexico are home to tuna, blue marlin, tarpon and a host of other species. Louisiana resident saltwater licenses are $5.50 for the season; nonresident licenses are $8.50 for two days. Both are available at the state **Wildlife and Fisheries Building,** 300 Chartres Street, open Monday through Friday from 8 a.m. to 4 p.m. (568-5636).

Several fishing guides in the New Orleans area offer charter boat trips. Among them:

Captain Nick's Fishing Charters

1052 Sandalwood Dr., Harvey
• 361-3004

Boats leave Joe's Landing in Lafitte, about 45 minutes south of New Orleans, to fish Barataria Bay and offshore islands for redfish, speckled trout, striped bass and flounder, returning at 2 p.m. Tackle is provided and fish cleaning, food, lodging and transportation to the dock are available.

Departures daily 6 a.m. Cost $75 per person.

Pete Poole

229 St. Anthony St., Raceland
• 537-3263

Larry Robichaux

P.O. Box 463, Larose
• 693-7474

Both charters set out from docks along Bayou Lafourche and ply the coastal marshes in search of redfish and speckled trout. Tackle is provided.

Cost $95-$125 per person.

Phil Robichaux

4037 Hugo Dr., Marrero
• 348-3264

The charter sets out from Joe's Landing in Lafitte and seeks redfish and speckled trout in inland waterways to Grand Isle. Tackle is provided.

Cost $70-$125 per person; more expensive package includes fuel, sandwiches, drinks and fileting and bagging of catch.

The **Venice Marina** (1-534-9357), in a small town about a 90-minute drive south of New Orleans, is home to an array of charter boats and guides. Bass boats for one or two fishermen, with a guide, are available for $100 to $150 a day and troll the marshes; larger boats for these inshore waters, carrying up to five fishermen, are available for $150 to $300 a day. Big boats that can carry more than a dozen anglers to the blue water offshore run $350 to $600 a day. High-rolling anglers can take an overnight trip to a fishing camp on the coast.

Louisiana Fishing Lodge
P.O. Box 507,
Golden Meadow
• 798-7117

Accommodations on uninhabited offshore island with access to coastal and deep-water fishing. Licenses available at lodge. Includes bus and boat transportation from New Orleans International Airport, lodging, meals and equipment.
Cost $195 per day. Air transportation $150 round trip additional.

For more modest, do-it-yourself ventures, small boats for marsh excursions can be rented closer to the city. Fishermen must provide their own gear. Two rental outlets near the city are:

Gulf Outlet Marina
Paris Rd.,
Chalmette
• 277-9980

About 20 miles from the city. Flat-bottom skiff (fifteen footer) with fifteen-horsepower motor, $30 a day, gas extra.

Gilbert Cousin's
US 11 south of Slidell
• 1-643-5432

About 25 miles from the city. An eighteen-foot flat-bottom skiff with a seven-and-one-half-horsepower motor and gas will cost $25; a ten-horsepower motor about $30.

There's also surprisingly good bass fishing in the middle of New Orleans, from dawn to dusk in the lagoons of City Park, where no boat is required. A one-day park fishing permit is $1.50 for adults and $1 for children under 16, available at the Casino building in the park (483-9371). Strictly speaking, state fishing licenses also are required; the casino sells seasonal freshwater licenses for residents for $5.50; non-resident licenses are available at the state Wildlife and Fisheries Building, 300 Chartres St., for $8.50 for two days and $10.50 for seven days (568-5636). The lagoons are off-limits for a short time in spring spawning season.

GOLF

Both of the city's easily accessible major parks operate public golf courses.

Audubon Park
• 861-9511

Eighteen holes.
Greens fee $8 weekdays, $10 weekends.

City Park
• 483-9396

Four eighteen-hole courses.
Greens fee varies; Adults $6-$7.75 weekdays (students & senior citizens $5), $8-$10 weekends. Driving range, $2.25-$3.50; lessons available.

HORSEBACK RIDING

Cascade Stables in Audubon Park offers guided, hour-long trail rides of two miles through the park for $20 a horse, and pony rides for small fry for $2. Daily from 9 a.m. to 4 p.m. 891-2246.

HORSE RACING

Fair Grounds

1751 Gentilly Blvd., Gentilly
• 944-5515

Thoroughbred racing, since 1872.
Open Nov.-Apr. Post time Wed.-Thurs. & Sat.-Sun. at 1 p.m., Fri. at 3 p.m. General admission $1; reserved grandstand seats $1 weekdays, $1.50 weekends and holidays; club house admission $4. General parking $2; valet parking $3 additional.

Jefferson Downs

1300 Sunset Blvd., Kenner
• 466-8521

Thoroughbred racing in the suburbs.
Open Apr.-Nov. Post time 6:30 p.m. Wed.-Sun. Apr. & May, Thurs.-Sun. June-Nov. Grandstand admission $1, clubhouse $2.

TENNIS

Both of the city's easily accessible major parks operate public tennis courts.

Audubon Park

• 895-1042

There are ten synthetic clay courts.
Open 8 a.m.-sundown. Cost $6 per hour.

City Park

• 483-9383

There are 39 courts and equipment rentals.
Open 7 a.m.-10 p.m. (until 7 p.m. in winter). Cost $4 per hour 7 a.m.-6 p.m., $5-$6 per hour 6 p.m.-10 p.m.

TOURS

BUS TOURS

Gray Line

2345 World Trade Center, Central Business District
• 587-0865 (information), 587-0861 (reservations)

Departures and ticket office by Jackson Brewery and Toulouse Street in French Quarter. Major hotel pickups. Reservations required. Basic two-hour city tour hits French Quarter, St. Charles Avenue, the Garden District, Lake Pontchartain and spots in between.

Gray Line also offers a night city tour with a restaurant dinner, as well as long and short plantation tours, combination bus/boat tours of the river and of swamps and a bus/boat/streetcar tour of Audubon Zoo and St. Charles Avenue. Prices, duration and departure times vary.

Departures of basic city tour at 9 a.m., 11:45 a.m. & 2:30 p.m.; $15 adults, $8 children.

Machu Picchu Tours

4450 General DeGaulle Ave., Ste. 1117, Algiers
• 392-5118, 392-4865

The firm offers a standard city tour of three hours, departing at 9 a.m. and 1 p.m. It also offers a plantation tour and a swamp tour. All tours available in Spanish, German, French and Italian.

Standard tour cost is $20.

Tours by Isabelle

P.O. Box 740972, New Orleans
• 367-3963

A three-hour city tour is available. Others include swamp and plantation tours of various lengths and combinations. Narration is available in Spanish, German, French and Italian.

City tour cost is $20.

RIVERBOAT TOURS

The poor man's riverboat tour is the ferry that crosses the Mississippi River from the foot of Canal Street on the east bank to the Algiers neighborhood on the west bank. It affords a great view of the central business district skyline—and it's free for pedestrians (cars $1 round trip). Departures every half hour from 6 a.m. to 9 p.m. 364-8100.

Several excursion companies offer tours of one to five hours on boats departing from wharves in the French Quarter and Central Business District, and many operate tour desks at the major hotels. Among them:

Audubon Express

The Audubon Express, a high-speed catamaran, makes eighteen-minute trips between the Aquarium of the Americas and the Audubon zoo.

Cajun Queen

New Orleans Paddlewheels, International Cruise Ship Terminal, Poydras St. Wharf • 524-0814

The *Cajun Queen* takes a one-hour cruise of the harbor and Chalmette Battlefield.

Departure at 3 p.m. from Riverwalk shopping center, foot of Poydras St. in Central Business District. Adults $10, children $6.

Cotton Blossom

New Orleans Steamboat Co., Ste. 2340, World Trade Center • 587-0740, 586-8777, (800) 233-2628

The Cotton Blossom sternwheeler cruises seven miles upriver to Audubon Park and zoo (zoo admission extra).

Departures from foot of Canal Street at 9:30 a.m., 12:15 p.m. & 3 p.m. Adults $8.50 round trip, $5.50 one way; children 2-12, $4.25 & $3.25.

Creole Queen

New Orleans Paddlewheels, Inc., New Orleans International Cruise Terminal, Poydras St. Wharf • 524-0814

The sternwheeler takes a three-hour narrated harbor cruise with a stop at Chalmette Battlefield; narration tapes are available in Spanish, French, German, Italian and Japanese. Also, night cruises with jazz and dinner depart at 8 p.m.

Daily departures from Riverwalk at 10 a.m. & 2 p.m. Day cruise: adults $12, children 3-12 $6. Dinner cruise $34.

Natchez

New Orleans Steamboat Co. • 586-8777, (800) 233-2628

The *Natchez* takes a two-hour narrated cruise of the harbor. It also makes a two-hour dinner cruise departing at 6:30 p.m. nightly, $29.75 and $15, and a two-hour moonlight dance cruise departing at 10 p.m. Saturday, $10.75.

Daily departures of two-hour cruise at 11:30 a.m. & 2:30 p.m. from Jackson Brewery at St. Peter St. Adults $10.75, children 3-11 $5.50.

WALKING TOURS

National Park Service

916 N. Peters St., French Quarter • 589-2636

French Quarter tours daily at 10:30 a.m., 1 p.m. and 3 p.m., beginning at the visitors center at 916 N. Peters Street; a St. Louis Cemetery No. 1 tour daily at 9:30 a.m., beginning at the vistors' center (reservations required); a *tour du jour*, with subjects changing daily, at 11:30 a.m., beginning at the visitors' center; and a Garden District tour, daily at 2:30 p.m., beginning at the corner of St. Charles Avenue and First Street. All tours free.

Friends of the Cabildo

701 Chartres St., French Quarter • 523-3939

Beginning at the Presbytere in Jackson Square, the tours are conducted by a private museum support group and publisher of historic architecture texts. The price includes admission to two of three Louisiana State Museum buildings: Presbytere, 1850 House or Old U.S. Mint.

French Quarter tours Tues.-Sat 9:30 a.m. & 1:30 p.m., Sun. 1:30 p.m. Adults $7, senior citizens & guests 13-20 $3.50.

OUT OF NEW ORLEANS

CAJUN COUNTRY

Despite what Hollywood would have you believe, New Orleans is not Cajun (although, like other places, it has been recently inundated with instant "Cajun" restaurants, dance halls and other exotica). Cajun culture is essentially rural, native to the swamps, bayous and grassy prairie of southwest Louisiana. Its fringes reach toward New Orleans, but its heart is in the region centered on the city of Lafayette, just under three hours west.

The first Cajuns were French refugees exiled from Nova Scotia, Canada, by the English in 1765. They called their homeland Acadie (Acadia in English) and themselves *les Acadiens* (Acadians), later corrupted to 'cajuns, or Cajuns. French and Catholic, they were alienated from the English-speaking Protestants who filled up northern Louisiana, and they were cut off from the rest of the world by a watery geography that made land travel difficult. They developed and sustained a distinctive folk culture, marked by richly spiced cooking based on crawfish, turtle, alligator and other local fare, an infectiously rhythmic music played with fiddle and accordion, and strong bonds of kinship and community. Ironically, as their core culture has been eroded by the onslaught of twentieth-century communication and transportation technology, their food and music have become popular across the country, with upscale Cajun cafés sprouting from New York to Los Angeles, and zydeco in every record store.

Because Cajun culture is simple and rustic, it is not easy to see: it did not produce impressive architectural monuments à la Jackson Square (although there are a couple of noteworthy antebellum mansions in the area), and even the fabled cooking is more at home in farmhouse kitchens than restaurant dining rooms.

LAFAYETTE

Lafayette, the unofficial capital of Cajun country, was a roaring boomtown during the oil bonanza of the 1970s that transformed the region; the subsequent price collapse brought severe unemployment and recession. Lafayette includes the tourist attraction called **Acadian Village** (200 Greenleaf Rd.; 318-981-2489 or 318-981-2364), a re-creation of a nineteenth-century community with restored period buildings and a museum, open from 10 a.m. to 5 p.m. daily, with adult admission $4 and $1.50 for children aged 6 to 14 . Also in Lafayette is the authentic **Grant Street Dance Hall**, for doing the down-home two-step (113 Grant St.; 318-237-8513). The town hosts the **Festival International de la Louisiane** in late April, featuring dance, drama and music from French-speaking countries around the world, and **Les Festivals Acadiens** in mid-September, which offers music, food and folk crafts. Near the city, outside Carencro on Interstate 49, is **Enola Prudhomme's Cajun Café** (4676 Northeast Evangeline Throughway, 318-896-7964), run by the sister of the celebrated New Orleans chef, Paul Prudhomme. It's open from 11 a.m. to 10 p.m., Tuesday through Saturday, and from 11 a.m. to 2:30 p.m. on Sunday.

OUT OF LAFAYETTE

The little towns and villages around Lafayette are closer to the real thing. **St. Martinville**, twelve miles to the south, is a throwback to the old days, with Cajun French spoken alongside English in the streets and shops. It was the setting for Longfellow's poem "Evangeline," the tale of ill-fated love in exile. St. Martinville includes the 1844 **St. Martin du Tours Church**, known as the mother church of the Acadians, as well as an antebellum courthouse and hotel. The Longfellow-Evangeline State Commemorative Area in St. Martinville is host to no fewer than three festivals: the one-day **Journée de Famille** in mid-April, which includes storytelling, hayrides and zydeco music; the **Louisiana Parks Potpourri** in mid-May, a state festival of historic crafts; and **Fun on the Bayou** in mid-June, with pirogue races on Bayou Teche and boat-building displays.

Breaux Bridge, six miles east of Lafayette, is home to **Mulate's** (325 Mills Ave.; 318-332-4648), a famed restaurant and dance hall. The owner is hoping to open franchises around the world. It's open from 7 a.m. to 10:30 p.m., Monday through Saturday, and from 11 a.m. to 11 p.m. on Sunday. The town's annual crawfish festival in early May salutes the inimitable mudbug in food, eating and peeling contests, a parade and musical performances. In **Henderson**, twelve miles east of Lafayette, they dish up Cajun crawfish specialities at **Robin's Restaurant** (Hwy. 352; 318-228-7594), open from 9 a.m to 10 p.m. daily.

Natural attractions in Cajun country include **Avery Island** (318-365-8173), where the McIlhenny family of Tabasco sauce fame has developed a wildlife park and luxuriant tropical garden atop a salt dome rising from the surrounding marsh. The park and garden are open from 8 a.m. to 5 p.m. daily; admission is $4.50 for adults and $3.50 for children ages 6 to 12. The hot-pepper-sauce factory is there, too, open for free tours Monday through Friday from 9 a.m. to 3:45 p.m. and Saturday from 9 a.m. to 11:45 a.m., although the machinery doesn't operate on the weekend.

The **Atchafalaya River Basin**, 25 miles to the east of Lafayette, is a vast expanse of tangled swamp, the archetypal setting for the (now only remembered) rough-hewn cabins of Cajun trappers and fishermen. **McGee's Landing** in Henderson (Rte. 5 [Box 689], Breaux Bridge; 318-228-8519 or 318-228-2384) offers two-hour tours of the basin at 10 a.m., 1 p.m., 3 p.m. and, in the summer, 5 p.m. The cost for adults is $7.50, with children ages 2 to 12 $4; reservations are recommended. A similar excursion is offered by **Basin Boat Tours** at Whisky River Landing in Henderson (c/o Whiskey River Landing, P.O. Box 111, Cecilia; 318-228-8567) at the same departure times, with adults $7 and children under 12, $4.

Shadows-on-the-Teche is a gracious, restored antebellum plantation home in **New Iberia**, twenty miles southeast of Lafayette (317 E. Main St., New Iberia; 318-369-6446), open daily from 9 a.m. to 4:30 p.m.; admission is $4 for adults and $2 for children aged 6 to 11. **Chretien Point**, at a century and a half one of the oldest Greek Revival plantation homes in the state, is twenty miles north of Lafayette in **Sunset** (Rte. 1 [Box 162], Sunset; 318-662-5876); it's open from 10 a.m. to 5 p.m. daily, with a $5 admission charge for adults and $2.50 for children under 12.

CHALMETTE BATTLEFIELD & ST. BERNARD

Jean Lafitte National Historical Park, Chalmette Unit

8606 W. St. Bernard Hwy., Chalmette
• 589-4430

New Orleans and the Louisiana Purchase had been in American hands just a dozen years when the city was threatened by an invading British army during the War of 1812. General Sir Edward Pakenham and 5,300 of His Majesty's finest troops landed south of the city. On January 8, 1815, at Chalmette Plantation, they met a hastily asssembled American force of 4,000 men, including Kentucky backwoodsmen, Louisiana militia, Choctaw Indians, free men of color, some pirates led by Jean Lafitte and just a few hundred regular troops, all under the command of General Andrew Jackson.

The Americans gathered behind a muddy rampart, stretching from the Mississippi River to a cypress swamp, and the British obligingly marched out of a thick fog directly into Jackson's line, to be mowed down by American sharpshooters. Pakenham was killed and his force suffered 2,000 casualties; American losses totaled six dead and seven wounded. Neither side knew that a peace treaty had been signed in Europe weeks before (although it was not ratified until after the battle). The victory made Jackson a national hero and put him on the road to the White House.

Today, the battlefield is a national historical site. Located six miles south of the French Quarter on La. 46 just over the New Orleans–Chalmette line, its 164 acres include a small museum, and markers showing battle lines and

troop movements, as well as a reconstruction of the American rampart. The visitors' center is housed in a classic white-columned antebellum plantation home.
Open daily 8 a.m.-5 p.m. Admission free.

Jean Lafitte National Historical Park, Islenos Unit

1357 St. Bernard Hwy. (La. 46), St. Bernard • 682-0862

The vestiges of one of the more unusual chapters in Louisiana history lie down La. 46, deep in St. Bernard Parish: the story of the Islenos. It dates to the period of the Spanish ownership of Louisiana, from 1763 to 1801. In the late 1770s, fearing British reprisals for Spanish aid to American colonists in the Revolutionary War, Spain sponsored a migration of several thousand settlers to Louisiana from the Canary Islands, which lie 500 miles west of Morocco in the Atlantic Ocean, and which had been colonized by Spain in the fifteenth century. Four settlements of islanders, or Islenos, were established to guard the approaches to strategic points in south Louisiana, but the need for the settlements soon faded and the settlers were left to their own devices. The remote St. Bernard settlement along Bayou Terre-aux-Boeufs retained its cultural identity the longest, although the immigrants turned to fishing and trapping to make their livelihood, as their marshy territory was well suited to those pursuits. Other than a sizable number of Perezes, Nunezes, Morelos and the like among the old families of St. Bernard, there are few traces of Isleno heritage today. The small museum occupies a modest home about twelve miles south of the Chalmette Battlefield, and there's an old cemetery farther down the road, on the other side of Bayou Terre-aux-Boeufs.

The settlements in which the Isleno descendants clustered still offer a glimpse of the vanishing way of life of south Louisiana fishing villages, for years isolated by bayous, marshes and bad roads. About 40 minutes from New Orleans at the very end of La. 300, a spur of La. 46 below the museum, is the community of Delacroix. The mobile homes and modest ranch houses that straggle alongside its single street aren't much to look at, but the bayou side of the road is lined with fishing boats, and an endless expanse of glimmering marsh stretches to the horizon.
Open daily 8:30 a.m.-5 p.m. Admission free.

PLANTATIONS

New Orleans has always been a very urban place, but it is very deep in the Deep South, and the aura of moonlight and magnolias still lingers not far away. In fact, several of the city's neighborhoods were developed from classic Southern plantations. The landed gentry were French, rather than English or Scotch-Irish, and the crop was sugarcane rather than cotton, but the economics were the same: vast holdings with large slave labor forces produced immense wealth, a portion of which was spent on stunning mansions that rival anything Georgia or Alabama has to offer.

In south Louisiana, most of the estates fronted on the natural highway of the Mississippi River, and the great steamboats would pull right up to the plantation dock. Today, the route to the fabled past reaches west from New Orleans, along the river roads on either bank of the Mississippi. Several glorious temples to an age gone by are within easy driving distance of the city.

EAST BANK

Ashland–Belle Helene

7497 Ashland Rd., Geismar
• 473-1328

Ashland–Belle Helene is one of the most richly evocative plantation homes in the state, lying on a little side lane off the river road. Its haunting appeal comes not so much from its columned grandeur as from its state of mouldering decay. The 1841 mansion has not been much restored: the grounds are untidy, the pearly stucco is fading and some of the floors are rotted away, but there's still an intact central hallway and a three-story spiral staircase (only the upstairs has been completely restored).
Open daily 10 a.m.-5 p.m. Adults $4; children 12 & under free.

The Cabin Restaurant

Hwy. 44 & Hwy. 22 (Box 85), Burnside
• 473-3007

11/20
CAJUN/TRADITIONAL CREOLE

Between Houmas House and Tezcuco, and a mile inland, is The Cabin Restaurant, which began in a 150-year-old slave cabin from the defunct Monrore Plantation. The original cabin has been enlarged with the addition of another authentic slave hut, and other cabins have been brought to the property. Dining rooms are decorated with antique tools. The Cabin serves a regional menu of fried seafood, po' boy sandwiches, gumbo and red beans as well

as fish and steak entrées, with dinner prices up to $24 per couple, including wine.
Open Mon.-Wed. 8 a.m.-3 p.m., Thurs. 8 a.m.-9 p.m., Fri.-Sat. 8 a.m.-10 p.m. & Sun. 8 a.m.-6 p.m. No cards.

Destrehan

9999 River Rd. (Box 5), Destrehan
• 764-9315

The oldest intact plantation home in the lower Mississippi Valley, Destrehan is about 25 miles west of New Orleans, fewer than 10 miles beyond the airport. Built in 1787, the hip-roofed mansion on four acres features a graceful row of smooth columns, supporting a broad gallery shading large windows on the two-story facade; the West Indies–influenced architecture, designed to be cool and breezy, is typical of early Louisiana plantation houses. The flanking *garçonnières*, which were bachelors' apartments for the owner's sons, were added in 1812.
Open daily 9:30 a.m.-4 p.m. Adults $5, senior citizens $4, children 6-11 $3.

Houmas House

Rte. 1 (Box 181), Convent
• 562-3929, 473-7841

Houmas House comes close to the romantic ideal of what a plantation should be. About an hour's drive from the city, it is a good choice for a single quick dip into the *Gone With the Wind* past. The large and imposing Greek Revival mansion sits on a broad sweep of lawn, shaded by towering, ancient, live oaks. The big mansion is attached by a carriageway to a modest house behind it that dates from the 1700s. The period furnishings include a large collection of Louisiana wardrobes, or armoires. Houmas House was built at the outside point of a hairpin bend in the river, and erosion has taken away much of the original long drive from the house to the water's edge. A high grassy levee keeps the river in check now, but it also blocks the view. A walk to the top of the levee reveals a magnificent panorama, with two long arms of the Mississippi reaching into the distance.
Open daily Feb.-Oct. 10 a.m.-5 p.m. & Nov.-Jan. 10 a.m.-4 p.m. Adults $6, children 13-17 $4 & children 6-12 $3.

Ormond

8407 River Rd., Destrehan
• 765-8544, 885-3317

A mile and a half or so farther from the city than Destrehan, Ormond, a late eighteenth-century plantation, recently opened for tours. Ormond began to serve lunches and dinners of Lousiana cuisine and offer bed-and-breakfast service in mid-1990.
Open daily 10 a.m.-4:30 p.m. Adults $5, senior citzens $4 & children 6-12 $2.50.

San Francisco

Hwy. 44 (Drawer AX), Reserve
• 535-2341

With its flamboyant color scheme, elaborate gingerbread work and overwhelming cornice, San Francisco is a striking contrast in style to the restrained elegance of most of the other plantation homes in the area. The look is called Steamboat Gothic because of its resemblance to the gaudy sternwheelers. The mansion's name is a corruption of a French slang term alluding to the enormous cost of the home when it was built in 1856. The interior features impressive ceiling frescoes and period furniture, while the small grounds include two large cisterns for rainwater and a gazebo.
Open daily 10 a.m.-4 p.m. Adults $5.50, children 12-17 $3.75 & children 6-12 $2.50.

Tezcuco

3138 Hwy. 44, Darrow
• 562-3929

About an hour west of New Orleans, on a stretch of the river road, is this raised 1855 Greek Revival cottage, with roof dormers and a front gallery graced with wrought iron railings.
Open daily 10 a.m.-5 p.m. Adults $5, children under 12 $2.50. Overnight cottages rent for $60 to $125 a night, double occupancy, including full breakfast and tour.

WEST BANK

The west bank is "the other side of the river" from New Orleans, reached by the Huey P. Long Bridge in Jefferson Parish, the Hale Boggs Bridge at Luling-Destrehan and the Sunshine Bridge near Donaldsonville and Convent, or by free ferries at Reseve-Edgard and Lutcher-Vacherie. Crossings can be woven into a plantation tour route to combine the best of both banks.

Lafitte's Landing Restaurant

Access Rd. (Box 1128), Donaldsonville
• 473-1232
CAJUN/TRADITIONAL CREOLE

Lafitte's Landing, about a half hour west of Oak Alley, combines French finesse with Cajun zest, in a relocated 1797 house. From the rich and spicy gumbo or crawfish bisque and the quail, veal or shrimp to the bread pudding or butter-pecan cheesecake, the homey restaurant consistently shines. Lunch specials range from $4.95 to $15, entrées from $12.95 to $19.95. Dinner for two should run around $80, including wine. (See also review on page 59.)
Open Mon. 11 a.m.-3 p.m., Tues.-Sat. 11 a.m.-3 p.m. & 6 p.m.-10 p.m., Sun. 11 a.m.-8 p.m. Cards: MC, V.

Madewood

Rte. 2 (Box 478), Napoleonville
• 369-7151

A detour off the river road about fifteen miles down Bayou Lafourche leads to Madewood, a gracious 1848 home, with fluted Ionic columns supporting a grand neoclassical pediment. Madewood specializes in overnight accommodations, serving wine and cheese in the library, and an old-fashioned candlelight plantation dinner, family-style, to guests gathered around a large table in the main house, which includes nine guest rooms.
Open daily 10 a.m.-5 p.m. Adults $4, students $3 & young children $2. Overnight lodging from $85, with Continental breakfast, to $150, with dinner and a full breakfast, double occupancy.

Nottoway

Box 160, White Castle
• 545-2730, 545-2409, 346-8263

Nottoway is a grandiose and lavish Italianate mansion, one of the largest in the South, and it strains the archetypal form. Its 53,000 square feet comprise 64 rooms, including a 65-foot grand ballroom. The stupendous home took a decade to build and was finished in 1859, at the close of the great plantation era.
Open daily 9 a.m.-5 p.m. Adults $8, children 12 & under $3. Overnight lodging $120 a night double occupancy, including full breakfast and tour.

We're always interested to hear about your discoveries, and to receive your comments on ours. Please feel free to write to us, and do state clearly exactly what you liked or disliked.

Oak Alley

Rte. 2 (Box 10), Vacherie
• 523-4351 (New Orleans), 265-2151

Oak Alley lives up to its name, in spades. The handsome Greek Revival house, dating to 1839, lies at the end of a spectacular tunnel of 28 massive arching oaks, planted by an unknown French settler 100 years before the house was built. The owners rent the plantation's cottages to overnight visitors, at reasonable rates.
Open daily Mar.-Oct. 9 a.m.-5:30 p..m. & Nov.-Feb. 9 a.m.-5 p.m. Adults $5.50, children 13-18 $3 & children 6-12 $1.50. Restaurant open daily 9 a.m.-3 p.m. Overnight cottages from $80 to $107 double occupancy, including Continental breakfast.

SWAMPS & BAYOUS

New Orleans was hacked out from the fetid swamps and murky bayous of South Louisiana, a marshy land created by the alluvial deposits of the Mississippi River. Today, nearly 275 years after the founding of the city, much of New Orleans has been drained, dried or filled in, although some of the original landscape—or waterscape—remains, complete with alligators, snakes and other slippery creatures.

Bayou Jean Lafitte Cruise

New Orleans Steamboat Co., 1300 World Trade Center
• 586-8777, (800) 233-2628

The Bayou Jean Lafitte takes a five-hour narrated trip downstream, into the canals of the west bank and along Bayou Barataria and back again. Food and drinks are available on board.

Departures daily 11 a.m. from the Toulouse Street wharf near the Jackson Brewery in the French Quarter. Adults $13.75, children 6-12, $7.

Cajun Bayou Cruise

538 Madison St., Apt. D
• 244-7811, 583-8759

Cajun "Papa Joe" Ordogne takes travelers on a one-hour drive to his 30-foot open-air boat to cruise through the lush Bowie Swamp near Vacherie. His folksy narrative comes in English, Spanish or Cajun French. The six-hour trip includes Papa Joe's home-cooked lunch and a visit to his native village.

Hotel pickup by appointment at noon. Adults $40; children with parents $35.

Cajun Queen

New Orleans Paddlewheels, International Cruise Ship Terminal, Poydras St. Wharf
• 524-0814

The big boat heads downriver and then penetrates the canals and bayous of the west bank on a four-hour cruise. Food and drinks are available on board.

Departures daily 10:30 a.m. from the Riverwalk dock in the Central Business District. Adults $14, children 3-12 $7.

Cypress Swamp Tours

622 Napoleon Ave.
• 581-4501

The company's three-hour half-day tour includes a van ride across the Mississippi to the west bank and then a two-hour boat ride along Bayou Segnette. The seven-hour full-day tour includes a short van tour of the French Quarter and St. Charles Avenue, the Bayou Segnette boat ride, and then a drive to lunch (additional charge) outside Oak Alley plantation and a ferry ride to the east bank for a tour of San Francisco plantation (tour admission included).

Half-day tours by appointment at 8:30 a.m. & 12:30 p.m.; adults $35, children 3-12 $25. Full-day tours at 8 a.m.; $45 per person.

Honey Island Swamp Tours

106 Holly Ridge Dr., Slidell • 1-641-1769.

The Honey Island Swamp, an outstanding example of a freshwater bottomland hardwood swamp, lies along the Louisiana-Mississippi border about 45 minutes from New Orleans. The two-hour flatboat tours of the swamp are organized by Paul Wagner, a wetlands ecologist who lives near the swamp, and narrated by him or his assistants.
Open by appointment. Adults $35, children under 12 $20, with hotel pickup (less without transportation to the swamp).

Jean Lafitte National Historical Park, Barataria Unit

7400 Hwy. 45, Marrero • 689-2002

The park, located about 45 minutes from the French Quarter, on the west bank of the Mississippi River, offers an easy way to get an informed look at the area's unusual ecology, courtesy of the U.S. government. The spacious park includes an array of ecosystems: hardwood bottomland forest, cypress swamp, palmetto swamp, freshwater marsh and, of course, a bayou or two (a bayou is a small stream, usually slow moving). There are walking tours narrated by park rangers, self-guided tours along wooden walkways raised above the wetlands, and canoe tours. A visitors center provides maps and sells nature books.
Open daily 9 a.m.-5 p.m. Guided walking tours at 11:15 a.m. & 3:15 p.m.; canoe tours Sat.-Sun. 8:30 a.m. (by reservation). Admission free; canoe rentals $25.

Louisiana Swampfari Guide & Expedition Service

P.O. Box 23194, Harahan • 733-0251

A van picks up guests from major hotels early in the morning and takes them to the park, where they paddle their own flat-bottomed canoes, known as pirogues, on a four-hour guided journey through the backswamp.
Open by appointment; $35 per person.

Louisiana Swamp Tours

908 N. Sibley St., Metairie • 467-8020

A van picks up travelers at hotels in the morning between 8:15 a.m. and 8:45 a.m. and makes a second pickup in the afternoon between 12:30 p.m. and 1 p.m. There's a 45-minute ride to the boat landing in Crown Point and then there are two hours in a boat, with food served on the morning outing only.
Open by appointment. Adults $35, children under 12, $17.

New Orleans Tours, Inc.
4220 Howard Ave.
New Orleans
• 482-2077

Round-trip transportation to the park is provided, with hotel pickup at approximately 9 a.m. and the return at 1 p.m.
$20 per person.

Voyageur
Canal Street Dock
• 523-5555

The *Voyageur* takes a cruise downstream to the Chalmette Battlefield from the foot of Canal Street and then crosses the river to ply canals and bayous on the west bank, returning after five hours. Sandwiches and drinks are available on board.
Departures 10 a.m. daily from the Canal St. Dock in the Central Business District. Adults $9.50, children 6-12 $4.75.

CITYLORE

New Orleans was founded on an investment hoax so corrupt that today's insider trading scandals pale by comparison. John Law, a professional gambler from Scotland, became private adviser to Philippe, the Duke of Orleans, in the early 1700s. The duke allowed Law to establish a private bank and the Company of the Indies, through which Law then conducted a ruthless sales campaign to convince noblemen and rich businessmen in France to buy shares of stock in Louisiana land in return for gold, silver and diamonds from the New World. He then turned to the poor and rural people in Europe, offering them free land, housing and transportation if they would emigrate to Louisiana and work on developing the city of New Orleans.

When gold and diamonds did not materialize and takers for the plan were not as plentiful as needed, Law hired kidnappers to clean out the streets and dungeons of Paris, bringing their victims to ships, where they were shackled to the bulkheads, to be taken to Louisiana. Hundreds perished during the transatlantic voyage. The land was much harder to develop than expected, and skirmishes with the local native tribes, disease and discontent all worked against Law's scheme. In 1718, New Orleans was settled as a new city, named in honor of Law's patron. Two years later, the bubble had burst and Law fled Paris as a bankrupt fugitive. It is to the credit of Jean Baptiste LeMoyne, Sieur de Bienville, who governed Louisiana in those trying times, that the forests were cleared, sheds and barracks were built on stilts in the swampy terrain, and the small, struggling settlement on the curve of the Mississippi River managed to survive as the city of New Orleans.

COLORFUL POLITICS

Perhaps because of this inauspicious beginning, the city has always attracted a variety of adventurers, outlaws and speculators. Nonetheless, by the 1720s, New Orleans had attained a decidedly virtuous reputation. The Ursuline nuns were brought from France to operate a military hospital and to teach young girls of the colony; a busy port had developed along the river; the Code Noir, a set of laws that governed the owning and treatment of slaves, was in place; and the city became the capital of the whole Louisiana Territory.

Those early days did, however, establish Louisiana's freewheeling politics, a tradition that has lasted to the present. One of the early governors, the Chevalier de Kerlerec, dubbed *Chef Menteur* ("Chief Liar"), is honored today by Chef Menteur Highway, a major thoroughfare in eastern New Orleans. Two hundred years later, Governor Edwin "Silver Fox" Edwards fought for his political life against racketeering charges and narrowly won in a series of federal trials in New Orleans. Most famous, perhaps, is Governor Huey P. Long, the Kingfish, who built up one of the most powerful political machines in the United States with his "share the wealth" programs of the early 1930s. When, in 1934, the New Orleans mayor closed City Hall in opposition to Long and his machine, the Louisiana National Guard was sent to the city to reopen it forcibly under Long's supervision. The mayor could do nothing to stop him.

PEOPLE GUMBO

Because of its location on the river, and sandwiched as it is between Texas and Florida, New Orleans has become an international city. The laissez-faire attitude for which it is known derives from a mixture of cultures, languages and customs. Like one of its most famous dishes, New Orleans is itself a gumbo. The thick, browned-flour base, flavored with filé (ground sassafrass root), represents the original Native American, French, Spanish, African and Caribbean influences of the eighteenth century; the okra, sausage, chicken and seafood that form the bulk of this delicious stew are the Americans of British and Scotch-Irish ancestry and immigrants throughout the nineteenth century—German, Irish, Chinese and Italian laborers. The rich spices that give this gumbo its tongue-tingling flavor are the more recent immigrants from Latin America, Cambodia, Vietnam and the Soviet Union. All these nationalities, blended for years over a slow fire, imbue the New Orleans of today with its unique, rich flavor. Since tradition is deeply revered in this city, there are, naturally, a place and time for every culture to showcase its talents and contributions to the city's life. Hence the many festivals and parades that spring up each year like the ubiquitous banana trees in neighborhoods and city wards.

The Mardi Gras "Indians" (often called Black Indians) deck themselves out in their brilliantly colored handcrafted Indian costumes and dance along Orleans and Claiborne streets. The Italians take the spotlight on St. Joseph's Day, with a tour of fabulous altars to that saint in various homes and churches in Mid-City; Italian-American families prepare the homemade breads and foods weeks in advance in order to honor their patron in style. The Irish host a massive parade and street party on St. Patrick's Day in the Irish Channel, with young men, slightly inebriated, stopping to kiss the ladies along the route and hand them each a paper (or real) carnation. In New Orleans East, a lively outdoor Asian market materializes every Saturday, and once a year an Asian-American festival is held, during which first-generation Asian-American children imitate the dances and customs of their parents. This is to name but a few of the ethnic and cultural events forming part of the nonstop parade that is New Orleans.

THE OLD SQUARE

The wonderful thing about New Orleans, distinguishing it from many other American cities, is that much of its original center, the Vieux Carré (Old Square), or French Quarter, remains intact today. Although only one or two buildings date back to the 1720s, when Bienville first settled the area, the balconied facades that line the Quarter's narrow streets look today very much as they did during the 1800s, when they were built. This area came very close to being demolished in the early 1900s, but thanks to the foresight of several influential women, headed by Elizabeth Werlein, a commission was finally formed in 1936 and a moratorium declared on tearing down the formerly sumptuous Creole homes. Strict laws were passed regarding renovation and preservation of the area. No neon or flashing signs are permitted (except on Bourbon Street), buildings must be repainted in their original colors, and nothing can be altered on the exteriors of buildings. While property owners today sometimes chafe under the Vieux Carré Commission's inflexible standards and its meticulous attention to detail, everyone agrees that were it not for the conscientious enforcement of those standards, little, if any, of the Quarter would have been preserved for posterity.

The Quarter could easily have become a museum to the past if a vibrant residential and business community had not pulled together and continued living and working there, investing in the Quarter's future. Today, fortunately, that investment is paying off, and it is that lived-in quality that so attracts visitors to the Old City.

THE CREOLE CONTROVERSY

Creole cooking, Creole tomatoes, Creole gumbo—just what *does* Creole mean? In Louisiana, the term is often debated with an intensity normally reserved for political scandals or the pros and cons of instituting a state lottery. Historically, the name Creole was given to children born in the colony to French and Spanish settlers in the early 1700s. As the first generation of Creole children set up households, their belongings, including their African slaves, took on the name Creole. Thus, there were Creole horses, Creole carriages and Creole slaves. The food prepared by the family cooks became known as Creole cuisine, which today continues to be based on the original flavors and ingredients used by those families.

As the years passed, there was some mixing of young French men and free women of color in New Orleans under the socially accepted institution of *placage*, the placement of a young, free woman of color in the care of a French suitor. These liaisons frequently resulted in several children before the Frenchman went on to marry a woman of his own race and class. In the late 1700s there were large immigrations of Roman Catholic, French-speaking people, both white and of color, who were also known as Creoles.

The white Creole society as a unique social unit in New Orleans began to lose its status in post–Civil War days, when the city became thoroughly Americanized, but the Creoles of color maintained their own community well into the 1960s and the civil rights era. For that reason, you may still hear light-skinned African-Americans today in New Orleans referred to as Creoles, whereas white descendants of the French and Spanish settlers no longer call themselves Creoles. A "Creole townhouse" in the French Quarter, for example, inevitably refers to a house built for and occupied by white Creoles, and a "Creole cottage" refers to a house most often built for and occupied by Creoles of color. While the distinctions can be quite confusing to visitors, New Orleanians take them for granted, although the debate still rages locally as to whether the term "Creole," as applied to various things today, really means black or white, or both.

CREOLES VERSUS AMERICANS

In New Orleans, people refer to the median strip in the many wide avenues as a "neutral ground," and for good reason. There was a time, shortly after the Louisiana Purchase in 1803, when Canal Street served literally as a neutral ground between two rival governments and police forces, those of the Creoles in the old French city (today called the French Quarter) and those of the interloping Americans on the other side, where today you find the Central Business District and the Garden District, which they built.

To the Creoles, who had kept to themselves for a century and who had developed *la haute culture* of French opera, theater, fine arts and genteel style of living, these new English, Scotch-Irish and German settlers were brash, shamelessly aggressive and, above all, less cultivated—in short, not at all welcome. In the early 1800s, New Orleans was a divided city, and it was not unheard of for Creole gendarmes to conduct shooting forays across Canal Street at their opponents, and vice versa. Fortunately, this rift in city politics was eventually healed; today, all that remains of that era is the persistent term for the crepe myrtle–bedecked medians, the "neutral grounds."

INDIANS & PIRATES

From its earliest days, New Orleans had two adversaries—the Native American tribes who roamed the area, and the pirates, who waylaid ships on their way up the Mississippi. The Indians—the Acolapissa, Choctaw, Tunica, Natchez, Chitimacha, Houmas and Tangipahoa tribes, among others—had a working relationship with the founders and early settlers of the city. As in other areas of the country, Native Americans served here as guides through the swamps, introduced local foods to the Europeans, traded pelts and furs, and even on occasion sold their daughters to white men to be their homemakers. As late as the 1880s, Native American women were to be seen in and around the French Market with their woven baskets, vending herbs, spices and medicinal mixtures. But, as the Native Americans became less in demand economically, especially as they proved to be impossible as slaves, the French and Spanish saw them as a threat and built primitive walls around the city to ward off attack. Today, the street that marks the back of the French Quarter is still known as Rampart Street.

Wars against Europeans and intertribal skirmishes, disease and a diminishing food supply decimated the various Native American tribes in the eighteenth century. What remains of their once considerable influence is the filé (ground sassafrass root used in gumbo), and many place names (such as Tchoupitoulas Street), the term *bayou* for a natural water canal, and the name of the Mississippi River.

The pirates fared even worse than the Native Americans, and left even less written evidence to prove they ever had existed. For many years in the early 1800s, Jean Lafitte was the undisputed leader of a vast and nefarious network of outlaws in the many-channeled delta that lies between New Orleans and the mouth of the Mississippi River and the Gulf beyond. Lafitte, whose name is memorialized by a town in southern Louisiana, and by a street and a building in New Orleans, masterminded the hijacking of hundreds of ships entering the river, often killing or imprisoning the crew, and stealing the ships' cargoes to sell in his own black markets, set up throughout the swamps.

In an ironic twist of history, the colorful Lafitte turned patriot, and became a key player in the Battle of New Orleans in 1814 to 1815. General Andrew Jackson recruited him and his pirate band to alert the Americans about the British troops approaching from the mouth of the river, a crucial bit of intelligence at the time. Lafitte and his men were promised full pardons in exchange for their help, and Jackson, with some chagrin, was made to honor his promise after the war.

CAJUN CRAZE

A sure sign of a tourist is someone expecting to find Cajuns all over New Orleans. Although there are some recent restaurants and night spots in the city that specialize in Cajun food and music, the Cajun people have never lived in New Orleans or been part of its history. In 1755 and again in 1758, the Acadians (French colonists) were expelled from their Canadian homeland, Acadia, called Nova Scotia by the British. Some wandered for a long time down through the Louisiana Territory, following the Misssissippi River, and settled finally in areas south and southwest of New Orleans, around St. Martinsville. Their odyssey was beautifully recounted in 1847 by Henry Wadsworth Longfellow in his epic poem "Evangeline," about two lovers separated by the journey and eventually reunited in Louisiana. For the next century and a half, the Cajuns, as they came to be called, kept to themselves, fishing and trapping in the bayous and wetlands, which were somewhat similar to the coastal lands they had left in Canada. They had only minimal contact with the French settlers in New Orleans, and were considered a rural and isolated people.

The Cajun craze that has brought these resilient shrimpers and trappers into the national limelight in the past decade is due largely to the public relations aptitude and entrepreneurial skills of several Cajuns, including the rotund cook of blackened-redfish fame, Paul Prudhomme, musicians such as Doug Kershaw and Bruce Daigrepont and comedian Justin Winston. Even Hollywood has started to make several films on the bayou country and its quaint, accented inhabitants. With all this publicity, the lines between what was once Creole and Cajun began to blur, though to locals in New Orleans the distinction remains clear—a *fais do-do* (Cajun dance) with fiddles and accordions still has no resemblance to a Dixieland jazz session, though both are good times.

SPORTING HOUSES

A port city, New Orleans naturally inherits the reputation of an open, no-holds-barred sort of place. From the days of the keel-boat operators and the Kaintucks in the early 1800s to the multinational sailors of the modern shipping industry, men have drunk, brawled and loved in New Orleans.

Sporting houses, as they were called in a former era, or brothels, were a logical answer to the demand for wine, women and song. Beyond the gambling halls, the drinking establishments and the cribs where cheap prostitutes plied their trade, the sporting houses were the mainstay of the city's lucrative sex trade. These institutions were large, often elegantly furnished, Victorian houses, operated usually by an astute madame, who hired her own guards and paid off the police to protect her. The better places were known as parlor houses, and employed their own musicians to provide entertainment as the guests feasted at sumptuous tables, eventually stealing upstairs with whichever woman they fancied.

By the end of the nineteenth century, sporting houses had become so widespread in New Orleans that the municipal government passed a bill, introduced by alderman Sidney Story, to relocate all such houses, along with the accompanying gambling joints and bars, to a specific district on the outskirts of the French Quarter. Police would not patrol the area, but prostitutes would be required to register, pay taxes and submit to periodic medical examinations. Storyville, as the district was dubbed by locals, much to the chagrin of family man Story, became the first red-light district in the United States to be sanctioned and regulated by the government. A guide to the houses and entertainment in the district, the *Blue Book*, was published annually. Storyville lasted for a brief two decades (1897–1917), but its name lived on. Today, a government housing project stands on the land where

Storyville was situated. All the buildings, including some lavish sporting houses, were destroyed; a marker in the middle of Basin Street is now the only sign of the notorious district's former existence.

The tales of the goings-on in the sporting houses can more than fill a book. There was madame Kate Townsend, who kept two dozen girls in a luxurious house and was known for being able to drink liquor like any man. She and her live-in lover, Treville Sykes, had nasty fights, and in 1882, Townsend was found dead of stab wounds at the hand of Sykes. She was buried in a $600 dress, and fine Champagne was served at her wake. Miss Josephine Icebox was said to be the most frigid woman in the district. Prizes were offered periodically for the suitor who could "defrost" her. It is not known if any man succeeded. One of the house's names survives today, Lulu White's Mahogany Hall, in a jazz bar now located on Bourbon Street. In Storyville days, Lulu White, an octoroon (a person of one-eighth black ancestry, and thus fair-skinned) of West Indian heritage, operated one of the most celebrated brothels in America. She offered exotic women of mixed race, immortalized in such songs by her nephew, Spencer Williams, as "Mahogany Hall Stomp" and "Basin Street Blues." Her elegantly furnished pleasure palace was the last of the Storyville buildings to be torn down. Only the poignant photographs of the women of Storyville made by an enigmatic local photographer, Ernest B. Bellocq, give us a peek into the famous demimonde that was the district.

ALL THAT JAZZ

The development of jazz dates back before Storyville, but it became widely known only in the era when jazz musicians from across the city met to play in the sporting houses and bars of the district. Jazz greats such as Jelly Roll Morton, King Oliver, Kid Ory and Bunk Johnson, and, some say, even Louis Armstrong as a teenager, were hired to play in the sporting houses. In 1914, for example, statistics show that Storyville supported 750 working women, 300 pimps, 200 musicians, 500 domestic workers and 150 saloon employees. When Storyville was uprooted, in 1917, many of the musicians went upriver to St. Louis and Chicago to find work, taking with them that bawdy New Orleans sound that would eventually be recognized as the only indigenous American music. To identify jazz with Storyville alone is, however, not historically accurate, for there were many places outside the district where the music was created, played and refined.

BOURBON STREET

Although Bourbon Street, named for the Duke of Bourbon and not the drink, is today the center of French Quarter adult entertainment, it was once a quiet residential area, interspersed with small shops. After Storyville was closed down in 1917, the madames and their women, the saloon keepers and the gamblers spread out into the French Quarter, especially along Conti Street. Eventually, lower Bourbon developed into the nine-block stretch of strip joints, bars and music halls that it remains today, dubbed by some journalists the "'playground of the South."

VOODOO QUEEN

If you wander through St. Louis Cemetery No.1, behind the French Quarter, the tomb of Marie Laveau, famous voodoo queen of the 1800s, will greet you. Unlike any of the other aboveground vaults so typical of the city's burial places, her tomb bears a series of X's, made in chalk and shards of brick by present-day devotees who continue to evoke her power.

This is the most visible sign of a religion brought to the city in its earliest days by immigrants from the West Indies. In Catholic New Orleans, the potions and rituals of voodoo were exotic, but tolerated, and at the height of her reign, Marie Laveau is said to have attracted more white than black followers. A light-skinned black woman (and a hairdresser by trade), she was reputed to have extraordinary psychic powers, putting curses on her enemies and causing miracles of romance, riches and health for those who followed her intricate instructions. The elder Laveau was replaced by her daughter, who bore the same name and resembled her remarkably, thus giving devotees the belief that she was immortal. Today, although one often sees voodoo dolls with pins in them in gift shops, and although a voodoo priestess has an office in the French Quarter, it is rare to find people openly practicing voodoo as a religion. A close study of voodoo and the more recent santeria shows evidence of these Caribbean religious influences overlapping with Catholicism here as well as in Latin America.

MARDI GRAS

New Orleans is synonymous with Mardi Gras, and to read some accounts you would think that every day in the city is Carnival. Actually, Mardi Gras occurs only once a year, in the week leading up to Fat Tuesday, the day before Lent, which falls sometime between early February and early March. But the true New Orleanian spends much of the rest of the year preparing for this one citywide blast. Costumes have to be designed, elaborate balls planned, marching bands and majorettes trained, and money saved for the massive floats that ride through certain downtown and suburban streets night after night prior to Fat Tuesday.

Much of the uniqueness of New Orleans is in some way related to Mardi Gras. It is the only city in the country where children are let out of school and most businesses and offices close for a three-day span around Mardi Gras Day. King cake, a special circular braided loaf decorated with gold, purple and green (the colors of Mardi Gras), is sold in bakeries for several weeks leading up to Carnival Day. A small plastic baby hidden in the king cake brings delight to whomever discovers it, but it also means that that person must provide the next king cake the following day. Plastic beads, brightly decorated plastic cups and large metallic coins called doubloons are tossed by revelers from the floats during the parades; anyone who has gotten caught up in the madness of trying to catch one of these perfectly useless items and risked an arm or a leg in the jostling crowds to do so, inevitably winds up later wondering, "Why on earth did I do that?" Yet the fascination to join in the chant "Throw me somethin', mister!" is irresistible to even the most rational person.

Mardi Gras is the world's largest free party—the whole city joins in on Fat Tuesday, and the celebration lasts well into the night. Along St. Charles Avenue and into the French Quarter winds a river of people in the wildest costumes imaginable, all jovial, friendly and having a wonderful time. While it is true that Rex, King of Mardi Gras, is chosen from an exclusive club to ride through the streets on his throne and toast his queen, there is also some truth to the local saying that on Mardi Gras, everyone can be king or queen for the day.

BARONESS PONTALBA

In the 1840s, when the city was fast becoming Americanized, the most valuable land in New Orleans, the area around Jackson Square, fell by inheritance into the hands of a young and highly spirited woman, the baroness Micaela Pontalba. She was living at the time in Paris, where she had gone from her native New Orleans to marry her first cousin. They had been separated for some time, and when the baroness decided to return to Louisiana with her sons and claim her legacy, she was intercepted by her irate father-in-law. In a meeting in his private chamber, he shot Micaela three times; thinking her dead, the elder Pontalba pointed the rifle at himself and committed suicide.

Micaela recovered and was able to make the voyage to her home town. There, she directed the mammoth project of erecting two long brick apartment buildings, with ornate balconies and millwork, patterned after popular buildings in Paris of the day. Jenny Lind, the famous singer, was in town in 1850 when the apartments were dedicated. The baroness put Lind up in one of the apartments, had her conduct a concert from the balcony, and later sold every piece of furniture and all the linens Lind had used to collectors for a handsome price. No wonder Andrew Jackson, in the equestrian statue of him that decorates the center of Jackson Square, is situated so that he is tipping his tricornered hat in the direction of what was once the baroness's apartment!

WHERE Y'AT?

Don't be surprised to hear very little Southern accent in New Orleans. In fact, visitors often note that many people sound as though they have come straight out of Brooklyn, New York. Due to history, geography and immigration patterns, the N'Awlins accent is unique; most movie actors who try to imitate it fail. The *oi* vowel sound comes out as an *er* sound, "oil" becomes "earl" and "boil" becomes "burl." Yet, strangely, the *er* sound as a word ending is usually shortened and rounded, as in "motha" and "fatha." There are so many terms, phrases and designations used by New Orleanians that a booklet has been published to explain them all. "I stay by my sister's" translates as "I live with my sister"; "rench de close in de zink" means "rinse the clothes in the sink"; "makin' groceries by Swagman's" refers to going grocery shopping at a popular supermarket, Schwegmann's. A "po' boy dressed with lots of my-a-nez" means a thick sandwich on crisp French bread, with lettuce and tomato and lots of mayonnaise. "Suck da heads an' pinch da tails" is much less risqué than it first may sound—it instructs the visitor how to enjoy eating boiled crawfish (and yes, they're called *craw*fish, not *cray*fish, here!). Even directions have their own nomenclature in New Orleans. The curving river renders east-west and north-south indicators useless; more often, you'll be told to go two blocks toward the river or toward the lake. Apartments for rent are listed "above Canal" (Street) or "below Canal." Uptown and downtown are used to designate areas of the city, but there are so many other terms, such as Mid-City, Faubourg Marigny, Black Pearl, Gert Town and Gentilly, or designations by housing project (Desire, St. Thomas, Iberville), that finding your way is often confusing. If lost, you might try out the local greeting on a passerby—"Where y'at?" But don't expect an answer, because the question in New Orleans means, simply, "Hi!"

LANGUOR & CHARM

Much of the languour and charm of the deep South still survives in New Orleans. There really are moss-draped giant oak trees, mirrored in lagoons in the parks; horse-and-carriages still wend their way through the streets of the French Quarter; a lovely carousel with handpainted horses delights children and adults alike; the streetcar, just as in the 1930s when Tennessee Williams wrote *A Streetcar Named Desire* in his Royal Street apartment, still runs along the riverfront and up and down past St. Charles Avenue; and people carry parasols against the glaring sun or sit on iron-lace balconies sipping mint juleps and gin fizzes. Duels, settled in the days of the French by saber under the oaks in City Park, are still fought, but the weapon of choice is more often a handgun, the venue a housing project, and the victim a poor black youth. Like every other American city, New Orleans grapples with the problems of urban blight, pollution and unemployment. It's just that here, where the humidity is usually 90 percent or higher, where a big thirst can be quenched at drive-through daiquiri stands, and where a cavalier sense about doing things just as easily tomorrow as today reigns, the typical response to a problem, to anything, is *laissez les bons temps rouler!* Let the good times roll!

BASICS

AT YOUR SERVICE

ADDRESSES & TELEPHONE NUMBERS

- **American Express**, 158 Baronne St., Central Business District, 70112; 586-8201
- **Amtrak**, Passenger Station, 1001 Loyola Ave., Central Business District, 70113; 528-1610. **Reservations**, 800-872-7245 (800-USA-RAIL).
- **Chamber of Commerce**, 301 Camp St., Central Business District, 70130; 527-6900
- **City Hall** (mayor's office), 1300 Perdido St., Central Business District, 70112; 565-6400

CONSULATES

- **French**, 3305 St. Charles Ave., Uptown, 70115; 897-6381
- **Italian**, 630 Camp St., Central Business District, 70130; 524-2271
- **Japanese**, One Poydras Plaza, 639 Loyola, Ste. 2050, Central Business District, 70112; 529-2101
- **Mexican**, World Trade Center, Central Business District, 70130; 522-3596
- **Spanish**, World Trade Center, Central Business District, 70130; 525-4951

- **Greyhound-Trailways** bus lines, 1001 Loyola Ave., Central Business District, 70113; 525-9371

HOSPITALS

- **Uptown**, Touro Infirmary,1401 Foucher, 70115; 897-7011 (physician referral, 897-7777)
- **Southern Baptist**, 2700 Napoleon Ave., 70125; 899-9311 (physician referral, 362-8677)
- **Central Business District**, Tulane University Medical Center, 1415 Tulane Ave., 70112; 588-5263

- **Charity** (public), 1532 Tulane Ave., 70140; 568-2311
- **Emergency** (ambulance, fire, police), 911
- **Police routine**, 715 S. Broad St., Mid-City, 70119; 821-2222

POST OFFICES

- **Central Business District,** 701 Loyola Ave., Central Business District, 70113; 589-1136, 589-1036
- **French Quarter,** 1022 Iberville St., 70112; 524-0072
- **Uptown,** 3923 Carondelet St., 70115; 891-2816

- **Public Library,** 219 Loyola Ave., Central Business District, 70140; 529-7323, (529-READ)
- **Superdome ticket office,** Sugar Bowl Drive, Central Business District, 70113; 587-3800

TAXIS

- **United Cab,** 522-9771
- **Yellow-Checker Cabs,** 525-3311
- **White Fleet,** 948-6605

- **Tourist information,** 529 St. Ann St., French Quarter, 566-5031; airport 467-9276
- **Weather,** 465-9212

CRIME

For all its charm, New Orleans still is a large, twentieth-century American city, one with more than its share of poor neighborhoods plagued by drugs and violence. Although most dangerous areas are unlikely to be on a visitor's itinerary, and paranoia is unwarranted, prudence and caution are advised everywhere, as they would be in New York or Washington, D.C., for example. Crooks don't take vacations: an inebriated tourist reeling down the backstreets of the French Quarter late at night is a mugger's dream.

DIRECTIONS

The points of the compass are rarely used in New Orleans when giving directions. The city and its network of streets are defined by the geography of the Mississippi River and other bodies of water, and directions refer to them. "Uptown" as a direction, means upstream or upriver, while "downtown" means downriver. The other directions are "toward the river," referring to the Mississippi, and "toward the lake," meaning Pontchartrain. For example, the location of the Commander's Palace restaurant would never be referred to as the northeast corner of Washington Avenue and Coliseum Street, but rather as the downtown lake corner. As a very general rule, riddled with exceptions, "uptown" from the heart of New Orleans is more or less west, "downtown" is east, "toward the river" is south and "toward the lake" is north. (New Orleans is not alone in this method of telling directions. If you've been to Honolulu, you'll recognize the technique—in America's 50th state, directions are "toward the mountains," or "toward the ocean," and so on.)

It's also handy to remember that Uptown (capital U) and Downtown (capital D) are places within New Orleans, as distinct from directions. Uptown is the broad sweep of the city, stretching upstream from Canal Street, that includes the venerable residences of much of the social and economic elite of New Orleans. Downtown is a little trickier to define: historically, it meant the less prosperous, but more French-flavored, neighborhoods downstream of Canal; more recently it is heard, as in other parts of America, in reference to the main commercial area, which straddles Canal. Most New Orleanians are comfortable applying the term Central Business District to the commerical hub, or CBD for short.

The traditional points of the compass do appear in names of streets and some other features, but they often have nothing to do with reality. Streets that cross Canal Street without changing their names are known as North Whatever Street on the downtown side of Canal and South Whatever on the Uptown side, regardless of their orientation. For instance, the major street of North-South Claiborne Avenue runs mainly east-to-west. The interstate highway system does stick to the nationwide norm, with the route to Baton Rouge known as I-10 West and the way to Mississippi as I-10 East. Also, the side of the Mississippi River that includes the French Quarter, the Central Business District and most of New Orleans is known as the east bank, while the other side is known as the west bank, which makes sense only from a continental perspective—it is possible to watch the sun rise over the west bank from large sections of the east bank.

Mercifully, the street numbering system is quite regular. Addresses go up by 100 for each block away from Canal Street or the river, depending on the direction of the street. For example, 130 St. Charles would be in the first block off Canal, 215 in the second block, and so on. For streets running off the river, the pattern usually holds street to street (the 600 block of Conti Street, for instance, backs onto the 600 block of St. Louis Street), but because the river twists and turns, the address is not an absolute guide to distance from the water; for the same reason, the pattern is broken every so often to reset to zero and put the 100 block on the riverbank.

MORE *GAULT MILLAU* "BEST OF" GUIDES

The guidebook series known throughout Europe for its wit and savvy now reveals the best of major U.S., European and Asian destinations. Gault Millau books include full details on the best of everything that makes these places special: the restaurants, diversions, nightlife, hotels, shops and arts. The guides also offer practical information on getting around and enjoying each area. Perfect for visitors and residents alike.

Please send me the books checked below:

- ☐ The Best of Chicago $15.95
- ☐ The Best of France $16.95
- ☐ The Best of Hawaii $16.95
- ☐ The Best of Hong Kong $16.95
- ☐ The Best of Italy $16.95
- ☐ The Best of London $16.95
- ☐ The Best of Los Angeles $16.95
- ☐ The Best of New England $15.95
- ☐ The Best of New Orleans $16.95
- ☐ The Best of New York $16.95
- ☐ The Best of Paris $16.95
- ☐ The Best of San Francisco $16.95
- ☐ The Best of Washington, D.C. $16.95

PRENTICE HALL TRADE DIVISION
Order Department - Travel Books
200 Old Tappan Road
Old Tappan, NJ 07675

In the U.S., include $2 (UPS shipping charge) for the first book, and $1 for each additional book. Outside the U.S., $3 and $1.

Enclosed is my check or money order made out to Prentice Hall

Press, for $__________

NAME ______________________________

ADDRESS ______________________________

CITY ________________ STATE ________________

ZIP ________________ COUNTRY ________________

313/90

DRINKING LAWS

New Orleans is a party town, and it shows in the city's laws governing alcohol—or the lack of laws on the subject. Booze of every kind is sold over the counter at any time, day or night, in supermarkets, convenience stores and even gas stations. Bars can stay open 24 hours, and a number of them do; most others go several hours after midnight before last call. Virtually all bars offer customers plastic "go cups" for take-out drinks, which legally can be consumed on the street (but not from glass containers). The drinking age is 21, but anyone 18 and over seems able to buy drinks without much trouble. It's legal to drink while you drive, but it is against the law to drive while drunk, and the police are serious about enforcing that one.

FOREIGN EXCHANGE

The **Whitney National Bank** exchanges currency at its main office at 228 St. Charles Avenue in the Central Business District 70130, Monday through Friday from 9 a.m. to 2 p.m., and in the lobby of the New Orleans International Airport, Monday through Thursday from 8:30 a.m. to 3 p.m. and Friday from 8:30 a.m. to 5:30 p.m. (586-7272). **Deak International**, a private trading company, exchanges currrency at its office at 111 St. Charles Ave. in the Central Business District, Monday through Friday from 8:30 a.m. to 5 p.m. (524-0700), and on Concourse *C* at the airport, daily from 8 a.m. to 6 p.m. (466-4219).

LATE-NIGHT SERVICES

All of the companies listed below offer their services 24 hours a day, unless otherwise noted.

Babysitter

- **Kinder Friend** (469-5059) provides a 24-hour sitter referral service for any age child or adult in home or hotel room.

Car Repair

- **Mechanic on Wheels** (394-0157) provides anytime road service for minor repairs.

Dentist

- **Dr. Daryl Byrd**, at 10050 Morrison Rd., Eastern New Orleans, offers 24-hour emergency dental service for all ages; 244-8484.

Doctor

- **The Doctors Urgent Care** clinic at 4300 Houma Blvd., Metairie, offers 24-hour emergency care; 456-5780.
- **Doctors Home Care, Ltd.**, Ste. 305, 3715 Prytania St., Uptown, is open from Monday to Friday from 8 a.m. to 5 p.m., and staffed by doctors who make house calls; 899-6361.

Limousine

- **A Touch of Class**, 522-7565
- **London Livery**, 944-1984
- **Carey**, 523-5466
- **New Orleans Limousine**, 529-5226

Locksmith

- **City Wide Locksmith**, 525-7072
- **Rolland Locksmiths**, 586-1824
- **ABC Locksmith**, 581-6114

Newsstand

The 24-hour newsstand appears to have gone the way of the nickel phone call, at least in New Orleans, but **Lakeside News** (3323 Severn Ave., Metairie) is open round the clock (no phone). In the city, **Riverside News** (620 Decatur St., French Quarter; 522-6675) is open daily from 10 a.m. to 10 p.m., and **Sidney's News Stand** (917 Decatur St., French Quarter; 524-6872) is open daily from 8 a.m. to 9 p.m.

Pharmacy

- **Eckerd Drugs**, 3400 Canal St., Mid-City; 488-6661

Photocopying

- **Kinko's**, 762 St. Charles Ave., Central Business District; 581-2541

Pickup & Delivery

- **United Cab** (522-9771) has radio-dispatched cabs that can make pickups and deliveries 24 hours a day.

GETTING AROUND

AIRPORT

New **Orleans International Airport**, in suburban Kenner, is located within easy reach of the city, thirteen miles and twenty minutes west of the Central Business District via Interstate 10, where it has stood since the 1940s. Although it has expanded several times, it is still relatively small and fairly easy to get around. Like many airports, however, it always seems to be undergoing renovation, making for unusual traffic patterns and touches of Early Plywood decor.

Taxis provide the most convenient transportation to and from the airport. The fare is set at $18, plus tip, between the airport and most of the city, for up to three passengers; additional riders cost $6 apiece. **Rhodes Limousine Service** (943-6621 in New Orleans; 469-4555 at the airport) operates a van service at the airport. They pick up departing passengers at most hotels in the city and make the same stops on the way in; sometimes, they'll drop people off at in-between spots along the way. They take a little longer than taxis, but the vans are comfortable and the fare is only $7. **Park & Ride** (566-1010 or 800-874-5999) offers direct service by Cadillac limousine ($45 to airport, $55 from airport), touring van ($45-$55) and motorcoach ($75-$85). **Louisiana Transit** (737-9611) operates a bus between the airport and the corner of Tulane and Loyola avenues in the Central Business District, from about 5:30 a.m. to 6 p.m. The fare is $1.10, in exact coin change.

CAR

The usual array of rental cars is available at the airport and in the city. Many visitors won't need cars: most of the city's leading sight-seeing attractions, hotels and shopping areas, along with many of the top restaurants and nightspots, are in the French Quarter and adjoining Central Business District, which are covered easily on foot, or in neighborhoods a short streetcar or taxi ride away. For extended excursions to plantation or Cajun country, a car is recommended.

PUBLIC TRANSIT

The **Regional Transit Authority** operates buses throughout the city, as well as streetcars on the historic St. Charles Avenue line and the new Riverfront line. Bus service is extensive and convenient. Most buses, mercifully, are air-conditioned, and there also are some "kneeling" buses offering easy access for the handicapped. The **RTA Rideline** (569-2700) provides information (from an actual living person) on schedules, routes and the best way to get from here to there; for information on handicapped service, call 523-5428. The fare for most buses and the streetcars is 60 cents, exact change, with transfers to intersecting lines an extra 5 cents. Express buses, available only on certain routes, cost 75 cents, with, again, an extra 5 cents for a transfer. The **Easy Rider** shuttle bus, which loops through the Central Business District on Canal and Poydras streets, is 25 cents.

TAXIS

Hailing a cab in the street can be difficult. **United Cab** (522-9771) operates a large fleet of radio-dispatched taxis that can be summoned quickly. There are usually cabs available at the taxi stands in front of major hotels and at the airport. The fare is an initial $1.10, and then 10 cents for each additional tenth of a mile. Taxi drivers usually will provide pickup and delivery service. As befits the spirit of their city, New Orleans cabbies tend to be considerably more laid-back than their kamikaze counterparts in other parts of the country.

GOINGS-ON

MARDI GRAS

Called the "Greatest Free Show on Earth," it is all that and more, at once a grand public spectacle and a closely guarded local tradition that plays a major role in defining the city's sense of itself. Mardi Gras, which is French for "Fat Tuesday," is the day before Ash Wednesday, and the onset of Lent and self-denial. It is the frenzied culmination of a weeks-long period beginning January 6 (Twelfth Night), that is known as Carnival. The word "carnival" itself means, loosely, "farewell to meat." (In common usage, "Mardi Gras" and "Carnival" are almost interchangeable.) Carnival is the peak of the social year for established New Orleans society, and various Carnival clubs, called "krewes," stage formal private balls throughout the season.

The first of dozens of Carnival parades begin soon after Twelfth Night in outlying suburbs, but the big city parades start on the weekend ten days before Mardi Gras, with a parade each weekend day, and every night, through Mardi Gras itself. Mardi Gras parades are not like most other parades: they are put on by various krewes, which range from neighborhood clubs to elite blue-blood fraternities, and the krewe members toss plastic beads, aluminum doubloons and other trinkets from the moving floats to the surging mobs below. It is a hard-hearted spectator who does not get caught up in the excitement, screaming "Throw me something, mister!" and scrambling frantically to capture a worthless bauble.

Parades by old-line aristocratic krewes, such as Momus (Thursday night before Mardi Gras), Proteus (Monday night) and Comus (Mardi Gras night), feature torchbearers and krewe "dukes" on horseback. The giant nighttime parades by the newer, more democratic krewes of Endymion (Saturday before Mardi Gras) and Bacchus (Sunday) are phantasmagoric processions, with dozens of brightly lit floats and hundreds of costumed float riders bedecked in dazzling plumage and sequins.

Mardi Gras Day brings more parades, with the popular black krewe Zulu kicking off its funky parade early in the morning, followed by Rex, a big, old-line krewe, which honors one of its members as the King of Carnival, and, finally, at night, by Comus, the most elite krewe. The real show is in the streets, flooded by hundreds of thousands of costumed merrymakers as the city shuts down to party. The French Quarter is choked with crowds, especially where the gay Mardi Gras queens strut their elaborate finery.

All in all, it is an astonishing performance. Tales abound of visitors who came to New Orleans for Mardi Gras, fell in love with the place and never left. Those who do visit at the peak of Carnival should be advised that it is a hectic time, with traffic frequently tied up by the endless parades, and is ill suited to a leisurely sampling of the city's charms.

OTHER FESTIVALS

Louisiana is a festival-mad state. Given almost any excuse, folks will get together and celebrate with food and music, the twin staples of most festivals. The state tourist office says Louisianians put on more than 300 festivals a year. Most are pretty simple, with a few food booths (often serving the event's theme dish), some arts and crafts and a couple of live bands. They're very folksy, and offer visitors a chance to mingle with the natives.

Listed below are the major festivals in New Orleans or within about an hour's drive from the city, as well as other cultural events in the city. Festivals usually are held on weekends, so the precise dates vary from year to year. For further information on Louisiana festivals, call the **Louisiana Office of Tourism** in Baton Rouge at 342-8119.

JANUARY

- **Battle of New Orleans Re-enactment**, Chalmette. History buffs dress up in period uniforms to re-enact 1815 battle against British invaders. With food festival nearby.
- **Sugar Bowl**, New Orleans. College football on New Year's Day in major postseason bowl game. Superdome.

MARCH

- **Amite Oyster Festival**, Amite. Oyster eating, music.
- **Shemp Festival**, Donaldsonville. Campy tribute to the third of The Three Stooges, after Moe and Curly. Pie throwing.
- **Spring Fiesta**, New Orleans. Parade, historic house tours.

- **St. Joseph's Day**, New Orleans. Italian-Americans celebrate with French Quarter parade and, in the days before, by building distinctive cookie-and-cake altars in their homes, many of which welcome visitors. Real folk culture.
- **St. Patrick's Day**, New Orleans. Catch cabbages thrown from flatbed truck floats in an unpretentious but lively (and very New Orleans) parade through the Irish Channel neighborhood.

APRIL

- **French Quarter Festival**, New Orleans. Outdoor jazz brunch in Jackson Square, music and other events on stages in the Quarter.
- **Isleno Heritage and Cultural Festival**, St. Bernard. Arts, crafts, food, music in salute to eighteenth-century Canary Island immigrants.
- **Italian Festival**, Luling. Food, music, rides.
- **Jefferson Downs** race track opens. Thoroughbred racing to November, in Kenner.
- **Louisiana Crawfish Festival**, Chalmette. Crawfish races, crawfish to eat, and music.
- **Magnolia Festival**, Schriever. Beauty pageant, food and rides in a small town.
- **Ponchatoula Strawberry Festival**, Pontchatoula. Berries, bands and rides.
- **USF&G Classic**, New Orleans. PGA golf tournament. English Turn Country Club, Algiers (west bank).
- **New Orleans Jazz and Heritage Festival** (last weekend in April through first weekend in May). The Jazzfest is far more than just a run-of-the mill festival. It is a sprawling celebration of music and food that draws visitors from across the country and overseas; many of them return year after year to get down and get funky, New Orleans–style. The heart of the action is at the Fair Grounds racetrack during the day on Friday, Saturday and Sunday of both weekends. An incredible array of musicians, from obscure regional groups to nationally known performers, play jazz, rock, Cajun, gospel and other styles continuously on ten outdoor stages and in huge tents. The food is almost as big a draw, with dozens of booths serving regional specialities, such as crawfish, gumbo, red beans, catfish, shrimp and oysters, as well as many other offerings. The party spills over to nighttime concerts at clubs and auditoriums throughout the festival, which energizes much of the city. Admission to all the action at the Fair Grounds is $10 a day for adults, $2 for children aged 12 and under (advance tickets are $7 and $1.50). Parking costs $2 a day, while food and drink are extra. The gates open at 11 a.m. Tickets for nighttime cost from about $15 to $28.50. For information, call 522-4786 (or Ticketmaster, 800-535-5151).

MAY

- **Greek Festival**, New Orleans. Greek music, food and dance instruction.

JUNE

- **La Fête, New Orleans**. Intermittent celebration of food and culture.
- **Great French Market Tomato Festival**, New Orleans. City's top chefs compete in tomato cook-off. Plus food and music.
- **Jambalaya Festival**, Gonzales. Lots of the spicy rice casserole, music.
- **Kentwood Dairy Festival**, Kentwood. Booze-free tribute to dairy farmers.
- **Louisiana Antique Festival**, Ponchatoula. Old stuff, plus food and music.
- **Louisiana Catfish Festival**, Des Allemands. Famous catfish, plus music.

JULY

- **Louisiana Oyster Festival**, Galliano. Oyster-eating contests, music, rides.

AUGUST

- **New Orleans Saints** football (exhibition and regular season) begins and continues through December. Superdome.

SEPTEMBER

- **Harahan Railroad Fair**, Harahan. Salute to a New Orleans suburb's railroading past, with food, music and rides.
- **New Orleans Symphony** season begins. Performances to May. Orpheum Theater, 129 University Pl. 565-3680.
- **Le Petit Theater** season begins. Community theater performances, to July. Le Petit Theater du Vieux Carre, 616 St. Peter St., 522-2081.
- **Tangipahoa Black Festival**, Hammond. Wide range of music, exhibits, lectures.
- **Tulane University Green Wave** football begins. Home games at Superdome, to November.

OCTOBER

- **Andouille Festival**, LaPlace. Chicken andouille (it's a zesty Cajun sausage) gumbo and music.
- **Festa d'Italia**, New Orleans. Food, entertainment.
- **The Gumbo Festival**, Bridge City. Lots of music, lots of gumbo across the river.
- **New Orleans City Ballet** season begins. Four productions per season, in October, December, March/April and May. Theater of Performing Arts, Armstrong Park, 522-0996.
- **New Orleans Opera Association** season begins. Four productions per season, in October, November, December and March. Theater of Performing Arts, Armstrong Park, 529-2278.
- **Renaissance Festival**, Metairie. Musicians, magicians, dancers and troubadours in suburban New Orleans.
- **Slidell Food and Fun Fest**, Slidell. With baby contest and crafts.
- **Sorrento Boucherie Festival**, Sorrento. Parade, music, food.

NOVEMBER

- **All Saints' Day**, Lafitte. On the night of November 1, Cajun country folk gather in simple bayouside cemeteries, decorating the whitewashed tombs with flowers and candles and catching up on family news. Authentic Louisiana culture, worth seeing.
- **Destrehan Plantation Fall Festival**, Destrehan. Food and crafts on grounds of antebellum home.
- **Fair Grounds** racetrack opens. Thoroughbred racing to April in New Orleans.

DECEMBER

- **Plaquemines Parish Fair and Orange Festival**, Fort Jackson. Luscious fruit, crafts, kids' games.

MAPS

90
WILLOW ST.
CLARA ST.
MAGNOLIA ST.
ROBERTSON ST.
FRERET ST.
LA SALLE ST.
LIBERTY ST.
SIMON BOLIVAR ST.
SARATOGA ST.
RAMPART ST.
DRYADES ST.
BARONNE ST.
CARONDELET ST.
ST. CHARLES AVE.
PRYTANIA ST.
MELPOMENE AVE.
EARHART BLVD.
ERATO ST.
Louisiana Superdome
JULIA ST.
LIBERTY ST.
Union Passenger Terminal
CLARA ST.
DERBIGNY ST.
MAGNOLIA ST.
FRERET
ST.
LA SALLE ST.
POYDRAS ST.
GRAVIER ST.
TULANE AVE.
CLEVELAND AVE.
PERDIDO ST.
COMMON ST.
GRAVIER ST.
UNION ST.
PERDIDO ST.
POYDRAS ST.
GIROD ST.
RAMPART ST.
LAFAYETTE ST.
JULIA ST.
BARONNE ST.
CARONDELET ST.
HOWARD AVE.
ST. JOSEPH ST.
ST. CHARLES AVE.
Lafayette Square
Lee Circle
CAMP ST.
CAMP ST.
MAGAZINE ST.
ST.
LAFAYETTE ST.
NOTRE DAME ST.
GIROD ST.
TCHOUPITOULAS
JULIA ST.
HOWARD AVE.
POEYFARRE AVE.
CALLIOPE ST.
GAIENNIE ST.
DIAMOND ST.
SO. FRONT ST.
MAGAZINE ST.
CONSTANCE ST.
ERATO ST.
Greater New Orleans Bridge
Louisiana Convention Center
ANNUNCIATION ST.
THALIA ST.
Public Parking
TERPSICHORE ST.
RACE ST.
98
Gondola Route

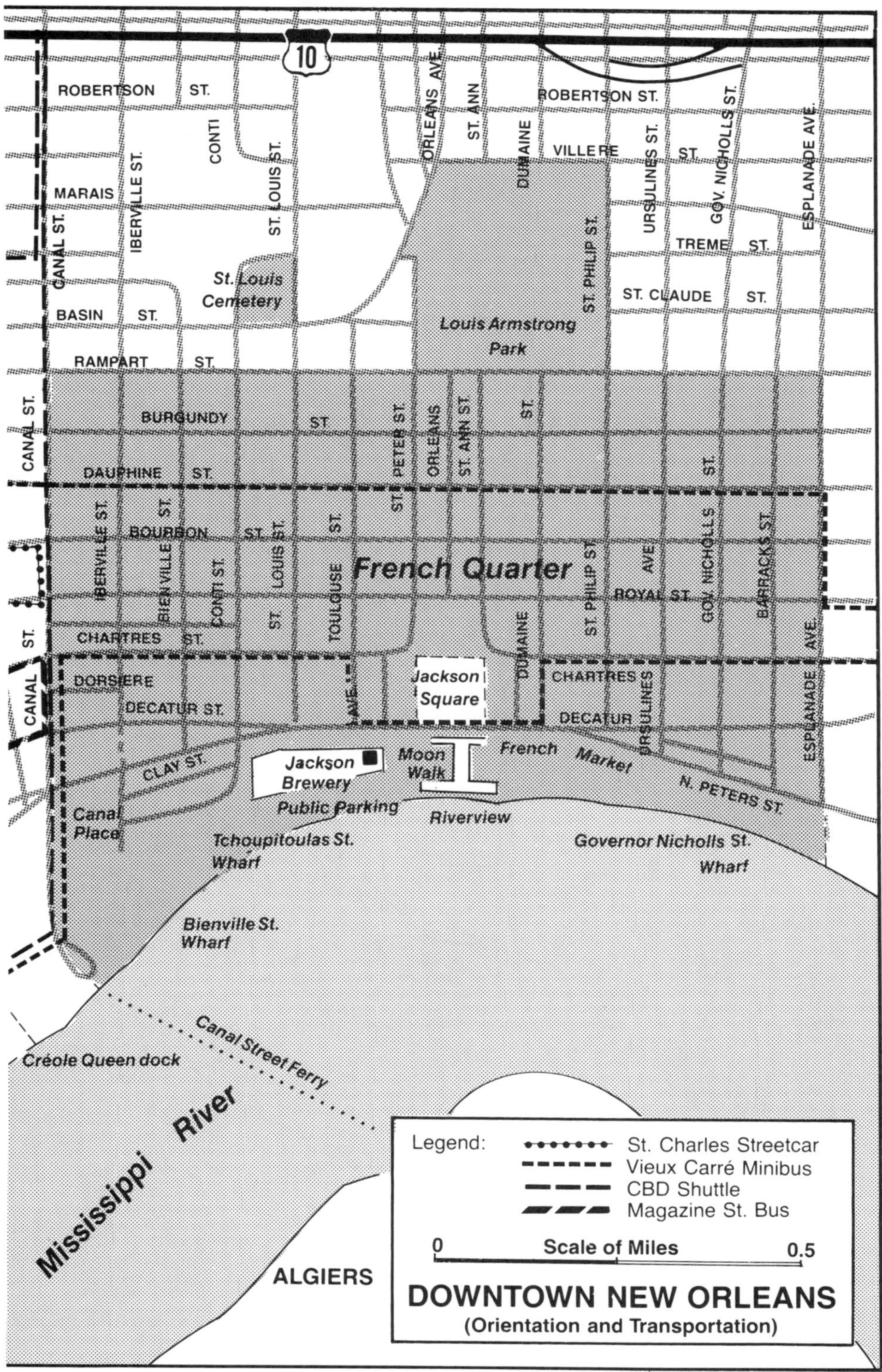
10
ROBERTSON ST.
ROBERTSON ST.
ORLEANS AVE
ST. ANN
DUMAINE
VILLERE ST.
URSULINES ST.
GOV. NICHOLLS ST.
ESPLANADE AVE.
CONTI
ST. LOUIS ST.
IBERVILLE ST.
MARAIS
CANAL ST.
TREME ST.
ST. PHILIP ST.
St. Louis Cemetery
ST. CLAUDE ST.
BASIN ST.
Louis Armstrong Park
RAMPART ST.
BURGUNDY ST.
ST. PETER ST.
ORLEANS
ST. ANN ST.
ST.
CANAL ST.
DAUPHINE ST.
ST.
BOURBON ST.
IBERVILLE ST.
BIENVILLE ST.
CONTI ST.
ST. LOUIS ST.
TOULOUSE ST.
French Quarter
ST. PHILIP ST.
AVE.
GOV. NICHOLLS
BARRACKS ST.
ROYAL ST.
DUMAINE
CHARTRES ST.
AVE.
ST.
CANAL
DORSIERE
DECATUR ST.
AVE.
Jackson Square
CHARTRES
DECATUR
URSULINES
ESPLANADE
CLAY ST.
Jackson Brewery
Moon Walk
French Market
N. PETERS ST.
Canal Place
Public Parking
Riverview
Tchoupitoulas St. Wharf
Governor Nicholls St. Wharf
Bienville St. Wharf
Créole Queen dock
Canal Street Ferry
Mississippi River
ALGIERS
Legend:
St. Charles Streetcar
Vieux Carré Minibus
CBD Shuttle
Magazine St. Bus
0
Scale of Miles
0.5
DOWNTOWN NEW ORLEANS
(Orientation and Transportation)

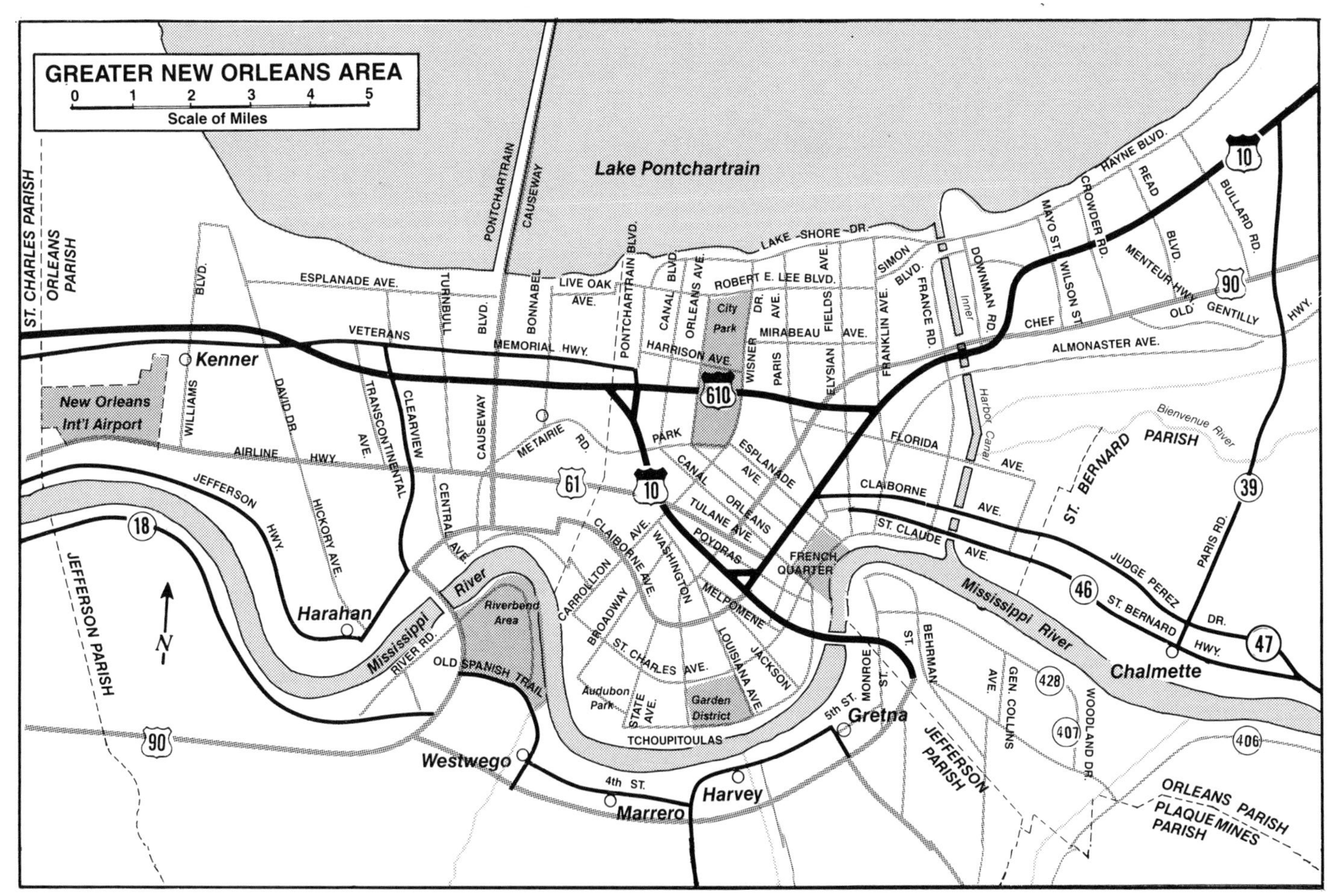

GREATER NEW ORLEANS AREA
0
1
2
3
4
5
Scale of Miles
Lake Pontchartrain
ST. CHARLES PARISH
ORLEANS PARISH
JEFFERSON PARISH
ST. BERNARD PARISH
ORLEANS PARISH
PLAQUE MINES PARISH
New Orleans Int'l Airport
Kenner
Harahan
Westwego
Marrero
Harvey
Gretna
Chalmette
Mississippi River
City Park
FRENCH QUARTER
Garden District
Audubon Park
Riverbend Area
Inner Harbor Canal
Bienvenue River
PONTCHARTRAIN CAUSEWAY
ESPLANADE AVE.
VETERANS MEMORIAL HWY.
WILLIAMS BLVD.
DAVID DR.
TRANSCONTINENTAL AVE.
CLEARVIEW
HICKORY AVE.
AIRLINE HWY.
JEFFERSON HWY.
TURNBULL
CAUSEWAY BLVD.
CENTRAL AVE.
BONNABEL
LIVE OAK AVE.
PONTCHARTRAIN BLVD.
METAIRIE RD.
CANAL BLVD.
ORLEANS AVE.
HARRISON AVE.
ROBERT E. LEE BLVD.
LAKE SHORE DR.
WISNER
PARIS AVE.
MIRABEAU AVE.
ELYSIAN FIELDS AVE.
FRANKLIN AVE.
SIMON BLVD.
FRANCE RD.
DOWNMAN RD.
MAYO ST.
CROWDER RD.
WILSON ST.
READ BLVD.
HAYNE BLVD.
BULLARD RD.
MENTEUR HWY.
CHEF
OLD GENTILLY HWY.
ALMONASTER AVE.
FLORIDA AVE.
CLAIBORNE AVE.
ST. CLAUDE AVE.
PARK
ESPLANADE AVE.
CANAL
ORLEANS
TULANE AVE.
POYDRAS
CLAIBORNE AVE.
WASHINGTON
CARROLLTON
BROADWAY
MELPOMENE
ST. CHARLES AVE.
LOUISIANA AVE.
JACKSON
STATE AVE.
TCHOUPITOULAS
RIVER RD.
OLD SPANISH TRAIL
4th ST.
5th ST.
MONROE ST.
BEHRMAN ST.
GEN. COLLINS AVE.
WOODLAND DR.
JUDGE PEREZ DR.
ST. BERNARD HWY.
PARIS RD.
10
610
90
61
18
39
46
47
428
407
406
N

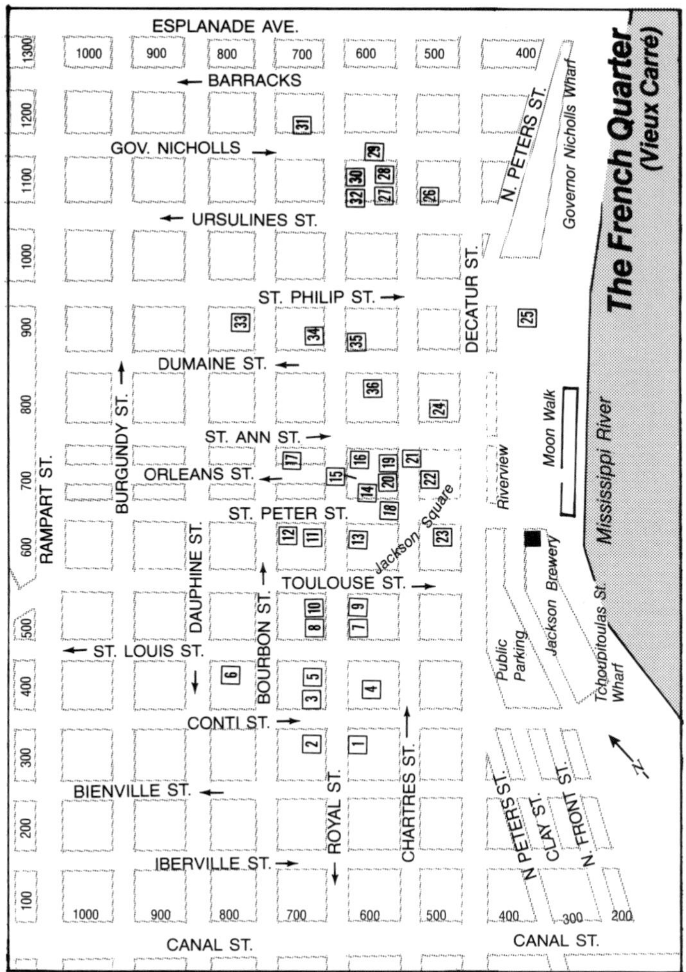

KEY TO THE NUMBERED REFERENCES: 1. Old Bank of Louisiana; 2. Old Bank of the U.S.; 3. Old La. State Bank; 4. New Orleans Court Building; 5. Casa Faurie; 6. The Hermann House; 7. Maison Seignouret; 8. Merieult House; 9. Casa de Comercio; 10. Court of Two Lions; 11. LeMonnier House; 12. Maison de Fléchier; 13. Maison LeMonnier; 14. Spanish Arsenal; 15. LaBranche House; 16. St. Anthony's Garden; 17. Salle d'Orléans; 18. Père Antoine's Alley; 19. The Presbytère; 20. St. Louis Cathedral; 21. The Cabildo; 22. Pirates Alley; 23. Pontalba Buildings; 24. 1850 House; 25. Court of the Two Sisters; 26. Old Ursulines Convent; 27. Beauregard House; 28. Soniat House; 29. Clay House; 30. LaLaurie House; 31. Thierry House; 32. The Gallier House; 33. Lafitte's Blacksmith Shop; 34. cornstalk fence; 35. Miltenberger Houses; 36. "Madame John's Legacy."

INDEX

A

We're always interested to hear about your discoveries, and to receive your comments on ours. Please feel free to write to us, and do state clearly exactly what you liked or disliked.

B

C

D

E

F

G

H

I

J

K

L

M

N

O

P

Q

R

We're always interested to hear about your discoveries, and to receive your comments on ours. Please feel free to write to us, and do state clearly exactly what you liked or disliked.

S

T

U

V

W

Y

Z

QUESTIONNAIRE

The Gault Millau series of guidebooks reflects your demand for insightful, incisive reporting on the best (and worst) that the world's most exciting destinations have to offer. To help us make our books even better, please take a moment to fill out this anonymous (if you wish) questionnaire. Return it to:

Gault Millau Inc.
P.O. Box 361144
Los Angeles, CA 90036

1. How did you hear about Gault Millau guides: bookstore, newspaper, magazine, radio, friends or other ? (please specify) ______

______

2. What cities (and/or countries) are you most interested in seeing covered in a Gault Millau guide? Please list in order of preference:______

______

______

3. Do you refer to Gault Millau guides only on your travels, or do you use the Gault Millau guide for your own city, too?

☐ Travels ☐ Own city ☐ Both

4. What are the three features you like most about Gault Millau guides?

1.______
2.______
3.______

5. What are the features, if any, you dislike about Gault Millau guides?

______

______

______

6. Please list any features you would like to see added to Gault Millau guides.

______

______

______

Continued →

7. Do you use any other travel guides in addition to Gault Millau? If so, please list below:

____

____

____

8. If you use another guidebook series, please list the features you enjoy most or find most useful about it:______________________________

____

____

9. How many trips do you take per year?
Business trips: Domestic ________ International ________
Pleasure trips: Domestic ________ International ________

10. Please check the category that reflects your annual household income:

- ☐ \$20,000–\$39,000
- ☐ \$40,000–\$59,000
- ☐ \$60,000–\$79,000
- ☐ \$80,000–99,000
- ☐ \$100,000–\$120,000
- ☐ Other (please specify)________
____

11. We thank you for your interest in Gault Millau guides, and we welcome your remarks and recommendations about restaurants, hotels, nightlife, shops and services around the world.

If you have any comments on Gault Millau guides in general, please list them in the space below.